GLOBAL THEOLOGICAL VOICES

I0880023

Jesus and the Cross

Reflections of Christians from Islamic Contexts

Global Theological Voices

Series Preface

The latter part of the twentieth century witnessed a global level change in Christian dynamics. One significant development was the rise of the churches in the global south, not only in their number but also in their engagement with their socio-cultural contexts. As theology is a dynamic interaction between the Christian message and the contemporary life of God's people and the world, it is natural to expect creative theological reflections from the southern churches. Global Theological Voices is a Regnum series exclusively dedicated to such theological explorations by the churches in Africa, Asia, Latin America and Eastern Europe. Through the provision of this credible international platform, the series empowers southern theological scholars whose voices are often not granted space by western publishers. The editors, therefore, invite theological seminaries and universities both in the West and in the "South" to submit relevant scholarly dissertations for possible publication in the series. Global Theological Voices will serve the global church by bringing the creative southern theological voices into a global dialogue with the existing western theological voices. Ultimately the editors and the publisher pray that the publications in this series will encourage the southern churches to make an important contribution to the shaping of a healthy future for global Christianity.

Series Editors

A full listing of titles in this series appears at the end of this book

GLOBAL THEOLOGICAL VOICES

Jesus and the Cross

Reflections of Christians from Islamic Contexts

Edited by
David Emmanuel Singh

Foreword by Lamin Sanneh

First published 2008 by Regnum Books International

Regnum is an Imprint of The Oxford Centre for Mission Studies,
P.O. Box 70, Oxford, OX2 6HB
www.ocms.ac.uk/regnum
and Paternoster Press
P.O. Box 300, Carlisle, Cumbria, CA3 0QS, UK
and
P.O. Box 1047, Waynesboro, GA 30830–2047, USA

09 08 07 06 05 04 03 8 7 6 5 4 3 2 1

British Library Cataloguing in Publication Data
A catalogue record for this book is available from the British Library

ISBN: 978-1-506478-06-7

Typeset by BB Ltd

The financial assistance of Robin and Nancy Wainwright of Middle East Fellowship toward this publication is gratefully acknowledged.

Distributed by 1517 Media in the US and Canada

Contents

FOREWORD

Lamin Sanneh

Dr Lamin Sanneh is D. Willis James Professor of Missions and World Christianity at Yale University, USA

In the encounter of religions and civilizations, none is more consequential and more urgent than that between Islam and Christianity, and in that encounter nothing is more fundamental than the question of the crucifixion of Jesus. That Good Friday event has stymied relations between the two religions, and because of its decisive role in the shaping of the West's cultural consciousness, it has bedevilled the encounter of the West with the Muslim world. At face value, the crucifixion as an historical event is simply dismissed a priori by Muslim tradition as inconsistent with the nature of an immutable transcendent God, and, therefore, as factually implausible. How could mere mortals defy the will of an omnipotent God by cornering Jesus and pinning him to the cross as a trophy of divine impotence? If such a thing were allowed to come to pass it would demonstrate the illogicality of human defiance prevailing against divine omnipotence, and for that reason it must be repudiated lock, stock, and barrel.

Consequently, evidence for the crucifixion in the Christian scripture must be evidence of fabrication and corruption. *Tahrif* is the Islamic term for the corruption of the scriptures by Jews and Christians as asserted in the Qur'án. There are two kinds of *tahrif*, *tahrif ma'nawí* (corruption of the meaning), and *tahrif lafzi*, corruption of the words. As far as the claim for the crucifixion is concerned, a double transgression has been committed, with textual corruption accompanied by falsification of meaning. Thus, beyond the face-value integrity of factual evidence there lies the equally serious matter of religious confusion among Christians, which explains why, in the words of al-Ghazali, biting with their wisdom teeth, Christians persist in manifest error against all common sense and theological reason.

The abstract quality of Muslim objections to the crucifixion sets up an obdurate barrier to attempts at dialogue and understanding. At every turn in the road we encounter a recurrent obstacle in the form of an a priori objection to what God is not allowed to permit. It hands Muslims a foolproof defence of God's prerogatives. Yet it does so by an implicit restriction of the bounds of divine sovereignty, so that defending God against a Good Friday-derived definition of divine suffering saves God from an undeserved fate – and human beings from grave error. Muslims are adamant that the weakness and humiliation of the crucifixion are unworthy of God and fatal to the success of God's will and design for the social order. That is the scandal – the affront - of the cross: a scandal to the Muslim religious temper, and a scandal to worldly wisdom.

Muslim and Western civilizations remain deadlocked on this religious frontier, with movement occurring only with the aid of contrived strategies of evasion, suspension, appeasement, and tactical concession. There has been no strategic surrender, at least not officially. The cross remains central to an appreciation of the complex heritage that is Western civilization to the same degree that its rejection has defined the response of the Muslim world to the West. There was a time in the post-World War II era when a secular compromise was thought to offer a neutral common ground for intercultural encounter, but that idea evaporated in the heat of the Arab-Israeli conflict and its aftermath. Meanwhile the OPEC upheaval of the 1970s, culminating in the 1979 Iranian revolution, brought to power in the Muslim world the forces of anti-secular conservatism whose ascendancy diminished considerably liberal prospects of a rapprochement with the West. Any remaining hopes were dashed with the string of terrorist attacks beginning with the attacks on New York and Washington, D.C. in September, 2001, and continuing with the bombings in Madrid in March 2004, and in London in July, 2005. In response, America's military invasion of Afghanistan and Iraq has only stoked the embers of radical fury and fanned the flames in new breeding grounds in immigrant communities in the West itself.

It remains, surely, one of the supreme ironies that the suffering that radical violence wishes to inflict on the West is in the name of a God who is immune to suffering and yet who will reward sacrifice on His behalf. Right-minded people must press this contradiction and ask how morally plausible it is to lay down one's life for God when God is forbidden to lay down His Life for humanity. The logic of extremism hands religious fundamentalism a warrant that does not exempt innocent civilians, including ordinary Muslims, and all this in the knowledge that extremism has incurred little Muslim public stigma. Radicalism infers an implicit endorsement in the silence of the Muslim public, fed by the lingering effects of the estrangement Muslims feel from a cross-bearing Western church. Few of those Muslims who denounce the methods of radical terror have been willing to reject the end for which it is being undertaken, which is the punitive drive to convert an infidel West. It gives the radicals little incentive to cease and desist.

The intercultural tension has been festering in spite of the fact that a liberal West has declared its wish to be considered as religiously non-aligned, willing in the process to abandon any adherence to the teachings of the church, including the cross. Yet that has not, alas! appeased Muslim radicals. After all, a liberal West still remains committed to something other than Islam, namely, secularism, something conscientious Muslims regard as a false absolute, as an idolatry, which is no less objectionable than the claim for the crucifixion. The barrier to intercultural reconciliation has remained intact in large part due to the symbol of the cross. Only by bringing the cross down in deference to Islam can the West earn the confidence and gratitude of the Muslim world.

Given the momentous events of the recent past and their sequel in global politics and international security, this volume of collected essays is extremely timely. The essays offer a range of views on the cross in Muslim tradition and history and in missiological endeavors in the Muslim world. The apostles and disciples found themselves confronted with the stark reality that the crucifixion and the resurrection took place against their own expectations and ideas, and those historical events demanded a response. To deny the events does not resolve the challenge they pose: the events would have no meaning whatsoever if they did not happen.

The response required involves a fundamental alteration of ideas of God's justice, and that in turn changed the way the followers of Jesus understood the nature of historical direction. God in Christ had displayed the cross at the heart of universal history, and defined the divine mission by the merits of the cross. There are premonitions, as it were, in the Qur'án itself where it speaks of Jesus as God's mercy, as God's *rahmah*, a claim not so alien to how St. Paul described Jesus as God's righteousness (Rom. 3: 25), the righteousness of cross-bearing redemptive merit, not the righteousness of finite human wisdom (1 Cor. 1:30, 1 Cor. 3: 18ff). Shakespeare shows how majesty is not negated by condescension when he writes of mercy that "'Tis mightiest in the mightiest; it becomes/The throned monarch better than his crown;/His sceptre shows the force of temporal power,/The attribute to awe and majesty,/Wherein doth sit the dread and fear of kings;/But mercy is above this sceptred sway,/It is enthroned in the hearts of kings,/It is an attribute to God himself." Shakespeare's point here is that the temporal majesty of natural law gives us little clue into what divine majesty is really like. Earthly power ill equips us for mercy as God's sovereign attribute. The restricted human character of power renders us blind to the true scope of the divine measure.

Gregory of Nyssa (d. c. 395) joins the debate when by several centuries he anticipates and responds to the Islamic Christological objection in insisting that the transcendent and omnipotent power of God is "the condescension to the weakness of our nature" so that "sublimity is seen in lowliness and yet the loftiness descends not." Divine humility is testimony to divine omnipotence in Gregory of Nyssa's view. To deny that option to God would be to infringe on God's prerogative to be God and to our grave moral detriment. The book is an invaluable resource for reflection and study of the meaning of the cross in the world of Islam and in intercultural relations. I cannot recommend it too highly.

INTRODUCTION

David Emmanuel Singh

Dr David Emmanuel Singh is a member of faculty at the Oxford Centre for Mission Studies, UK

Reflecting particularly on the increasing conflicts around the world, a large corpus of academic work is appearing within what can be described as Conflict and Peace Studies.[1] Many of these revolve around the idea of sacrifice in religion. Our premise here is not new: the Cross is the principal symbol of sacrifice and reconciliation. The story of this sacrifice is the Good News for all as it proclaims the end of hostilities from the point of view of the one who was wronged in the first place. Representing what God did through Jesus, the Cross invites all peoples to experience reconciliation in its fullness and potentially undermines the very roots of violence and conflict in society and between peoples of different faiths.

In this context, this book represents the increasing recognition and celebration of the tradition of Christianity as a faith in Jesus Christ, the Lamb of God, who takes away the sins of the world. The Cross reminds us that the sins of the world are not borne through the exercise of power but through Jesus Christ's submission to the will of the Father. The papers in this volume are organised in three parts: Scriptural, Contextual and Theological. The central question being addressed is: how do Christians living in contexts where Islam is a minority or majority religion, experience, express or think of the Cross? This is, therefore, an exercise in listening. As the contexts from where these engagements arise are varied, in drawing scriptural, contextual and theological reflections the papers offer a cross-section of Christian thinking about Jesus and the Cross.

Part One contains four papers which assume continuity between the Old Testament (OT) and the New Testament (NT) and belong to the mainstream Christian tradition that recognises the centrality of the Cross as the fulfillment of the OT narratives of the 'suffering patriarch, Prophet-Servant.' Jules Gomes' paper uses the metaphor of the 'Lamb of God' as the means by which violence

[1] See for example, Brombley D.G. and Melton J.G. (ed.), 2002; Jackman 2001; Scott, 2000; Childester, 1991.

is 'displaced' and 'deflected'. The innocent are thus spared the wrath of God and protected from exercising their tendency to act violently towards their oppressors. Eliya Mohol dwells particularly on the notion of the suffering Prophet-Servant referred to by Gomes. However, he highlights the idea that the Prophet-Servant prefigures the Christ in the Hebrew scripture as he is called to receive the Word and embody it. Suffering is a necessary corollary of this informing of the Word. Babu Immanuel's paper argues that the Gospels represent the Cross at two levels: as a culmination of the conflicts between Jesus and the Jewish leaders and as an eternal divine plan. Thus, the Cross was neither an accident nor simply the result of the combined will of the Jewish leaders to undermine Jesus, but a volitional act of Jesus' love for sinful humanity and obedience to the holy, all-knowing and all-powerful God. Kenneth Cragg argues persuasively that the Qur'anic and Biblical accounts are not 'unsympathetic' but there is 'sympathy in contrasts'. The idea that prophets were bearers of the word of God is common to both scriptures but there is a parting of the ways. Thus, whereas the Biblical prophets/prophecies were fulfilled in Jesus and the Cross, the prophetic witness in the Qur'an remained susceptible to 'despair' leading to the Hijrah by which a 'quest for the deployment of power' was realised. By contrast, the NT response was 'Christ crucified'.

Part Two contains 'Reflections from Contexts' which include, in particular, Afghanistan, Indonesia, East Africa, India, Pakistan, Egypt and Palestine. These are set against the background of the early discourse on the Cross by Muslims and Christians. David Thomas argues that early Christians living in the new Islamic Middle East enjoyed a fair amount of freedom in doing theology in relation to Islam. Whilst they recognised Islam to be of divine origin, they believed that the 'absence of the Cross' in Islam was fully realised through the Jesus of the Gospel. In this sense, they assumed continuity between the Islamic and Christian revelations. Mark Beaumont focuses on the examples of early Christian debates with Muslims on the Cross. The Muslim arguments were threefold: firstly, the Qur'an denied it, secondly, God cannot allow His messenger to suffer and be humiliated and, thirdly, God's eternal character is threatened by the suffering of His messenger. These, therefore, became the themes of Christian debates with Muslims.

The regional reflections begin with Len Bartlotti's 'The Gospel in Afghan Poetry, Proverbs and Folklore'. This is an excellent case study of a 'folklorist' approach to contextualisation, examining elements within Afghan poetry, proverbs and folklore that reflect the Cross. Bartlotti selects three themes for such an examination: separation-reunion, friendship and reconciliation. Jonathan Culver writes about Indonesia and particularly looks at the 'feast of sacrifice' in Islam which commemorates the Qur'anic narrative on the 'sacrifice of Ishmael'. Culver distinguishes 'folk' from 'traditional' Islam. He suggests that in folk Islam the feast of sacrifice is not just enabling performers to rememeber but expresses a deep desire for atonement. This reminds us of

Gomes' suggestion that sacrifice is a means of 'displacing' and 'deflecting' violence. The Biblical account where Isaac replaces Ishmael is not necessarily suggesting that the Qur'anic account is false, but that in choosing Isaac for the sacrifice, the violence is deflected or displaced. Isaac thus becomes a prototype of Jesus who takes someone else's death upon himself. Sacrifice can be, therefore, a powerful means of reconciliation. Salim Munayer gives us a concrete example of how the efforts towards reconciliation made by the Musalaha Ministry in Israel are being realised. John Chesworth examines how the theme of the Cross is used in the so-called 'outreach literature' in East Africa by Muslims and Christians. His conclusion is that the old themes in Muslim-Christian debates are repeated, and despite centuries of such debates, the tracts do not reflect any development in thinking on either side. Jose Abraham examines the Girardian theory of sacrifice with a view to understanding interfaith violence in India. The author challenges us to review events of violence from the perspective of the victim, whereby one can see that the victim is often a scapegoat wrongly accused of guilt. Moreover, this realisation can be not only a basis for the cessation of conflicts but also a basis for reconciliation. Writing about Pakistan, Pervaiz Sultan suggests that the Pakistani Christian experience of poverty and of being a minority leads to an appreciation of the Cross and its potential for peace and reconciliation. Arne Fjeldstad writes on the centrality of the Cross both as a concrete object and as a spiritual concept. As an object the Cross occupies a central place in Coptic piety as an outward sign of Egyptian Christian identity and an outward symbol of the inner faith. The Cross is displayed, worn and etched permanently on the body as a symbol of their Lord's suffering and of their suffering. Coptic Christians do not run away from their daily cross but rather accept it with joy as this unity with Christ in suffering holds the promise of life eternal. In the final paper of this section, Hwa Yung argues for a contextually relevant approach to Muslims which rises above the usual theological impasses that characterise Christian-Muslim dialogue. He concludes by suggesting that Christians should seriously take into account the Asian ideas of 'shame' and 'honour' in place of 'guilt' or 'sin'.

Part Three consists of papers with substantial 'Theological Reflections'. Ida Glaser's paper uses Kenneth Cragg's idea of 'cross-reference' to suggest that theology must refer to the context of faiths and people of faiths. Central to this theology is the Cross. The Muslim denial of the Cross has provoked different sorts of Christian responses. She argues for a theology of love for Muslims as a particular approach that satisfies the demands of Christ's own suffering love for humanity. Rollin Grams reflects on the Islamic idea of God as the beneficent and merciful in relation to Jesus' Cross and calls for a movement from abstract to concrete theologising. Liberal theology and Islam dismiss the Cross and both 'suffer from theological abstraction.' Like Ida Glaser, he argues for a theology of love manifested in the Cross of Jesus Christ. It is on this Cross that the idea of God being beneficent and merciful is fully realised. Clinton Bennett revisits his own struggles as a Christian to encounter the absence of the Cross in Islam. He attempts to offer 'a positive contribution' to 'cross-reference theology' for a possible theological rapproachment between Christian and Muslim. Simply stated, his position is that the language of death and blood is appropriate given the background of the NT writers. It was not meant to be an absolute as God is capable of loving sinful people 'without a price being paid.' To him Jesus did die on the Cross but the Muslim interpretation of the Cross challenges the Christian over-emphasis on the need for the 'sacrificial, substitutionary, atoning death', which Christians regard as the 'bed-rock of Christian faith.' Undoubtedly this is not consistent with the historic Christian witness of the Cross and, therefore, will be controversial. For this reason, I have sought to include a critique of this argument by Kenneth Cragg. Cragg's paper returns the Cross to the centre of the historic Christian faith. Reminiscent of Bennett's rejoinder about the Cross not being the 'bed-rock of Christian faith', Cragg speaks of the Cross being the 'very focus of its (Christian faith's) sacramental *anamnesis*...(and) the central theme of New Testament witness....' Also, one of Cragg's main arguments is that the Cross is 'less absent' in the Qur'an than Bennett thinks. My own paper ends Part Three and takes a different approach to the Cross than those taken by the previous authors. I argue for a plurality of theological structures both 'Traditional' and 'Alternative'. Fundamental to the Alternative structure is the notion of a 'Complex Unity', which is assumed to be the 'hidden' aspect of the traditional Islamic notion of a 'Simple Unity'. The main argument is that the Traditional structure with its strict separation of God and man makes incarnation impossible to conceive of, whereas the Alternative structure influenced by Greek Neoplatonism is more amenable to it. The idea of the Perfect Man is evidence of the radical nature of the Alternative structure. In this context, the Cross is not too radical a possibility.

PART ONE

THE CROSS IN THE SCRIPTURES

ECCE, AGNUS DEI: THE CROSS IN THE OLD TESTAMENT

Jules Gomes

Rev Dr Jules Gomes is Coordinating Chaplain to the Old Royal Naval College, University of Greenwich and Trinity College of Music, London

> 'As he (the Lamb) spoke his snowy white flushed into tawny gold and his size changed and he was Aslan himself, towering above them and scattering light from his mane.' C.S. Lewis, *The Voyage of the Dawntreader*.

If the crux Christi is the apex of Christian belief and practice, and if the Christian New Testament is understood to be in theological, thematic and even textual continuity with the Hebrew Old Testament, is it possible to legitimately discover the crux of Christian faith in the crucible of the Hebrew Bible? The apostolic witnesses were confident that they could credibly construct the gospels as the fulfilment of the Hebrew Scriptures. This is especially seen in the passion narratives where attention has been paid to meticulous detail in drawing parallels between the passion narratives and OT texts[1] dominated by images of the suffering Patriarch (Genesis 22),[2] the suffering Prophet or the Servant (Isaiah 53)[3] and the suffering Psalmist (Psalm 22).[4] The gospel writers thus seek to portray the crucified Christ as the fulfilment of the entire Hebrew Bible - the Law, Prophets and Writings (cf. Luke 24:27).

But tracing the relationship between God's revelation in the Old Covenant and the New Covenant has never been trouble-free: 'Though it may seem hard to believe, the fact is that this basic and important question has scarcely been given a clear answer over the past twenty centuries of Christian living. And that fact has conditioned the whole of theology.'[5] Models of salvation history, tradition history, typology, promise and fulfilment, and continuity and discontinuity have been suggested as bridges across the exegetical impasse.[6]

---

[1] Moo, 1983, Brown, 1994: 1445-1467

[2] Rosenberg, 1965: 381-388, Daly, 1977: 45-75, Brown, 1994: 1435-1444

[3] Hooker, 1959

[4] Dillon, 1987: 430-440, Freed, 1983: 62-73, McCaffrey, 1981: 73-89, Reumann, 1974: 39-58

[5] Segundo, 1976: 487-88

[6] For an extensive study of these schemes and their main proponents see Baker, 1991. Also see, Westermann, 1963. Recognising that the relationship between the OT and the

One possible way of exploring a relationship between testaments is by association - identifying an important OT metaphor, theme, text or tradition that in the NT is so closely linked to the cross that it acts as a metonymy for the cross. After examining the legitimacy of the NT link, this theme or text can then be studied in its historical OT context and its meaning there discovered without arbitrarily superimposing later NT interpretations.[7]

An example of this is the representation of Jesus as the Lamb, which the gospel of John identifies with the crucified Christ.[8] In the fourth gospel, the Baptist introduces the first disciples to Jesus using the metaphor of the Lamb: 'Behold, here is the Lamb of God!' (*ecce, agnus dei!*) (John 1:36). Jesus has already been introduced as 'the Lamb of God who takes away the sin of the world' (John 1:29).[9] The Lamb is also alluded to in the passion narrative: at a time that is a few hours before the Passover meal (19:14-16), Jesus (the Lamb) is handed over to be crucified. The passion narrative concludes with the reference to the OT: "These things occurred so that the scripture might be fulfilled, 'None of his bones shall be broken'" (19:36). This is again a reference to the Passover Lamb (Exodus 12:10, 46; Numbers 9:12).[10]

It is also significant that the fourth gospel is intent on associating the Lamb with the OT Messiah. John's intention is primarily to show that Jesus really is the Messiah and the Son of God (John 20:31). The response to the Baptist's introduction of Jesus as the Lamb is the 'eureka' declaration of Andrew to Simon Peter: 'We have found the Messiah.' The declaration uses the Aramaic/Hebrew for Messiah, followed by a telling editorial note translating

---

apostolic witness to Jesus is not 'one of simple material correspondence' but is a dialectic process where 'Scripture reveals the meaning of events and that events reveal the meaning of Scripture, that is, they require that certain aspects of the received interpretation be set aside and a new interpretation adopted', the document by the Pontifical Biblical Commission on 'The Interpretation of the Bible in the Church' attempts to go beyond a traditional understanding of *sensus plenior*.

[7] See Nielsen, 1992: 121-132 who studies the use of metaphor (lamb) in the OT and shows how they can be reused in other contexts, opening the possibility of reinterpretation (Revelation).

[8] Though John cites the OT less frequently than the Synoptic gospels there are unmistakable allusions to Jacob's ladder and Jacob's well (1:51, 4:5-6) and to Abraham (8:31-58). Johannine typology also uses Moses' brazen serpent as a type of the cross (3:14). See Reim, 1974. Also see Summers, 1965: 35-43 for the centrality of the Lamb motif in John's gospel and Armerding 1942: 110-116 for the brazen serpent as a type of the cross.

[9] It must be noted that in vv. 29-31, different days in Jesus' first week are mentioned: 'the next day' in 1:29, 35, 43, and 'on the third day' in 2:1 clearly pre-empting the cross. There will also be a last week before Jesus' death (12: 1-19: 3-19). For a survey of how scholars have variously understood 1:29, see May, 1947: 50-91, Carey, 1981: 101-107, Du Plessis, 1986: 148, Sandy, 1991: 448-9

[10] Brown, 1994: 1184-86 discusses whether the reference is to the Lamb or the Psalmist in Psalm 34:21.

the term into Greek (John 1:41). The primary characterisation of Jesus as the 'Christ' (Messiah) is central to the relationship between the Testaments.[11] Hence, one way of attempting to study the 'cross' in the OT would be to examine the imagery of the Lamb in the Hebrew Bible.

Furthermore, early church tradition gives some justification to proceed in this direction. Justin Martyr depicted the paschal lamb as being offered in the form of a cross and claimed that this prefigured the crucifixion of Jesus. While Justin Martyr may have been thinking of the Samaritan Passover of his day, rabbinic evidence seems to show that in Jerusalem the Jewish paschal lamb was offered in a manner that resembled crucifixion.[12]

A Jew familiar with Hebrew traditions would detect in the catchphrase 'Lamb of God' a theological concept that spanned the scope of scripture. In Genesis, the lamb features in the story of Abraham and Isaac on Mount Moriah. In Exodus, the blood of the Passover lamb was applied to the doorposts of the Hebrew slaves in Egypt. In Leviticus, the sacrificial lamb was used in the burnt offering. In Isaiah, the lamb is the Suffering Servant of Yahweh who is led to slaughter. In the inter-testamental book of Enoch there is the image of a lamb sprouting a great horn, and battling with the enemy.

The story of Genesis 22:1-19, where a lamb is sacrificed in place of Isaac, starts a series of other 'Lamb' traditions in the OT. A few preliminary points may be noted. The literary placement of the story in Genesis 22:1-19 acts as a climax to the Abraham cycle by making Abraham pass the supreme test of faith. The Elohist's version of the story is without parallel in the Yahwist.[13] There is a debate as to whether vv.15-18 are a later addition;[14] I believe it to be part of the original story since it is both Abraham's obedience and his faith in God's promises which is being tested (cf. Hebrews 11:17). The reiteration of the promises to the obedient patriarch is well deserved.

In Genesis 22:7 the Hebrew word used is 'sheep' (*seh*) which is used almost synonymously for 'ewe' (*rahel*). This is seen in Isaiah 53:7: 'like a lamb (*seh*) that is led to the slaughter, and like a sheep (*rahel*) that before its shearers is silent….' However, what is then provided for the sacrifice is the 'ram' (Genesis 22:). In Akkadian *shu'u* is used for 'ram' and in Ugaritic ritual texts it is limited to 'ram' or 'he-goat'; elsewhere its use is more general, encompassing both sexes.[15] The LXX translates the word as *probaton*, which is in Greek used in the widest sense to denote all four-footed animals especially tame, domestic

---

[11] Some of the most important works on this theme are Mowinckel, 1956, Ringgren 1956, Clements, 1989: 3-19. In the NT, the Messianic declaration is the pivotal Christological confession of faith (Matthew 16:16, Mark 8:29, Luke 9:20, John 11:27) as is the cross.

[12] Tabory, 1996: 395-406

[13] See McEvenue, 1984: 315-332

[14] See Wenham, 1994: 2.96-118

[15] See Theological Wordbook of the Old Testament (TWOT), CD-Rom

ones. The word used for Jesus as lamb in John's gospel is *amno* (John 1:29, 36, Isaiah 53:7 LXX, cf. Acts 8:32, 1Peter 1:19). However, the primary use of the Hebrew *seh* (sheep) and its use elsewhere for a clean animal that may be eaten (Deuteronomy 14:4) and offered for a sacrifice; whose firstling belongs to Yahweh (Exodus 34:19; Leviticus 27:26), is to be roasted for the Passover meal (Exodus 12:3ff), is suitable for a guilt offering or a burnt offering (Leviticus 5:7; Leviticus 12:8) and is led silently to the slaughter (Isaiah 53:7) is sufficient to identify it with the lamb in the NT.

When examining specifically the function and meaning of the lamb in the 'binding of Isaac' story it is interesting to note that in the history of religions in Western Asia the 'lamb' is identified most closely with the human being since it is the most domesticated of all animals. "Sheep need human care as humans need human care, and this isomorphism of need proved a powerful stimulus to the religious imagination first of Ancient Israel and later of early Christianity," explains Miles.[16] "The equation of sheep with man is striking as well in the story of the binding of Isaac. 'God will provide the lamb,' Abraham says to Isaac (Genesis 22:8), all the while expecting to slay his son. Isaac believes his father, trusting just as the lamb, anthropomorphized, seems to trust when it is led unresisting to the slaughter ground."[17] It has been suggested that the story was originally an aetiology formally rejecting human sacrifice and explaining why it was no longer permissible in Israel.[18] Human sacrifice was supposed to expiate past transgressions and possessed a redemptive character. It also brought about atonement.[19] The term *olah* (Genesis 22:2) was also used to refer to child sacrifice (2 Kings 3:27). A judge like Jephthah sacrifices his only child - a virgin daughter - because of the vow he has made (Judges 11:34-40, cf. 2 Kings 17:17, Micah 6:7).[20] Snyder suggests that Abraham and his men reject the contemporary idealization of human sacrifice as the highest form of worship and so their proud and open return to the community becomes an exceptional act of courage.[21] The lamb, being closest to the human, could be thus seen as the ideal substitute or scapegoat that was killed in the place of the slaying of a human being.

In the Genesis story we are faced with an individual and not a communal sacrifice. Abraham is to offer Isaac as a 'whole burnt offering' *olah* (22:2); literally 'an offering of ascent' or an 'ascending offering'. This was so called

---

16 Miles, *ABD*-CD-Rom

17 Miles, *ABD*-CD-Rom.

18 Daly, 1977: 45-75, Cf. Wenham, 1994: 2.96-118

19 Read, 1987: 6.516

20 Tucker, 1999: 30-47 for a history of child sacrifice.

21 Snyder, 1988: 23-25. Contra Veijola, 1989: 236-244 who argues that signs of Yahwistic elements point to a post-exilic date for the final redaction which indicates that the message is not one explaining why Israel rejects child-sacrifice, but one of Abraham's unconditional obedience.

because the sacrifice was entirely burnt on the altar and its smoke ascended to the heavenly deity. This type of offering was the most widespread in ancient Israel - the phrase 'burnt offerings and peace offerings' could be used as merism for the entire sacrificial system.[22] Milgrom has argued that the *ola* was the earliest form of atonement sacrifice in the biblical materials.[23] Job 1:5 is good evidence of this: "Job would rise early in the morning and offer burnt offerings according to the number of (his sons) for he said: 'It may be that my sons have sinned and cursed God in their hearts.'" In Leviticus 1:4 it is said that the burnt offering 'shall be acceptable in your behalf as atonement for you'. In this case, what is Abraham making atonement for, if such is indeed the case?

Wenham convincingly demonstrates the literary parallel between the story of Abraham and Isaac (Genesis 22:1-19) and the preceding story of Ishmael's expulsion, but does not explain why the editor has dovetailed the two narratives as parallels.[24]

Ishmael	Isaac
God orders Ishmael's expulsion (21:12-13)	God orders Isaac's sacrifice (22:2)
Food and water taken (21:14)	Sacrificial material taken (22:3)
Journey (21:14)	Journey (22:4-8)
Ishmael about to die (21:16)	Isaac about to die (22:10)
Angel of God calls from heaven (21:17)	Angel of the LORD calls from heaven (22:11)
'Do not fear' (21:17)	'fear God' (22:12)
'God has heard'	'You have obeyed (heard) my voice' (22:18)
'I shall make into a great nation' (21:18)	'Your descendants will be like stars, sand,' etc. (22:17)
God opens her eyes and she sees well (21:19)	Abraham raises his eyes and sees ram (22:13)
She gives the lad a drink (21:19)	He sacrifices ram instead of son (22:14)

The background is the conflict between Sarah and Hagar for which Abraham is held responsible. Indeed, the term Sarah uses for the 'wrong done to me' (Genesis 16:5) is *hamas* which is best translated 'violence' and is used

22 Levine, 1974: 21

23 Milgrom, *ABD*-CD-Rom

24 Wenham, 1998: 2.76-89

elsewhere in the flood story to describe the earth 'filled with violence' which is why God decides to destroy the earth (Genesis 6:11,13).[25] It is not improbable that the story of Isaac's binding and the offering of the lamb in his place was intended as a means of resolving the conflict between the descendants of Isaac and Ishmael, at least in an earlier version. The story concludes with Abraham and his 'young men', presumably including Isaac, returning to Beersheba and living there (Genesis 22:19). The name of the place is mentioned twice in v. 19; earlier Abraham has sent Hagar away and she is left wandering in the wilderness of Beersheba (Genesis 21:14). Midrashic readings narrate how Ishmael accompanied Abraham and Isaac to Mount Moriah to witness the Akedah (Genesis 22).[26] When he dies Abraham is buried by Isaac and Ishmael (Genesis 25:9). The sons of Ishmael are accorded almost equal honour as 'twelve princes according to their tribes' (Genesis 25:16). This time it is the Priestly source or redactor who places the two sons together but without a word of explanation.

The role of Isaac as potential victim is also important. He is an example of a righteous sufferer - facing the possibility of a violent death for no fault of his own. He does not fully understand what is going on; although it is hardly conceivable that Abraham's tense demeanour would have not betrayed his foreboding. 'The fire and the wood are here, but where is the lamb for a burnt offering?' he asks (Genesis 22:7). Like a lamb that is silent before its slaughterer, the text does not record his protest but only his silence.

The literary turning point of the story is the halting of the human sacrifice and the provision of a vicarious substitute in the form of an animal, which as we have seen earlier, is closest in terms of its domestication to a human being. The provision of the lamb/ram substitute is hinted at in 22:8 where Abraham tells Isaac: 'God himself will provide the lamb for a burnt offering, my son' (NRSV). This can be rendered in a number of different ways. Can it be understood as: 'God will provide (for) himself a sheep for the whole burnt offering?' Or 'God will provide a sheep for the burnt offering, namely my son,' since 'my son' is not preceded by the mark of the definite object. Or, better still, if the imperfect is understood as a jussive here, it could be read as: 'May God provide a sheep'. This reading would not in any case undermine Abraham's faith, because he would still be trusting and hoping that the God who gave him a son through whom the prophecies would be fulfilled, would not take him away now. The 'test' with which the story is introduced (Genesis 22:1) could be the test of whether Abraham believed that God would indeed provide - all that was needed to fulfil his promises. The story proceeds to the aetiological explanation for the name of the mount Moriah, with an editorial note, 'So Abraham called that place, "The LORD will provide;" as it is said to

[25] The only other use of the word in Genesis is in 49:5 'Simeon and Levi are brothers; weapons of violence are their swords'.

[26] See Reiss, 2002: 253-256

this day, 'On the mount of the LORD it shall be provided'" (Genesis 22:14). The point is made and reinforced: a substitute victim is provided by God himself in the form of a 'lamb'.

The first detailed account of a patriarch offering sacrifice is significant for it has its echoes in later scriptural traditions. It may be seen as paradigmatic for the other climactic moments in the biblical story where the sacrifice or killing of human beings is carried out in tandem with the slaughter of a lamb, or negotiated by the substitute slaying of a lamb, or where the lamb is inseparably identified with the human victim.

The canonical context in the story of the Exodus is clearly one of systemic, even genocidal, violence that has been carried out against the Hebrews (cf. Exodus 1:15-16). There is liberation from the oppression of Pharaoh only after a pronouncement is made that 'Every first-born in the land of Egypt shall die, from the first-born of Pharaoh who sits on his throne to the first-born of the female slave who is behind the hand mill, and all the first-born of the livestock' (Exodus 11:5). The corollary is that the first-born sons of Israel are spared judgement. However, every father is expected as a result to dedicate his first-born son to Yahweh and to redeem him by offering a sacrifice (Exodus 13:13). "It may be that Genesis itself is implicitly comparing Isaac's rescue to that sparing of Israel's first-born sons in the Exodus and the ram Abraham offered to the Passover lamb," writes Wenham.[27] In later Jewish tradition (e.g., the book of Jubilees, 100 bc) a connection is made between Passover and the sacrifice of Isaac.

While the Exodus verses 12:1-13 have been assigned to P by most scholars, there is also a widely held view that the slaying of the Passover Lamb and the annual feast of Unleavened Bread (12:14-20-P) did not originally belong together in the story of the Exodus and were not included until the exile.[28] It has been proposed therefore, that both Passover and Massot traditions were part of pre-Israelite cultic practices and were later taken over by Israel and adapted to her own story.[29] Whatever the case may be, the Exodus event when spliced together with the Passover ritual and the slaying of the Lamb, represents an act of the displacement of violence. In the Exodus event, it is Yahweh and Pharaoh - representing the Egyptian god - who do battle. The Israelites are hardly active participants in the violence unleashed against the first-born of the Egyptians. The only act of violence the Israelites indulge in is the slaying of the Lamb. The blood has an apotropaic function here - it serves to protect the Israelites from the 'angel of death.' If the entire section is to be interpreted cultically and ritually, the slaying of the first-born of Egypt belongs to the Passover ritual and may be read as the liturgical enactment of violence rather than the actual performance of it. It is the slaying of the Lamb in the annual cultic ritual of the

---

[27] Wenham, 1994: 2.96-118

[28] Childs, 1974: 184-5, Durham, 1987: 3.150-164

[29] Childs, 1974: 187

Passover that deflects the community's tendency towards acting violently against their oppressors or aggressors.

The Suffering Servant of Isaiah, like Abraham, makes an offering and sees his offspring (Isaiah 53:10). But like Isaac, who silently consented to being sacrificed, he was 'like a lamb that is led to the slaughter…[yet] he opened not his mouth' (Isaiah 53:7). And like Isaac he offered himself, rather than anyone else. But unlike Isaac the servant actually dies (Isaiah 53:8). Rosenberg convincingly argues that the 'Righteous One' of Isaiah 53 and the concept of John's gospel of Jesus as the Passover Lamb reflect the concept that the sacrifice of Isaac was to be re-enacted by the 'new Isaac'. He finds the origin for the tradition in the ancient Canaanite cult of Jerusalem, in which periodically the king, or a substitute for the king, had to be offered as a sacrifice so that the power of the deity might be renewed and his wrath diverted from the people.[30] It is worth noting that the noun *hamas*, most often used to describe systemic violence in the Hebrew Bible, is used to emphasize the innocence of the victim and the contrast with the violence done against him: 'They made his grave with the wicked and his tomb with the rich, although he had done no violence (*hamas*), and there was no deceit in his mouth' (Isaiah 53:9). The Lamb-like suffering and sacrifice of the Servant results in an eschatological expectation that ends the spiral of violence and hopes that 'violence (*hamas*) shall no more be heard in your land, devastation or destruction within your borders; you shall call your walls, Salvation and your gates, Praise' (Isaiah 60:18).

Thus the initial act of human sacrifice to take away violence that is substituted by a lamb in the Genesis story, and is re-enacted again in a scene of horrific violence in the Exodus liberation story, climaxes with the violence done against the servant, its vicarious acceptance and its eschatological hope. It is this emphasis on the role of the Lamb in the mediation of violence that comes to final fruition in the New Testament in the Lamb of God who takes away the violence of the world by his death on the cross. It is this that is cultically remembered and ritually re-enacted in memory of him 'who made there by his one oblation of himself once offered a full, perfect and sufficient sacrifice, oblation and satisfaction for the sins of the whole world'. It is thus right and fitting that the public response to the Eucharistic Prayer is in these words: 'O Lamb of God that takest away the sins of the world, grant us thy peace'.

30 Rosenberg, 1965: 381-388

THE PROPHETIC RESPONSE TO SUFFERING

Eliya Mohol

Dr Eliya Mohol is Professor of Old Testament Studies at the Union Biblical Seminary, Pune, India

Introduction

Far from being a sign of weakness, suffering is immensely powerful when it is willingly accepted and experienced on behalf of others. Biblical witness suggests that this sort of suffering characterized the experience of Jesus leading to the Cross. To those who hold to the unity of the scriptures, the Old Testament prophets appear to prefigure the Cross. In this paper, I am focusing on the Prophetic response to suffering. Moses and Jeremiah, among others, are known to have suffered so much that they have become typological models of the Suffering Christ. To Moses and Jeremiah can be added the suffering Servant of Isaiah 40-55 (the Servant), who is also considered as a prophetic figure. In this paper the main focus will be on the prophetic triad of Moses, Jeremiah and the Servant.

Approach

Fretheim encourages scholars to approach the Bible as a whole and in a balanced way. Failure to do this can result in creating discord between 'God the Father of Jesus' and 'Jesus himself'. Some scholars have a view that Jesus is a friend and God is an enemy. The understanding of the atonement based on such a separation of Jesus from God appears twisted as it can see Jesus as the one who came to save Man from God.[1] Many scholars have followed this approach to the Bible in the past.[2] Without a comprehensive and deeper reading of the

---

[1] Fretheim,1984: 2

[2] The imbalanced approach to the Bible can be seen generally in Kraemer, 1938; Soper, 1943; Glover, 1946; Blauw, 2003; Taylor, 1980. They generally follow either a selective and/or a proof-text approach to the Old Testament. This is especially true of the works produced during 1938-1961. A recent example is in M. David's paper in M.T.B. Laing (ed.) 2002. Here Old Testament texts are taken as support for preconceived theological positions. This approach is selective and thematic and sacrifices the need for being

Old Testament text the understanding of God being different from Jesus in his response to humanity is rather too simplistic and is not fully borne out by a serious engagement with the scriptures. Suffering was an in important part of prophetic experience. One of the major ways God responded to suffering was through 'theophany'. The prophet was the theophany of God and thus, his suffering was not unconnected to God. There was a sense in which the prophets embodied God. Thus, their suffering was a reflection of the suffering of God.[3] Prophetic suffering demonstrated what happens to God even though people cannot see him. There was a decisive continuity of theophanies within the call of the prophets. God does not just manifest himself, speak a word and then depart; God leaves his word behind, imbedded in his prophets' hearts. God called the prophets to receive and embody the word from the moment of their call. The prophets, in response, were called to function as an ongoing theophany of their God.[4] God suffered through his prophets and used them to persuade the people to repent.[5]

Moses and Suffering

Moses was a prophet par excellence. Unlike other prophets God spoke to Moses 'face to face'. He was conscious of his special position as a prophet: 'The Lord your God will raise up for you a prophet like me from among your own brothers. You must listen to him' (Deuteronomy 18:15). This promise starts a prophetic tradition that embodies prophetic and servant roles, and finds its final fulfilment in the messianic prophet-figure of the Servant in Isaiah 40-55.

As the leader of the Hebrews, Moses often faced loneliness and isolation. Instead of supporting him, the people of Israel often complained about him. He had to undergo rejection and ridicule by his own people. The people rebelled against his authority (Numbers 14:9). His colleagues, the Levites, challenged his leadership (16:1-3) and his own brother and sister envied his special relationship with Yahweh (Numbers 12). Finally, Moses experienced the full force of the wrath of God on account of his peoples' rebellion. He was deprived of the fulfilling experience of entering the Promised Land (Deuteronomy 3:26). God, however, held Moses responsible for this: 'because you did not uphold my holiness among the Israelites' (Deuteronomy 32:51). He suffered on account of his responsibility and role as a prophet to stand between God and the people.

---

comprehensive and exegetical. Thus, as a result, no particular tradition or section of the literature including Prophetic and Wisdom books is given a proper hearing.

[3] Fretheim, 1984: 153

[4] Fretheim, 1984: 151

[5] Fretheim, 1984: 159

Vicarious Suffering

His suffering can be viewed as being 'on behalf of the people'. He offered his very life for them: 'But now, please, forgive their sin - but if not, then blot me out of the book you have written' (Exodus 32:32). Yet his suffering was not vicarious in the full sense of the word since the people of Israel had to pay the penalty for their rebellion. The privilege of seeing the Promised Land was taken away from them (Numbers 14:23). Fretheim calls this aspect of prophetic suffering 'for others' and not exactly 'vicarious', but sees its fulfilment or development in Jesus (Fretheim 163).

Moses suffered willingly. Though, initially, he was reluctant to go before Pharaoh (Exodus 3:11), after accepting the leadership, he began taking initiatives. He chose to intercede for Miriam: 'O God, please heal her' (Numbers 12:13), and for the rebellious Israel: 'In accordance with your great love, forgive the sin of these people' (14:9; cf. Exodus 32:11-14). He faced the suffering and persecution in faith (cf. Hebrews 11:24-27) and persisted in the task of ministry entrusted to him by God. He did not give up. As he continued confronting the people with God's word, he also defended his prophetic and priestly office. He knew of his great reward from God and he dealt with the suffering in the light of the hope of receiving the reward from God. He let God deal with his persecutors. He became angry but, as far as is known, he did not show it before the people; instead, he poured it out before God (Numbers 16:15).

Jeremiah and the Seventh Century Prophets

Insights into Jeremiah's suffering are in the following texts: 11:18-23; 12:1-6; 15:10-12; 17:14-18; 18:18-23; 20:7-13; 14-18. These verses are called 'confessions of Jeremiah' and are thus a source of the understanding of his sufferings and his attitude to them. Thompson prefers to call them 'Dialogues with Yahweh' (Thompson, 1980: 88).

Jeremiah resembles Moses since he suffered for and on account of his people. First, like Moses he identified himself with the suffering of his people. He was deeply conscious of his own human existence and was filled with the passion of God for his people. Secondly, he interceded for his people often weeping and wailing for them. That is why he is called the 'weeping prophet'. Thirdly, like Moses, he was deeply aware of his special standing with God as his prophet and the great responsibility it entailed. It is out of this sense of responsibility that Jeremiah proclaimed alarm and condemnation of Israel's great sins in the hope that this would elicit repentance (Jeremiah 4). He felt a continuous tension between his ordinary human existence and his prophetic office. This tension comes through clearly in 'the complaints' (known also as 'the confessions') he expressed before Yahweh. Fourthly, like Moses, he underwent suffering at the hands of his own people (11:18-19). His suffering goes beyond Moses' because not only did he face brutal physical abuse, but also he was excluded from his community celebrations and received explicit death threats (11:9, 18, 21).

As a young man he would have liked to marry, but Yahweh barred him from entering into marriage and participating in the important events of the ordinary life of human beings such as weddings and funerals. He was to be a stranger to the joys and sorrows of village life (16:1-9; 15:17). He was whipped and put in stocks (20:2; cf. 20:7-9; 14-18). He was seized and brought before the court of the king; only the support from Ahikam prevented his death (26:24). The officials sought to cut short his life by putting him in a cistern (38:1-6). These sufferings filled him with deep anguish and a sense of powerlessness comparable idiomatically to the 'lamb being led to the slaughter' or 'being cut off from the land of the living'(11:9). In one more aspect Jeremiah appears to stand on a higher plane than Moses, i.e. in his relation to the divine word: whereas Moses heard the word 'face to face', Jeremiah experienced the 'informing' of the word within himself (Jeremiah 1:9). He was dragged against his will to Egypt where he died. In these ways, his sufferings anticipate the suffering of the Servant (Isaiah 53).

His suffering at the hands of his 'enemies' caused him at times to call upon God to visit them with vengeance (11:20; 12:3; 15:15; 17:18), and on one occasion he asked God to deliver up their children to famine and give his foes over to the sword so that their wives might become childless and widowed (cf. Deuteronomy. 28). He always looked to God for vengeance, committing his cause and bringing his case before Him: 'to you I have committed my cause' (11:20) and 'I will bring a case before you' (12:1; cf. 20:7, 12). He became so identified with the cause of Yahweh that Yahweh's enemies became his own; yet, paradoxically, he prayed for his enemies and sought their welfare (15:11; 18:20).

Jeremiah viewed religious pluralism as the cause of his sufferings (44:2-3). The people who dragged him to Egypt had adopted religious pluralism as an ideology. Jeremiah believed that 'Jerusalem suffers because people worshipped other gods while they still owed their allegiance to Yahweh' (44:2-3). In contrast, the people believed that 'Jerusalem and we suffer because we stopped worshipping the queen of heaven as we continued worshipping Yahweh' (44:15-18). It is, however, through the Servant that God comes into contact with human suffering in the most physical and intimate way.

The Servant of Isaiah 40-55

The insight into the Servant's response to suffering is found in the four hymns called the Servant Songs: 42:1-7, 49:1-7, 50:4-9 and 52:13-53:12. The Servant stands in the Moses-Jeremiah prophetic tradition. While continuous with those who preceded him, his suffering appears to be volitional (willing) and vicarious (for the sake of others). Whereas, the Word was spoken to Moses, it was put into Jeremiah's mouth. The Word was also on the Servant's 'tongue' (50:4).

Through the Spirit, the Word found its abode in the Servant (42:1). It was embodied in the Servant. God who spoke the Word dwelt within the Servant in a special way through His spirit ('I will put my spirit in him' (42:1). The Servant's suffering was not very different from God's suffering. In the Servant, God suffered and this showed His salvific purpose for all creation, especially humanity.

The suffering motif runs through all the Servant Songs. The first song (42:1-7) does not contain explicit references to suffering. The hint to suffering is found in the Servant's determination to establish justice on earth at any cost: 'He will not falter or be discouraged till he establishes justice on earth (v. 4). The second song (49:1-7) also implicitly refers to suffering caused by the lack of response to his labours and the consequent frustration he experiences: 'I have laboured to no purpose; I have spent my strength in vain and for nothing' (v.4). The third song (50:4-9) explicitly refers to the Servant's suffering: 'I offered my back to those who beat me, my cheeks to those who pulled out my beard; I did not hide my face from mocking and spitting' (v.6). The fourth song contains the climax of the suffering in that it explicitly refers to his humble beginnings, his meagre possessions and simple (poor) lifestyle, and his disdain and rejection by society. It goes on to portray in a graphic manner the depths of humiliation, the mental and physical torture the Servant undergoes including, his death: 'he was cut off from the land of the living' (v.8).

The Response of the Servant to Suffering

The volitional element in the Servant's suffering is strong compared to the prophets. The Servant willingly accepts the suffering: 'I offered…' (50:6). Yet, at the same time, the suffering was given to him by God. It was God's will to crush him and cause him to suffer (53:10). Here God's sovereignty and human freedom work in perfect harmony. God's will blends with that of the Servant. There has been in theological circles a division between those who are hesitant to describe the Servant's suffering as vicarious and those who accept the vicarious nature of the Servant's suffering. The latter group endorses the Servant's suffering and death which were effective for the redemption of all who believe. The Servant took up 'our infirmities and carried our sorrows' (53:4); 'the Lord has laid on him the iniquity of us all' (v. 6); 'the Lord makes his life a guilt offering' (v. 10).[6]

The Servant views suffering as the means for accomplishing God's saving purpose. He seems to be conscious of his suffering as being part of God's saving purpose for humankind. Therefore, he exhibits an uncompromising resolve to undergo suffering: 'Therefore have I set my face like flint'. He knows that his stance will be vindicated: 'and I know that I will not be put to

[6] The guilt offering ('*asam*) was offered when restitution was required. The offender sacrificed a lamb. This offering can thus be viewed as a sacrifice of atonement.

shame.' The verb used here is normally used in forensic or legal contexts and means: 'showing someone to be in the wrong'. Its opposite (used here with the negative) means: 'showing someone to be in the right' or being vindicated. The Servant will be vindicated in his adoption of the way of suffering for the right cause of bringing salvation to humankind. This explains his firm resolve. Also, in the NT, the suffering of Jesus is seen as part of the salvific plan of Yahweh (Acts 2:23; 4:28).

The confidence or determination with which the Servant takes up suffering paradoxically verges on rejoicing. He is so confident of his vindication and triumph that he begins to experience satisfaction and joy in undergoing suffering. The song-writer already views the Servant as the victorious king who divides the spoils with the strong (53:12). He is pictured as the one who has conquered even death not only for himself but also for many who believe (53:1): '...my righteous servant will justify many, he bore the sins of many' (v. 11b, 12b).

Thus, the servant here takes the 'floggings of men' on behalf of David's son, restoring the sonship and eternal rule to the true Israel (all who believe as did Abraham; 2 Samuel 7:14-15; Isaiah 55:3). His suffering demonstrates his Father's faithful love. It cuts open his Father's heart that bleeds with passion for people. It is through the everlasting covenant, mediated through the Servant/Redeemer figure that the blessings of David and Abraham are passed on to the members of the new Zion, i.e., those who believe. The Servant's suffering transforms the rebellious children of Isaiah 1 into the obedient servants of Isaiah 56-66. It is through the suffering of the son of man that the saints of the most high receive holiness and dominion in Daniel 7.

From the New Testament perspective, the Servant is Jesus, the living personal incarnate Word whom God the Father sent to communicate with man. The prophet's life as the embodied word of God was partial and broken. In the prophet there is continuity with what occurs in the Christ event. God's act in Jesus Christ was the culmination of a long-standing relationship between God and the world that is much more widespread in the OT than is commonly recognised. In Jesus both the prophetic and Servant's offices are fulfilled. So God tackled the suffering of the existential world by becoming part of it, i.e. from within, and by his suffering and triumph set in motion the process of transformation of the world. Just as He sent Jesus, Jesus sends us into the world of suffering and challenges us to transform it from within.

Conclusions

God suffers in and through His prophets. He appears through the prophet like a theophany when the Word is spoken and made known. The prophet embodies God's Word and His Presence within him. The embodiment of God's presence was more completely and clearly seen in the Servant. God suffered for humanity in and through the Servant. He intends to overcome suffering and eradicate it by eliminating death itself. Therefore, suffering is existential and not essential to human beings. God chooses to be present in the finitude and frailty of the human world. He identifies and experiences the mortal condition of humanity in order to work creatively for their salvation in a new world which knows no suffering: 'I will create new heavens and new earth...I will create Jerusalem to be a delight...the sound of weeping and of crying will be heard in it no more' (Isaiah 65:17-18); 'He will wipe every tear from their eyes. There will be no more death or mourning or crying or pain, for the old order of things has passed away'. (Revelation 21:4; cf. Ezekiel 37; Isaiah 54:13-14; 65:18-19)

The Cross in the Gospels

Babu Immanuel

Dr Babu Immanuel is Professor of New Testament Studies at SAIACS, Bangalore, India

Introduction

According to Cicero, crucifixion was 'the most cruel and repulsive, the most horrible form of death penalty.'[1] Therefore, 'The very name of the cross should never come near the body of a Roman citizen, nor even enter into his thoughts, his sight, his hearing.'[2] Hans Küng writes, 'The cross of Jesus was bound to strike an educated Greek as barbaric folly, a Roman citizen as sheer disgrace, and a devout Jew as God's curse.'[3]

In the Gospels and the book of Acts, it appears that the evangelists present the cross at two levels. At one level, it is the culmination of and an inevitable sequel to the various conflicts between Jesus and the Jews and their leaders. At another level, the cross is part of God's definite plan (he boule tou theou) and his foreknowledge. The purpose of this essay is to briefly study these two levels of the Gospels' (and Acts') presentation of the cross in order to draw some broad insights for conflict-ridden contexts.

The Cross and Conflicts

It is evident from the Gospels that Jesus was destined for conflict. Simeon had long before predicted that Jesus was '…destined for the falling and the rising of many in Israel, and to be a sign that will be opposed…' (Luke 2:34-35a). From the outset, Jesus' ministry inevitably leads him into conflicts of various kinds. As the end approaches, Jesus 'sets his face resolutely towards Jerusalem' (Luke 9:51). To his disciples he predicts that in the capital he will receive a final national rejection and crucifixion (Mark 9:12; Luke 18:31ff.): 'You rejected the Holy and Righteous One' (Acts 3:14). Crucifixion was, however, a necessity: 'I have a baptism to undergo, and how distressed I am until it is completed!' (Luke 12:50).

---

[1] Cited in Küng, 1977: 396

[2] Küng, 1977

[3] Küng, 1977: 397; Küng's emphases.

The rejection motif is poignantly presented in the Gospel of St. Matthew. Starting from the infancy narrative until the passion narrative, Matthew portrays Jesus as a rejected figure. In the birth story, Herod's killing of the male children could have prematurely ended Jesus' life, if there was no divine intervention (2:1-13, 22) but it appears as if Jesus is already on his way to the cross. At the trial scene in 27:25 the Jews bear the responsibility for and the consequences of Jesus' death sentence: 'Let his blood be on us and our children!' Therefore, Matthew blames 'all' (*pas*) for the death of Jesus (24:25).

In Acts' mission discourses, Luke makes it clear that it was tragic that the Jews repeatedly rejected and crucified Jesus:[4] 'You that are Israelites…this man (Jesus) handed over to you…you crucified and killed by the hands of those outside the law' (Acts 2:22-23). Although the 'lawless', i.e. the Romans, have physically crucified Jesus, Luke is persistent in maintaining that the cross of Jesus was the result of a free choice by the Jews: 'The entire house of Israel…this Jesus whom you (i.e., the ordinary Jews and their rulers [Acts 3:17]) crucified' (Acts 2:36; cf. 3:18; 13:27-29; 26:23).

Thus, the learned elders, the chief priests and the scribes (Mark 3:6; 8:31; cf. Acts 2:23; 3:12-14, 17) oppose Jesus, because they have been provoked by Jesus' words and deeds. Firstly, they were offended with the followers he chose[5] and the company he kept (e.g. Mark 2:16). One of them was a tax collector. Nothing that Jesus did gave greater offence than the choice of Matthew, the tax collector, to be a disciple. How could Jesus accept the servant of an invading and extortionist power (cf. Luke 3:12-13)? Besides, he associated freely with the lowest class of the population - with publicans, harlots, and sinners (Mark 2:13-17 and parallels).[6] When Simon the Pharisee was entertaining Jesus, he never doubted that, if Jesus had been a prophet, he would have known the identity of the woman who was touching him (Luke 7: 36-50, esp. 39).

Secondly, Jesus' seeming anti-Sabbath stance was amply clear as he was seen by all to be 'working' on the Sabbath (Mark 3:1-5). His rules for interpreting the Sabbath obligations touched the core of Jewish religious sensitivity and identity (Mark 2:23-28; 3:1-6 and parallels; John 5:1-18, esp. v.16). On several occasions, Jesus did not himself practice, nor encourage his

---

[4] See Tannehill, 1985: 69-85 for the tragic aspect of the Jews in Luke and Acts

[5] For instance, Simon the 'Zealot' (Luke 6:15; Acts 1:13): 'One of the twelve, therefore, was a member of the Zealots, the most aggressive advocates of rebellion against Rome.' See Burrows, 1977: 109. Perhaps the choice of Simon, the Zealot, was one of the points that Caiaphas raised in Jesus' trial linking Jesus with the criminal *kanna-im* (the Canaanite) movement, the Zealots. This was evidence, in Caiaphas' view, to Jesus' seditious tendency. See G. Thomas, 1987: 193

[6] Luke's account gives the impression that Jesus was inconsiderate. Perhaps Jesus actually ignored the niceties of polite behaviour on such occasions and preferred to act like the tax collectors and sinners with whom he usually mixed. Thus, it is likely that the Pharisees thought of him as a representative of that class. See Burrows, 1977: 173

disciples to practice many ritual observances, such as fasts and the washing of the hands before meals (Luke 11:37-54).

Thirdly, Jesus' claims to unique religious authority, and his promise of salvation to the Gentiles also contributed to the conflict (Luke 4:16-30). In addition, the so-called 'cleansing of the Temple' episode was a demonstration against those who profaned the sacred portals of the Temple by their commercialisation of religion (Mark 11:15-19). When Jesus appeared to have equated himself with God by claiming to be the Son of God or Messiah he provoked the utmost disquiet among them (Mark 1:1-12; 14:3-9; cf. Luke 7:36-50, esp. vv. 47-48; John 5:17-18; 1:1; 19:7). All of this jeopardised the status quo set by the religious hierarchy. These and other aspects in Jesus' public ministry, message, and activity confirmed the misgivings of the ritually pious and religiously learned Pharisees, who labelled him a 'social deviant' deserving death.[7]

Furthermore, the trial scenes of Jesus show that he was accused of being a messianic pretender (Matthew 26:63; 27:11, 17, 22, 27-31, 37), perverting the nation, forbidding people to give tribute to Caesar and an impostor (Luke 23:2-5). John adds that the whole body of the Sanhedrin presented Jesus to Pilate as a criminal (18:30). Malina and Neyrey consider such charges as unusual labels.[8] Labelling is a social name-calling, which is a type of interpersonal behaviour.[9] Names function as social labels by which another person comes to evaluate and categorise the person presented by the name either positively or negatively.[10] Of particular relevance to our present purpose is negative labelling such as 'the demon possessed' (Luke 11:15), 'perverting the nation', 'rebel' (Luke 23:2,5), and a 'criminal' (John 18:13). Conflict, then, can be expressed and monitored in the ways people use derogatory names and epithets against outsiders.[11] Such negative labelling or name-calling accuses a person of being a 'deviant' - someone radically out of social place.[12] It is evident then that Jesus was crucified because someone labelled him a deviant. The end of this process is called 'Status Degradation Ritual'[13], which in the case of Jesus describes his arrest and trial, public humiliation and crucifixion. His crucifixion, particularly his burial, 'marks the successful completion of the degradation ritual'.[14]

---

[7] Malina and Jerome, 1991: 97-122, esp. 110.

[8] Malina and Jerome, 1991: 99

[9] Malina and Jerome, 1991: 100

[10] Malina and Jerome, 1991: 99

[11] Malina and Jerome, 1991: 99-100

[12] Malina and Jerome, 1991: 100. Malina and Neyrey trace the Deviance Process in general and as applying to Jesus (based on Luke-Acts). See Malina and Jerome, 1991: 102-117

[13] Malina and Jerome, 1991: 107

[14] Malina and Jerome, 1991

The trial scenes also demonstrate that the protocol of justice had been totally flouted. In Acts 2:23, Luke affirmatively states that Jesus was 'crucified, and killed by the hands of those outside the law (*anomon*).' McGarvey sees *anomon* as simply a description of the 'wicked' (KJV) inclination of the Jewish leaders who influenced the Roman authorities to crucify Jesus.[15] But there may be more here than a mere reference to either Jews or Gentiles as such. *Anomos*, composed of a (without), and nomos (law), actually suggests one who acts outside the confines of law. They are 'Men without law, who recognize no law for their conduct, like men in high and low stations today who defy the laws of God and man.'[16]

In Acts 8:35, Luke further affirms, 'In his humiliation justice was denied him.' Plumptre feels that the meaning of the phrase is that Jesus, because of his refusal to defend himself, was robbed of justice.[17] The trial scenes show the egregiously flawed trial of Jesus with numerous moral and legal irregularities. Some even suggest as many as twenty-seven serious legal and ethical breaches of jurisprudence in the trial of Jesus.[18] Earle H. Wingo, a prominent criminal defence attorney concludes that the entire proceedings of Jesus' trial were no more than a mockery of the judicial system of Jesus' time and a farce.[19]

At the end of the deviance process and the trial, Jesus goes through what is called 'Status Degradation Ritual'[20] - his arrest and trial, public humiliation and crucifixion. His crucifixion, particularly his burial 'marks the successful completion of the degradation ritual'.[21] Jesus was rejected and that is clearly shown by the fact that his death occurred 'on a tree' (5:30; 10:39; 13:29), a symbol of rejection. In 13:29, the reference to the tree alludes to the accursed death described in Deuteronomy 21:23 (cf. Galatians 3:13).

Thus, from the point of view of the Jewish people and their leaders, Jesus' career had been ended prematurely before it sabotaged their preferred status quo (John 11:47-48). Ironically, however, they were deluding themselves that the cross marked the end of Jesus' career. The irony here is that the evangelists know and perceive more than the Jewish characters in the crucifixion story.[22]

From the Evangelists' point of view, in the story of the cross, the so-called 'Divine Contrast' was at work.

[15] McGarvey, 1963: 33

[16] Robertson, 1930: 29

[17] For instance, Plumptre, 1959: 53

[18] Corley, 1992: 851

[19] Wingo, 1954 and Goldin, 1952

[20] See Malina and Neyrey, 1991: 107

[21] Malina and Neyrey, 1991

[22] See Scholes and Kellog, 1968: 240

The Cross, Divine dei and Divine Contrast

The 'Messianic Pretender' in Matthew (26:63) is the righteous sufferer par excellence in Luke. Luke 23 makes allusions to Psalm 22:18; 31:5 where the Psalmist laments the suffering of a righteous person. Luke applies this pattern of suffering to Jesus and suggests that this was fulfilled in Jesus (Luke 23:34-36, 46). Throughout his Gospel, Luke maintains that Jesus is innocent (23:4, 14-15, 20, 22, 47). Luke 23:47 makes a climactic assertion that Jesus was innocent and yet he suffered despite his righteous status (*dikaios*).

Luke repeats the theme of righteous Jesus' suffering, particularly in the speeches in the book of Acts. According to Acts 2:23-24, the righteous sufferer is vindicated in his resurrection (Cf. Psalms. 18:4-5; 116:3-4). Acts 3:14-15 affirms that Jesus is 'the Holy and Righteous One.' Acts 4:10 and 5:30 repeat the same theme of the vindication of the righteous sufferer.

The story of the cross also shows that those who attempt to thwart the divine plan, actually act as catalysts for its actualisation. As Luke states, the cross is part of God's definite plan and foreknowledge (*he boule tou theou* [Acts 2:23]). The employment of the cause-and-effect sequence shows that it is God who ultimately determines Jesus' destiny and not humans. Therefore, the cross is not a scandal.[23] The same thought is reiterated by the evangelists, particularly Luke in their use of *dei* (it is necessary) or divine necessity.[24] The use of *dei* in Luke in relation to Jesus' death is significant. In Luke's scheme, certain things must precede Jesus' death. A Passover lamb must be sacrificed as Jesus and his disciples gathered for a final meal (22:7). The Son of Man or the Christ must suffer, be crucified in Jerusalem, and be raised (9:22; 13:33; 17:25; 24:7, 26; Acts 17:3). The scriptures must be fulfilled in that Jesus must be numbered with transgressors (Luke 22:37=Isaiah 53:12), and certain events predicted of Christ must occur (Luke 24:44), and finally, Judas' fall must happen according to Acts 1:16. Thus, the cross was not an accident. It was part of God's definite plan and foreknowledge (Acts 2:23). This is further highlighted by the fact that Jesus repeatedly showed his prescience about what was awaiting him (Mark 8:31; 9:31f.; 10:33f. and parallels; cf. John 18:4).

John's 'hour' motif is evidence of this preparatory process. In John 2:4, Jesus says to Mary, 'My hour has not yet come.' Necessarily, he will have to wait to go up to Jerusalem till his hour comes (John 7:6, 8). Even after he had gone up to Jerusalem, the Jewish authorities were not able to arrest him because his hour had not yet come (John 7:30; 8:20). Later, when some Greeks ask to see him, Jesus replies, 'The hour has come for the Son of Man to be glorified' (John 12:23). That Jesus refers to the 'hour' of his death is indicated by his statement that a grain of wheat must fall on to the earth and die in order to bring

---

[23] Haenchen, 1971: 180

[24] Grundmann says: 'The whole of God's will for Christ and for man is thus comprehended in the *dei*...' See also Cosgrove, 1984: 168-90

forth much fruit (v.24). In 13:1, John writes, 'Jesus knew that the time had come for him to leave this world and go to the Father.' Therefore, his arrest, trials, and crucifixion do not take him by surprise. Even Judas' betrayal was part of a grand plan since Jesus had predicted it much before his death (John 13:21-27). At several other points within the discourse Jesus alludes to his approaching death (John 13:36; 14:2, 12, 19, 28; 16:5, 16, 28). Later, he adds an explanatory note that it was for this very reason that he came to this hour (John 13:27). In 17:1, again, according to John, Jesus announces that his hour has come and he refers to the completion of the work God sent him to do (v. 4). The mission of Jesus always included the cross, and this cross lay before him from the beginning of his ministry. Thus, the use of 'the/my hour' (*hora*) in John from the very opening episode of his ministry is a means of narrating the whole ministry from the perspective of Jesus' death, or with Jesus' death in view. This means that in John's gospel the death of Jesus was no accident, but an integral part of God's plan for human salvation.

Finally, in the Garden of Gethsemane Jesus declares that the cup, meaning the cross, he was about to drink was God's will (Mark 14:36; cf. Luke 22:42). Therefore, for Mark, Jesus dies on the cross as God's Son (15:39). It is significant, however, that this recognition comes, not from Jesus' kinsmen, but from a Roman centurion, highlighting the fact that the implications of Jesus' death now exceed Jewish boundaries. Already Mark has informed his readers that Jesus inaugurated his mission as the Son of God (1:9-11) and now at the end of Jesus' life, Mark reiterates that Jesus is the Son of God (15:39). With this recognition, the Gospel of Mark assumes a coherent whole, an *inclusio*.[25]

The Divine Contrast Scheme in the story of the cross is also evident in the Gospels' portrait of the cross as vicarious and sacrificial.

Vicarious and Sacrificial Death of Jesus

The three passion predictions of Jesus in Mark 8:31; 9:31; 10:32-34 and the ransom saying of Jesus in Mark 10:45 underscore the crucial importance of the cross to God's plan of salvation, that is, without the cross, there is no ransom. Similarly, in Luke 22:20 and Acts 20:28, Luke speaks of Jesus' vicarious death. At the Last Supper, Jesus shared a cup that commemorated 'The new covenant in my blood which is poured out for you' (Luke 22:20). In Acts 20:28, Luke makes a retrospective reference to the cross. The church has been purchased with the blood of Jesus. Jesus is again portrayed as a sacrifice whose death gave birth to the new community, 'the church of God.' The Lukan picture or emphasis of the cross does not show or explain how the cross signifies forgiveness. Luke simply points out repeatedly that the cross has made it possible for humans to be related to God.

---

[25] 'An *inclusio* is a pattern in which a paragraph or longer portion ends in much the same way in which it began.' See Zuck, 1991: 140

In many places John employs the language and imagery of sacrifice in his account of Jesus' death. At the beginning of Jesus' public ministry John the Baptist declares that he is the Lamb of God (1:29, 36). John's qualifying statement, 'who takes away the sin of the world' in 1:29 is a clear indication of the sacrificial imagery present in the context. The vicarious nature of Jesus' death becomes much clearer in the Gospel of St. John. The outworking of God's plan of salvation is one of John's major emphases: 'For God so loved the world that he gave his one and only Son, that whoever believes in him shall not perish but have eternal life. For God did not send his Son into the world to condemn the world, but to save the world through him' (John 3:16-17). In the Bread of Life discourse (John 6:51), Jesus declares, 'This bread is my flesh, which I will give for the life of the world.' This verse looks at Jesus' death (i.e., the giving of his 'flesh') regardless of any secondary allusions that the statement may contain. Because this is said to be given for the 'life of the world,' a sacrificial motif is present here. Similarly, in 12:32, Jesus refers to his death, 'And I, when am lifted up from the earth, will draw all men to myself.'

As Jesus instructs his disciples to love each other as he has loved them (15:12), he gives concreteness to the nature of this love by defining its extremity as laying down one's life for one's friends (15:13). This is what Jesus will do. Probably, the basic salvific meaning of Jesus' washing of his disciples' feet is that it symbolises his vicarious death for them.[26] John's most extensive presentation of Jesus' death as a vicarious sacrifice occurs in the so-called parable (*paroimia*) of the good shepherd (10:1-16), which culminates in Jesus' identification of himself with this figure. The good shepherd is the one who lays down his life for his sheep. Clearly, this statement has been made with his sacrificial death in view.

Jesus' Cross and Glorification

Luke makes a passing reference to the cross being the means to glory: 'Was it not necessary that the Messiah should suffer…and then enter into his glory?' (Luke 24:26). But it is John who sees the glorious side of the cross more than any other evangelist. In his view, Jesus' death is the revelation of God's glory. John presents this by means of two terms, i) being glorified and ii) being lifted up. In John 3:14-15, reminiscing the story of the serpent in the wilderness (Numbers 21:4-9), Jesus explains that by looking at him in faith when he is lifted up on the cross one can be saved.[27] Jesus' death is the hour of his glorification (John 7:39; 12:16; 12:23; 13:31, etc.), in which his glory and the glory of God are revealed. When Jesus himself says that the hour has come for the Son of Man to be glorified (John 12:23), he is pointing toward his own death, now viewed as imminent (John 12:24-25), and to his death understood as

[26] See J.C. Thomas, 1991: 94f. citing Barrett, 1978: 441

[27] For more details, see Bennema, 2002: 116, 118 etc. and Bennema 2005: 135

a revelatory event: 'Father, glorify thy name' (John 12:28). The idea of being lifted up, exalted, is in John integrally related to glorification (John 3:14; 8:28; 12:32). Thus, the concept of glory (*doxa*) in the Fourth Gospel is intimately connected with Jesus' death.

Jesus' Response to Injustice

From the human point of view, the cross of Jesus epitomises injustice, betrayal, denial, dehumanisation, pain, and vulnerability. The cross exposes the mis-matching or the incongruity of values. Jesus stands for forgiveness (Luke. 7:47-48; John 8: 1-11), human equality and dignity (Mark 2:15), mercy more than sacrifice (Matthew 12:7), doing good (Mark 3: 4,5; Acts 10:38), and inner cleanliness more than social niceties (Luke 11:37-54). Does such a person deserve the cross? But Jesus' response to the injustice of the cross was determined by the Divine Contrast Scheme.

Luke sums up Jesus' response in one phrase, 'Father, forgive them; for they do not know what they are doing' (Luke 23:34). The elders and the chief priests and the scribes and the Jewish public did not know what they were doing because they failed to understand the true identity of Jesus. The person whom they have adjudged as a social deviant, and accursed (cf. Galatians 3:13) was actually the long expected Messiah, the Son of God. The convicted felon was God's only Son. If Jesus wanted, he could have taken full revenge on his enemies (Matthew 26: 53), but that was not his way. His attitude was one of infinite forgiveness (e.g., Matthew 18:22ff.). This is a deliberate reversal of the 'Lamech Syndrome' - to avenge seventy-sevenfold (Genesis 4:18-24; esp. v.24).

Conclusion

The argument of this essay so far has been that the cross of Jesus, viewed from the human point of view, is the culmination of and an unavoidable finale to the various conflicts Jesus had with the Jewish religious leadership. By crucifying Jesus, his opponents deluded themselves into thinking that they had won their case. From God's point of view, however, the cross is not a defeat, for the lifting up of Jesus plays a salvific role. What conclusions or insights can we then draw from the story of the cross for situations of conflict anywhere?

The first thing to note is that the way of the cross is the way of anyone who wants to follow Jesus. In Mark 8:22-10:52 (and parallels), Mark shows the correlation between the way of Christ and that of his disciples. The fate of Jesus is the fate of his disciples as well. The way of the cross is the way of the disciples as well: 'If anyone would come after me, he must deny himself and take up his cross and follow me' (8:34). If Jesus' mission is characterised by his suffering, then it automatically follows that the followers of Jesus must also situate their life and mission within the matrix of Christ-like suffering. Jesus asks John and James if they would drink the cup of the cross that he is about to drink (Mark 10:38-39). Discipleship is sharing Jesus' fate.

Secondly, Jesus' conflict with the Jewish religious authorities and the trial scenes reveal that the values that Jesus preached and championed were directly antithetical to those of the Jewish religious authorities. The cross is evidence to the fact that when like Jesus one stands for such values, often the opposition can come from insiders. The cross is also God's way of unmasking human hypocrisy - the travesty of professing to fulfil God's commandments but not subjecting oneself to them.

Thirdly, today's world is beset with socio-economic and political conflicts, fanatical ideologies, resurgent religious fundamentalism, commercialism and consumerism that often lead to conflicts at various levels. On the personal front, what does the Cross of Christ mean for people whose lives are intertwined with traumatic personal histories of abuse, depression, deprivation, and conflicts of various kinds?[28]

The conflicts that Jesus encountered and contemporary conflicts are not comparable. However, wherever justice is an issue and wherever human dignity is at stake, the Cross is present proclaiming the message of forgiveness and non-violent atonement. The dictum *christus victor* is correct, not politically, but theologically. The cross of Jesus is God's decisive act of questioning the legitimacy of violence, conflicts and injustice.

The cross is a prophetic voice against injustice. It invites us to live as he lived and taught. Even in the face of conflicts Jesus pointed a way to an alternative Kingdom of God and demonstrated in his own life that one can live as though one already belongs to it. His death shows that people caught up in situations of conflict and injustice can walk on the via dolorosa themselves and appropriate the story of the unjustly crucified Jesus as their story. They can find in it the power they need to survive. This death affirms their innocence, refutes the claims of supremacists, sanctifies their suffering and situates them within the cosmic drama. It also empowers them to continue to forgive and love. Jesus could not have put an end to violence and conflict without becoming a victim of it. This is the example his disciples ought to follow.

The cross reveals that when we stand for what Jesus stood for, we may end up in direct confrontation with the opposing values. The cross is the cost of standing up for the values and principles of the Kingdom, and yet, as John points out in his Gospel, the cross is the stepping stone to coronation and glory. Our context and values must be subjected to the criterion of the crucified Christ. This is the sole determinant for discerning the correct basis for Christ-centric and cross-based change.

---

[28] See Inkeles, 1999: 39. Inkeles states sociologists explain that the one dominant reason for most of the conflicts is 'the endless struggle between those without advantages, who wish to secure them, and those with privileges who wish either to get more or to prevent others from taking what is available.' See also Coser, 1956 and Galtung, 1959: 67-84

THE CROSS AND POWER: THE PARTING OF THE WAYS[1]

Kenneth Cragg

Dr Kenneth Cragg was the first bishop in Jerusalem in 1939 and is an internationally known speaker and writer on Christian-Muslim issues

Introductory

That there are 'sympathies' in contrasts is obvious enough when the central issue causing them is the same but is given a divergent answer. I have traced, in an earlier publication, the single Semitic, scriptural theme of a created order made susceptible to human management-in-trust and of that trust summoned by prophethoods into a directed, tutored fulfillment of autonomy thus pledged to the divine glory. Comparably, whether in the Bible or the Qur'an, that prophetic office found itself in the prolonged experience of a humankind chronically resistant to the vocation and perverse with the trust. Prophethood became a cumulative register of travail and 'burden', undergoing the harsh consequences of an unwantedness that brought frustration to its message and dismay or despair to its bearers. The divine 'means' in words, to convince, persuade, recruit and achieve the human concurrence, seemed to fail of its divine 'ends' in ordaining the 'deputy-ship' on which all turned, and that by explicit divine intent.

In their perception of this situation the Qur'an and the New Testament take radically contrasted courses in response.[2] The Qur'an's was the Hijrah, the deliberate quest for the deployment of power, despite the earlier clear and exclusive mandate for balagh and despite its own question: 'Do you think that you can compel men to believe?' (Sura 10.99) addressed to Muhammad himself.[3] The New Testament's response lay in a studied renunciation of power and an impulse for the saving principle of redemption, identified in the measure of 'Christ crucified'. Great controversy turns in both areas on the antecedents in either case and on the interpretations that were told to them in their respective

---

[1] See Cragg, 2004: 38-50. Reprinted with permission

[2] The study has to be of these two, not of the Qur'an and the Bible as a whole. Here we concentrate on where 'the parting of the ways' belongs.

[3] The confining of Muhammad to 'message' alone is frequent, as in Sura 5.99, 13.40, 24.53, 29.18, 36.17 and 42.48. The *hisab*, the 'reckoning' belongs to Allah. The 'sentness' is within its contents, not beyond them.

communities. Here the tașk is the exposition of the answers in either, and how, in their utter disparity, they were united as relating to a common divine/human ordering of a creation-in-trust.

The issue at stake might be expressed in the words of Paul to the Romans: 'Be not overcome of evil, but overcome evil with good' (Romans 12:21). Each, Qur'an and Gospel alike, were set to ensure that (negative) 'not overcome'. They would differently conceive of the second, more exacting (positive) that might 'overcome the evil', whether by the force that fails in 'overcoming' or 'overcomes' without being subdued, or by a redemption that left nothing unresolved. What, we have to ask, is the measure of 'the good' which effectively 'overcomes' the evil? The 'evil' thus far is merely verbal. It is what the Letter to the Hebrews called 'the contradiction of sinners' (Hebrews 12:3) using a rare Greek word *analogizomai*, meaning, exactly, hostile 'language' rebutting the 'saying' of the word-bearer. The Qur'an in many places makes almost a refrain of that encounter, 'They are saying... say thou.' Whether there or in the Gospels that verbal confrontation steadily threatens, on the public side, to pass into more than verbal exchange. What then does the word-bearer do? Have the 'word' speak in another language, as Jesus had long been doing in ministries of healing or, realising that the issue of his words is steadily creating a crisis around his person, take countering action? If so, what action is congenial with the words thus far and with the message they bring? It is useful to take the Qur'anic answer first, while holding in mind how the two situations agree as being 'the place for an answer'.

Hijra and Power

The answer in the Qur'an would seem to have been forming by the logic of the years around 619 of Muhammad's *sirah* or 'word-career'. There was something in his situation akin to that which kindled the prayer that ends the *te deum laudamus* in another liturgy: 'Lord, in Thee have I trusted; let me never be confounded.' For as Tradition narrates it, he was by then being very sharply 'confounded' in the seeming fruitlessness of his mission. The 'word' of the One, and omnipotent Allah was being refused in the name of non-entity deities whom the Meccans falsely invoked. Like the 'one who had learned' in Isaiah 50:4 and thereby given to carry a message 'ripe for hearing', he had incurred only calumny and reviling.[4] How was the contradiction, in such harsh terms, between his 'truth' and their 'falsehood' to be resolved?

That painful questioning was made the more urgent by his increasing

[4] The passage, among the so-called 'Songs of the Servant', is very apt to what is thought to be the 'way into being scriptured', i.e. a 'tuition' making the hearer 'one apprised of meaning', thanks to a diligent 'attention', as the condition of having a 'speaking tongue'. This 'wakening' is serialised 'morning by morning' or as often the Qur'an sees it 'night by night'. Truths come as 'dawnings'

loneliness following the deaths of Abu Talib, his uncle and stout protector and of Khadijah, his wife and mainstay in his vocation. Perhaps Mecca as his first locale was not to prove the scene of verbal success. Prospecting outside it, at least in the ill-fated venture up to Al-Ta'if, proved painfully barren. The only promise, and that not yet a sure one, lay in the interest shown by men from Yathrib during a visit to Mecca, when they had requested a preacher to come their way. When, the next year, a deputation returned and entered into a compact with Muhammad to afford him sanctuary, we may conclude from the Tradition that it represented what his perplexity logically, if not deliberately, sought as an answer by which 'non-confounded' he might be.

It was a drastic 'migration' on four counts. It would involve a seeming abandonment of Mecca, the decisive locale of his mission with the Ka'bah of Abraham's rearing and the environs of his personal call. Secondly, it would entail for most of his followers a rupture of their tribal bonds and a venture into the 'bond' of religion alone - a major crisis for them all.[5] Thirdly, there was much that was potentially precarious in the prospect of the Yathrib reception, seeing that the offer of sanctuary had been made only in the name of some Yathribites with goodwill towards him. These ansar as they would come to be named or 'aiders' could not ensure the welcome of the whole population. Fourthly, if not immediately apparent, the new venue would come to mean the end of the long powerlessness of the preaching years in Mecca, the prime period of 'defenceless' religion, left behind in a radical shift of character and definition as the price of a perplexity resolved and an ensured 'rescue' from impasse.[6]

Given how crucial the Hijrah was both in thought and deed, it is surprising that it seems nowhere to have been explicitly commanded in the Qur'an. By dint of the chroniclers of the *sirah*, we can locate two proximate references to the event and the miraculous preservation of Muhammad and his father-in-law companion Abu Bakr in the famous cave incident, thanks to the diligent spider.[7]

---

[5] This quality in the personal *hijrah* has often been stressed by recent writers. It was also a radical break with the strong tradition of tribal loyalty as this is registered in pre-Islamic poetry. *Silat al-rahm*, 'the tie of the womb' or 'blood relationship' was, in a desert society, the sole assurance of security. To belong to one's clan was the very heart of duty and survival. See, e.g., Guillaume, 1956: 41

[6] There is an interesting comment on the 'merit' of this Meccan powerlessness in Bashier, 1983. He concedes that 'in Mecca there was no ground for hypocrisy', whereas in Medina 'To be a Muslim was to ride a winning horse' Bashier, 1983: 71). Of the Meccan years, he writes: 'Perhaps it was that Islam needed a period of time in which to establish itself peacefully and on the merit of its own intrinsic spiritual and moral strength without the support of military force' Bashier, 1983 : 101). Why not so always?

[7] Some writers detect allusions to the 'cave' tradition in Sura 36:9 ('...they did not see...') and 9:40 where the word *shechinah* has been read in the sense of divine 'safeguarding'. Sura 59, however, is about another 'exile' or 'mustering' near Yathrib. Sura 18 is so named after the 'Seven Sleepers of Ephesus'.

Those had to do with physical risks. The deeper essential risks around those four issues proved also enduring and vindicated. The new 'religious' bonds availed well to discriminate the tribal ones. A new minority element would prove more than viable in its new haven so that Yathrib would be renamed *medinat al-nabi*, 'the city of the Prophet'. The defining choice of Mecca could in the sequel be at least partially retrieved. Notice would in time be served that migration from it had been in no way abandonment of it, nor of its vital significance.

It was around the fourth factor that, depending on how the factors are assessed (which is our core concern), questions painfully persisted. 'Powerlessness' would come to be a thing of the past but its being so would radically affect both the ethos of Islam, the themes of the Qur'an and, because of these, the historic perceptions of Muhammad.

At all events and on all counts, Hijrah was a pivotal event, apt to mark the outset of the Islamic calendar at 622 CE rather than a date of birth, or the occasion (unknown) of the Qur'an's first mediation. With hindsight and inter-faith assessments, the migration from Mecca to Medina has the significance the calendar indicates. For becoming empowered in steadily more political terms, Islam was transformed into what, hitherto by criteria of its first Meccan *balagh*, it had never been. The transformation came to be definitive for succeeding centuries, perpetuating the thirteen Meccan years in the Medinan form of contrasting 'empire'.

To be sure, the mediation of the Qur'an to Muhammad continued but it had a new temper and a new content, becoming concerned with the actual campaign and a running commentary on its vicissitudes, the recruiting of its resources both material and personal, and the ordering of its management in prisoners, ransoms, booty and martyrs.[8] A new will to enmity entered into Islam which had not been there before. Pre-Hijrah, there had indeed been fulsome and urgent language against the sins and ills of idolatry and a moral passion against infanticide and other *zulm al-nafs* in the pagan order. That religious intolerance developed into the passions of battle. What had been at stake between Allah and Meccan society became also what was at issue between the rival armed camps.

Of course, the situation was mutual. The Quraish had every reason to be more concerned about Muhammad 'at large' than when he had been within their own urban scene and subject to their vigilance, a vigilance only still about the impact of his words. Muhammad established in another abode, pledged to his protection, was a more suspect entity, one now liable as he had not hitherto been, to press his purpose in armed terms over hard terrain. The hostility of enemies which had already proved implacable in respect of the preacher, would inevitably become aggressive against a dangerous party that had eluded them.

---

[8] The last raises the issue whether 'martyrs' are 'made' in war when also taking victims, or only when 'witness unto death' is otherwise life-yielding.

That party would counter them in a mutual joining of the quarrel between them. So much the logic of the Hijrah ensured, but the consequences for the future expression of that original 'Let God be God and He alone' would be profound.

The power-equation brought its own implicit demands of 'hardness of heart' when arts and feats of war became 'the argument'. Courage to fight became proxy for will to witness and, with it, the snare of thinking these were one and the same. Did not the word shahid suggest both one who 'witnesses' and one who dies and the one who dies perhaps, as such, the one who kills? The Qur'an passed into a more strident tone. The resolve military engagement had to kindle had also to override misgivings drawn from human frailty, fear of death, and apprehensions about widows and orphans 'rawly left'. The shift can be readily measured in the transitions of a single word, *fitnah*, meaning whatever tempts, and so tests, the human spirit. These, of course, were one thing in the Meccan context, quite another in the Medinan. The earliest Muslims in the former had to contend with 'persecution', the customary lot of despised minorities exposed to adversarial power. With the onset of hostilities, that kind of *fitnah* becomes instead 'timidity' in the face of martial challenges. Muslims are no longer 'persecuted'. Their adversities are now those of war, on 'the suffering end' of things in war's differing terms. Being, perhaps, made casualties 'tempts' them to resist their leader's claim to their allegiance but they will only not be renegades in being ready volunteers. Later as victory ensures, *fitnah* becomes the 'sedition' to which successful causes are subject by those who conspire to undermine them. There are examples of these 'trials by base traitors' in the munafiqun of the Qur'an, of whom there were none in the Meccan years.[9] Persecutions attend minorities, seditions beset what invites the enmity or the envy of those who still oppose it.

These features were the necessary price of the 'manifest and great victory' which Medinan Islam attained.[10] Mecca at length capitulated by its own surrendering logic. Allah was vindicated as more powerful than its pagan deities who had conspicuously failed to better Him in battles. The keen failure of balagh in the impasse which the Hijrah had addressed in its own different terms had been totally reversed. Mecca had yielded. But in what terms had Islam been received? This question has been answered elsewhere.[11] What matters here is that religious faith had been historically fused with power, its means and ways, and that, therefore, something had happened which at least in

---

[9] People who sought the subversion of Islam from within by 'dissembling' a false allegiance. According to Sura 9:107-8 there was even 'a mosque of dissent' that had to be burned down. Note also the accession of 'pseudo-believers' (Sura 49:14) who had to be checked. 'Faith has not 'entered your hearts'.'

[10] The oft-repeated phrase that captures the achievement of *hajaru jahadu* 'they went forth and they strove'. The clear evidence of victory was an important dimension of it. The phrase, with one or both adjectives, appears some sixteen times.

[11] See chapter 5 in Cragg, 2004

respect of its inner assurance, was quite without precedent and would find perpetuation down the Islamic centuries as the telling model of a faith's legitimacy.

Precisely for that sequel and its long commendation to the counsels of religions, it is important to make the legitimation clear. The Hijrah, for all its 'Be hard with them where-ever you find them', was not sheer belligerence for its own sake. All that Yathrib becoming al-madinah symbolized was in the cause of the Meccan balagh. It was held to be the valid implementation of the divine quest by human means, via power, after word had failed. The lesson was that, if there is to be integrity, there must be this measure of intolerance. Incompatibles, when persistently proved such, must be subdued. There can be no honest exemption of the order of faith from the aegis of politics. Religion is right to equip itself with rulership. Prophethood was not called only to 'suffer fools (and pagans) gladly' but, at their charge and cost, to terminate their folly with the conclusive 'witness' of power and the necessary sanction of regime.

The validity of doing so derives wholly from the value and meaning of the message. The more critical the word, the more warranted the regime it takes up in its name. In appreciating Islam this must always be kept in mind. Medina was/is on behalf of Mecca and in its name. Of Meccan priority in the scheme of things there can be no doubt, both historically and essentially. Mecca had been evacuated by the Hijrah, only to be promptly re-instated there by the change of the old qiblah toward Jerusalem to convey all salat toward that umm al-qura, 'mother-city' of the faith. Hijrah, both by its personal challenge to the individual Muslim and in its definition of their Islam, gave proof that the thrust of the preaching about divine Oneness and human *khilafah* could brook no compromise. The Meccan faith must have its way and its sway. The 'reckoning', which was always proclaimed to be with Allah in line with the *balagh*, would come eschatologically 'in the end', but would also come historically in Medina's 'manifest victory'.

It is possible, as some have done, to surmise that there may have been discernible 'trials' of compromise between the Quraish and Muhammad. Before all became so far embittered there was the puzzling matter of 'the Satanic verses' on which only obscure light is thrown by the Tradition. Does Sura 53 imply that a modus vivendi was available to Muhammad, perhaps concerted by his uncle stressed by the tensions among kin and clans, a compromise whereby he would concede to the Quraish their plural worship, if they acknowledged the supremacy over them of his Allah, making his Islam a sturdy monolatry not an exclusive monotheism? (Sura 53:19-23)[12] If so, it did

[12] The 'incident' in the long Tradition is the theme of much controversy in which, either way, it is important to stress that if there was a parley Muhammad emerged strictly loyal. Some commentaries will not allow that he could ever have been thus tempted: others that, being so, he was all the more vindicated. The words 'they are but names...' 'inventions' (53:43) could fit either way, as a concessionary formula *or* as a rejectioning

not succeed. 'They are but names', Sura 53.23 insisted, human 'inventions', non-entities that Islam could not, would not, abide. If there had been a parley, Muhammad emerged from it steadfast in his *la ilaha illa-Allah*.

The second occasion, it might be argued, was at Al-Hudaibiyyah when Muhammad came, by mutual agreement unarmed, on his second bid to do pilgrimage at the still, *de facto*, pagan Ka'bah he held to be *de jure* Abrahamic. Might this measure of negotiated 'tolerance' have been sustained, seeing that on his first bid for access he had been well armed and now had agreed to come, vulnerable and dependent on Quraishi good faith? Something similar had been implicit when he had agreed that 'Muslims' reneging back to Mecca from Medina would not be returned to him, while he would return new muhajirin acceding to him - a ruling which much dismayed his faithful ones, as did his acceptance to sign the treaty merely as 'Muhammad ibn 'Abdallah', without his *al-rasul* title.

That was an empty gesture by the Quraish. For the whole treaty-making at Al-Hudaibiyyah had been a tactic anticipating final victory. It had no elements of permanence and was so soon overtaken by the climax of their surrender.[13]

The two 'compromise' episodes, if we rightly think of them as such, only confirm what the two cities symbolised in those post-Hijrah, pre-victory years, namely a faith requiring a necessary intolerance in its loyalty and a legitimate statehood in its cause. Both cities had their place in the affirming and confirming of Islam, and neither without the other. By their alliance, 'Lord, in Thee have I trusted' had its 'Let me never be confounded' for its satisfaction, and the genius of Islam would be known to the Hijri centuries.

The Cross and Power

It may seem odd to write of 'a parting of the ways'. For there is no evidence that the New Testament scenario played any part either in the logic or the event of post-Hijrah Islam, nor that 'the suffering Jesus as the Christ' was in any way present as a precedent being consciously rejected or ever positively applicable. 'Isa had been raptured to heaven and so retrieved from the hostility his mission aroused. That divine intervention made clear that he had needed it, in that clearly he had not pre-empted it by evading, or defecting, action on his own part. His readiness to have been a victim was plain enough in the very necessity

---

assertion. The passage underlies Rushdie's notorious and malicious *The Satanic Verses*; Rushdie, 1988.

[13] Though the apparent 'negotiability' of Muhammad keenly dismayed his most ardent followers who may not have recognised his strategy. For the moment access to Mecca turned on Quraishi compliance - a situation soon to end. 'Umar, for example, protested: 'Is he not Allah's Apostle and are we not Muslims and are they not polytheists?... Why should we agree to what is demeaning to our religion?' Ibn Ishaq, *sirat rasul allah*, Guillaume, 1957: 504

of his rescue. Jesus had never read himself in anything like Muhammad's situation so there was no actual 'parting of the ways'. However, in the formation of the faiths of Scriptures there most emphatically was. For some twentieth-century faith-negotiator, 'Muhammad and Jesus on the road together' might be a slogan[14] but 'the road' never historically trod was never the same road.

The crux lies in the theme of 'Messiah' so central to the New Testament's portrayal of Jesus' ministry and so far absent in the Qur'an's perspectives. Though regularly the Qur'an speaks of 'Isa (Jesus) as 'son of Mary, *al-masih*' the 'anointing' is meant as referring to his status as 'messenger', not in any way incorporating the sense of the word that gives definition to Christianity itself, namely 'the Christ of God', 'Redeemer of the world'. *Al-masih*, in that sense, is excluded from Islam's reckoning which is in line with the exclusively verbal, tutorial and legislatory form of Allah's relation with humankind in the given order of creation. Or, in the framework of any 'husbandmen parable' there are only 'messengers'.

The New Testament sees the Messianic vocation of Jesus as worked out in the day to day setting of his preaching and teaching ministry, his itineraries in Galilee and beyond, his comings to Jerusalem and the scenes of healing and compassion along his road. These all had to do with anticipations confusedly present in the popular mind-anticipations which stemmed from the long heritage of Jewish hope belonging to 'the land' and 'the kingdom', as these belonged in the mystery of 'covenant and people'. The contemporary context of Roman rule and oppression only made those hopes the more wistful and excited.

Jesus' ministry could only fulfil them by disabusing them of illusory political dimensions such as those most ardently held by the Zealots of the time. The teaching, caring ministry gave sign of a patient gentle Messianic quality - one which, for that very reason, could not fail to head into hostility and dispute because it so far disappointed. On other grounds, too, it incurred adversity for its characteristic by-passing of familiar 'establishment' notions of Scriptures and their 'official' interpreters. There was a freshness and a spontaneity about Jesus' commendation of 'your heavenly Father's' immediacy of relevance to human need and hope, as 'One who knows' and 'numbers all your hairs'.

For all the differences of time, locale and temper, we should discern 'a certain sympathy' - though with contrasted issue - between Muhammad's experience in Mecca and that of Jesus in the Gospels. Resentments grew in either case against what was perceived as inimical to tradition, disruptive of complacent ease, and fit to be opposed as uncongenial or pretentious. There were deeply local and popular factors in either case tending almost inexorably to rejection and dishonour.

---

[14] The title of Khalid, 1958, *ma'an 'ala-l-tariq muhammad wa-l-masih.*

The contrast, if we read respective Scriptures rightly, lay in that the adversities of Muhammad were taken by him as inducing the Hijrah and the process towards 'the political kingdom' which would bring 'power-success' to his preached message.[15] Those of Jesus were taken by him into the very definition of Messiahship and thence into its realisation in the self-giving of suffering love. The very evident onus there is in this contrast. For the case either made or makes reaches far into the nature of God and perceptions of humankind.

Despite contrary reading, it seems evident that Jesus deliberately turned away from Messianic patterns, whether those of the Zealotry that would militarily unseat the Romans as the Jewish Revolt decades later would attempt, or those of the ascetics who would withdraw into the desert in piety to await an eschatological hope. Jesus mingled readily with 'publicans and winebibbers' not disdaining neophytes of Rome nor forsaking human joys. Occasions 'by force to make him a king' he evaded something his popular following would joyfully have done (John 6:15).

Yet it is clear that Jesus had evoked potential hopes that could easily miscarry. As Matthew says: 'Until now the kingdom of heaven suffers violence and men of violence take it by force' (Matthew 11:12).

The 'violent' verb and noun are very harsh - 'plunder', 'seize', 'violate' almost, and denote an exercise of force born of excessive passion - something 'the kingdom' undergoes, not what it itself is doing.[16] These were zealous activists bent on diverting Jesus into seizing on their own aspiration and to activate his own mission by force. He did not do so, by deliberate repudiation of what he saw (in Qur'anic terms) as *fitnah*, a trap and a snare denying the authentic Messianic call. 'Until now' must be read as serving notice on this clamant delusion that it had no place in the days ahead as it never had in the authentic past. Hopes are often best fulfilled in being firmly denied.

The ultimate 'handing over' of Jesus in the garden of Gethsemane may well belong in this context of Messianic will in Jesus. Was Judas, by a sane conjecture on our part, seeking by his action to confront Jesus with an unavoidable decision by 'the kiss' that identified him in the darkness? Judas, who may well have been a zealot before, or still, may have reached final despair about ever having been a disciple of Jesus by that effeminate business over the 'woman with the ointment'. What had such puerile futility to do with

---

[15] Using a ready and popular adaptation of Matthew 6:33 about 'seeking first the Kingdom...' with the belief that only by power would 'the other things' be 'added'. This was the third 'temptation' offered to Jesus in the desert and rejected.

[16] It is not possible to translate *biazetai* as if the kingdom was forcing its way. The verb's form can only mean 'was being forcibly treated' (passive). It is not that 'the kingdom has been coming violently.' Cf. *harpazo* in John 6:14-15 and the always sinister sense in Luke 16:16. 'The Kingdom' was already so present as to have political activists try to adopt it to their own ends. 'Violence' does not describe God at work (cf. Matthew 11:29). For a contrary view, see Ladd, 1964: 155f.

'the Christ of God'? But if even he, this delaying, folly-indulging Jesus were at length faced with a situation he could not baulk, namely arrest, might he not at long last become a fighter, retaliate and usher in the longed-for riot that would initiate a saving rebellion? This seems a surer reading than the hint that Judas merely coveted 'thirty pieces of silver'. What were they to him?

It did not happen so and when Peter, with similar logic, drew out a sword, Jesus halted all belligerent ideas and accepted arrest after which there would be no averting the climax.

Enigmas remain in the story but what emerges, both from the logic of the whole ministry and from the subsequent reading of it in the nascent Church, leaves no reasonable doubt about 'the way that Jesus chose and went'.

There is no need to trace again the pressure of events in ministry toward this climax. At every point, something like incipient 'crosses' develop between Jesus and the priests, Jesus and the leaders, over, for example, the Sabbath, divine forgiveness, the authority of texts, the status of publicans and 'Gentiles'. They were 'crosses' in that there was a will to silence him, murmurs of ill-will towards him, urging counter-action going far beyond mere tacit disapproval.

If, inside the consciousness of Jesus, all this adversity was being pondered in the setting of Messianic vocation, how real was the precedent of suffering prophets from whose loyalties with truth that dream of 'Messiah' had come? The route seems clear from the journey of 'the suffering servant' in Isaiah to the garden of Gethsemane. 'The cup my Father gives' was how Jesus read vocation, as the very circumstances of its pursuit in place and time presented it to him, against the familiar backdrop of the travail of the prophets - the prophets from whose hope and story the Messianic theme itself had come to birth.

Throughout it has been right and honest to study the 'sympathy' between Muhammad's encounter with adversity and that of Jesus heading into his Gethsemane. It has, however, at this point, to be qualified by the crucial contrast in the two sequels. Muhammad's Meccan trauma led to Hijrah and Medina and all that ensued. Jesus' travail moved on toward the Cross. There had been in both cases a 'not being overcome of evil' through insistent fidelity. Whether there would be any 'overcoming of evil with good' would be what either, in their total contrast, would have to show.

To underline that open question and to truly appreciate the contrast, it is useful to note how the great Muslim sociologist Ibn Khaldun (1332-1406) argues in his Prolegomena (*al-muqaddimah*) that prophets must certainly organise and inspire asabiyyah, or 'collective spirit', or 'group ardour'. Jesus, therefore, ought to have let those 'men of violence', those 'enthusiasts', have their way and give them rein. A prophet needs 'prestige' among his people 'until he achieves the religious organisation God intended for him!' Otherwise there is no achieving due superiority.[17] For the New Testament community

---

[17] Ibn Khaldun, 1958: 187f and 322 and 414.

gathered by Jesus' 'prestige' it was a different order conceived in the sorrows through which it had passed in following him. How community was inseparable from faith had been assumed from the very nature of the 'witness'. Muhammad had striven to recruit disciples in Allah's Name so that *shahadah* ensued in ummah and the *kitab* found its ahl, the very 'people' of its bonding. Likewise for the Gospels it was axiomatic that the 'Messiah' would find, or found, a Messianic community. So it certainly proved in the New Testament story. What is noteworthy is how closely the pattern of defining origins was reproduced in the ensuing society.[18] The nascent Christian community proved as suffering-identified as its Lord.

Indeed there was, in the initial persecution of the newly formed Church, a clear continuity with the animus against Jesus which had culminated in the crucifixion. Saul's hostility to Stephen and those pioneers in Damascus only maintained the verdict Caiaphas had passed against Jesus. So much was evident in the meaning of his experience on the Damascus road, as presented in his friend Luke's narrative in Acts. 'Why are you persecuting me?' was the pointed question, so apposite as if the hearer's very venom concealed a struggling mind already half convinced against its own logic by virtue of Stephen's death and other factors. Much mystery clings to the drama but that surmise has a strong psychic element. 'I am Jesus whom you persecute', when the whole antipathy had been against the new community.[19]

That solidarity between Lord and people, if we rightly read it, was surely perpetuated in the sequel of three centuries of the suffering Church, victimised by Roman oppression, living under the likes of Caligula and Nero and unready and unable to challenge their imperium.

That founding condition of the Church has endured as its most fitting métier. When the 'Christian' word was first invented by jokers in Antioch it was linked with deliberate irony as denoting something despicable (Acts 11:26). The only two other uses carry a similar ignominy (Acts 26:28 and 1 Peter 4:16). Paul, in Philippians, read this situation as 'fellowship with the suffering of Christ' (Philippians 3:15), as also did Peter in 1 Peter 4:13. It was out of a sense of 'Messianic inclusion' that they explained this solidarity. The suffering Christ

---

[18] The same is true in the different faith-content and the community-shape of Islam. In its narrative of events, the Qur'an is also rehearsing what transpired in the identity-making of the faithful. The Hijrah, purposes in Yathrib, Badr, Uhud and beyond are alike sign-posts in the movement to completion of the Qur'an and of participatory Muslims in their allegiance. Each *fitnah*, for example, that occurs for them belongs in its themes.

[19] Further, the whole crux of his conversion lies in the fact that, as he recollected, the voice from heaven did not say: 'I am Christ' as any devout Jew might expect such a 'heavenly voice' to say, speaking from those 'heights' where precisely 'a Christ' could be expected to be 'riding on clouds of power'. The point was that 'the voice' from that 'Messianic' place actually identified itself with 'this Jesus' whom Saul 'persecutes'. The whole logic of what happened to him is in that clue.

was not merely the Master they preached but the one they emulated in reading their own condition in the world and their vocation. It translated into their own social relationships the perception of God expressed in Jesus' words: 'One there is who forgives...' They would do likewise, by something of the same self-expenditure, in their dealings between humans in the world. For those who believe themselves 'redeemed' are thereby called to live as 'redeemers', and only they who accept not to retaliate effectively 'redeem' thereby and draw the sting of enmity.

This inter-play between the saving story of Jesus and their conforming esteem of it is impressively evident in the way in which the New Testament literature is itself the creation of the New Testament Church. In this quality, there is no 'sympathy' at all with the Qur'an - a Scripture which its *ummah* possesses but which it did not itself compose.[20] One can only account for the New Testament as a document by virtue of the 'New Testament' as life. Those Gospels come about as texts because a community had memories. They are memories it had vital need to inscribe because the community was spreading widely in geographical expansion and coping with the passing of time. There would have been no ground for Gospel writing without communities concerned to know, because they were so distant from Galilee in Corinth and so far from Gethsemane in terms of time. Only a missionary Church could have necessitated and produced its own text.

The same factors obviously account for Letters educating this dispersed society in its own ethical life and the social expression of its faith-heritage. Dispersed it may be but it is not 'un-Messianic' and its essential character means its nurture by a monitoring apostolic authority, set as it is in a bewildering Roman and pagan world.[21] A centrifugal web of discipline belongs with a centripetal community in which the many are one by the necessity that they are many. This self-expressing quality of the Church across human frontiers, thus mirrored in its founding documents, stemmed only from its being preached. Its reach outside its Judaic birth into its 'Gentile' embrace was the direct sequel to its own content as 'historic redemption'. The hurdle it took in surmounting that long and stubborn Biblical divide was possible and achievable only by virtue of the inclusion it was able to read, of all and sundry, in the scope of the 'Messiah crucified'. All other versions of the Messianic meaning had confined themselves to 'Israel', whether as political zealotry, or Essene-style asceticism, or apocalyptic waiting. The embrace of the Cross was represented in its very shape as the gesture of divine inclusion and the unclenched hands, thrusting no fist into the air.

---

[20] Except insofar as the *wahy* from which it had mediation fused with the exchanges earlier studied, of charge and rebuttal, between the Quraish and Muhammad.

[21] So much in the impulse to 'epistle-writing' and sending is of this order, aiming to integrate the dispersed into a common discipline and to steer them through many cultural dangers.

Ibn Khaldun, at one point, opined that Christianity was 'not a missionary religion', because it pursued no Jihad, though later he agreed that it preached its balagh.[22] His instinct was that faiths were not inwardly fulfilled in the absence of a power dimension. Words, with no will to bring about a 'regime', were hardly self-consistent. Only an activism on their behalf could satisfy and vindicate their content as idea and truth. The spiritual telling was bound up with the political taking. By contrast, nascent Christianity, for three centuries, was innocent of power. Jewish Christians of that generation withheld themselves from all participation in the tragic Jewish Revolt of 670, despite great pressures on them to share the Jewish reading of the 'sacred' obligation and perhaps offset the seeming 'treachery' of their participation 'in Christ' with 'Gentiles'. In that respect, they were clearly exercising a deliberate choice, though, that context apart, one may argue that the Christian 'peace mind' was simply their option-less situation, Rome being so overwhelmingly entrenched in power. They were powerless anyway, so that there was no virtue in their acquiescence.

That case has often been made by Muslim commentary. Then the quite contrasted Arabian situation confronting Muhammad is evidence of the more ultimate vocation he was given - that of effectively subduing a feud-prone pagan society to single political control. That Jesus never enjoyed such a scenario becomes an aspect of his being 'pen-ultimate' to the Apostle for whom it was politically possible to attain and realise the ultimate reach of prophetic destiny and, once and for all, demonstrate its final, definitive shape.

The Qur'an, in its Meccan/Medinan sequence, would certainly be witness to that conclusion. For its whole ethos stands by it. In that different sense, it might resemble the New Testament, in being not the product but the register of its own mission. It effectively documents its own genius but does so in quite explicit terms of its own. Its human instrument was that of one recipient. It may be fair to say that the collective genesis of the New Testament as literature is, indirectly, the surest witness to 'the Messianic secret' according to Jesus which its community worked out in the world. For, without that origination in life and death in Galilee/Jerusalem, it would never have been.

The 'power-innocence' of the pre-Constantinian Church as more than mere de facto 'powerlessness' seems clear on further grounds. There, as one scholar writes:

> Nowhere do we hear anything of the voices of oppressed peoples who gave vent to their wrath against Rome's rapacity and destructive fury, in the manner of the King of Britain in Tacitus (Agricola 30)... nowhere the voice of painful boredom with which Rome's own writers and poets... recommended to the prudent the surrender of the capital city and flight to the country.[23]

---

[22] Ibn Khaldun, 1958: 1.473f. (note 15)

[23] Bornkamm, 1969: 21

Rather, there belongs with the Letters of Apostles a quiet presence in a harsh world, with inner resources of patience and hope. The heat, for example, in Galatians is reserved for matters of faith and moral loyalties. Where Paul is passionate it is because he is vigilant, and vigilant because he is anxious. Even in private with Philemon he handles slavery itself in the context of a de jure equality persisting 'in Christ'. If there is a 'tolerance' of what cannot be changed, there is tenacity in the light of it and sincerity enduring it. It was not an enmity-making faith, except in respect of those who disputed its Christ, for whom and with whom came the language of 'We beseech you...' or 'Ourselves your servants for Jesus' sake.' Otherwise, for their inward mood, their social order, they had 'let this mind be in you which was also in Christ' and 'Let the peace of God rule in your hearts,' where the allusion was not to an ever fleeting thing they had to guard, but a strong 'garrison' in charge of them.

To know it so is not to romanticise. There were blemishes aplenty in its story and dark shadows in its society. Yet it survived and grew in spite of Rome's rigours, for three arduous and turbulent centuries and weathered the strains its embrace of 'Gentiles' entailed especially after the devastating Fall of Jerusalem and the desperate demands of drastic self-preservation it induced in the Judaic community negotiating a parallel dispersion. Its defining formula 'in Christ' was its security until, for all its controversies of faith-definition and its human frailty, it looked attractive enough to a pagan emperor to suggest its enlistment into his imperial ambitions. That fateful turn of its privations early in its fourth century faced it with burdens and temptations that would quite transform its self-perceptions.

PART TWO

REFLECTIONS FROM CONTEXTS

Early Discourse

Denying the Cross in Early Muslim Dialogues with Christians

David Thomas

Dr David Thomas is Professor of Christianity and Islam in the Department of Theology and Religious Studies, University of Birmingham

Within a century of the death of the Prophet Muhammad in 632 AD, his followers had extended Islamic rule over a vast empire that stretched from the Atlantic Ocean in the west to the Indian Ocean in the east, and from Siberia in the north to the Sahara desert in the south. This empire absorbed vast populations of non-Muslims, including Christians, and such leading centres of Christian thought as Jerusalem, Damascus, Antioch and Alexandria. For centuries after this rapid expansion Muslims lived alongside Christians in these and the other great cities that sprang up as centres of Islamic culture, and the two faiths developed in parallel and to some extent interdependence.

It is a striking fact that at least in the early centuries of Islam Christians appear to have led their lives with little interference. Their status was defined by law, established on what came to be accepted as the agreement made between the second caliph 'Umar Ibn al-Khattab (d. 644) and Christian towns that capitulated to him. The broad lines of this pact stipulated that Muslims would protect Christians and other client communities, and in return these communities would pay a tax and recognise that they were protected people, *ahl al-dhimma* or *dhimmis*, by distinguishing themselves in public in their dress and demeanour, preserving the differences of faith and custom between themselves and Muslims, and generally deferring to Muslims in society. However, despite the clarity with which this status is defined in these terms, it seems that for much of the time under the Umayyad and 'Abbasid dynasties the regulations were ignored. Certainly, Christians were courted for their knowledge and skills as physicians, philosophers and translators, and such leading figures as the Nestorian Patriarch of Baghdad enjoyed direct access to the caliph's presence - in fact, in 781 the caliph al-Mahdi conducted a two day discussion about religious matters with the Patriarch Timothy I. Furthermore, there were churches and monasteries situated in and around the 'Abbasid capital Baghdad itself, and some caliphs were accustomed to take their courts there to enjoy the gardens and witness the spectacle of the liturgy.

The relative freedom enjoyed by Christians, despite the *dhimmi* status, is underlined by a complaint that has come down from the ninth century Muslim scholar Abu 'Uthman al-Jahiz, that Christians openly ignore the stipulations laid down by 'Umar, while Muslims applaud them for what they do, so much so that when a Muslim takes a Christian to court the judge treats them equally rather than giving the Muslim preference.[1] There may be some exaggeration in what is said here, but this complaint eloquently implies that the legal niceties that kept Christians and others distinct from Muslims in 'Abbasid society were routinely set aside.

In this atmosphere of relative social freedom for Christians (relative, because as Christians they must rarely if ever have felt total acceptance by Muslims) it is not surprising that Muslims showed considerable interest in Christian beliefs. It is no exaggeration to say that nearly all the leading Muslim religious thinkers who are known from early 'Abbasid times wrote at least one work on Christianity, and some are credited with two or more. While few of these have survived in their original form, it is evident from what has come down that many Muslims knew a great deal about Christian beliefs and had access to a surprising range of sources, including summaries of the doctrines of the major denominations that were found within the empire and accounts of great numbers of heretical sects. It would even appear that in a few cases Muslims were so expert in Christian beliefs that they could argue the merits of one denomination against another.

Christians and Muslims explored the differences between their beliefs at great length in the early centuries of Islam. On the Muslim side these explorations usually took the form of serial examinations of Christian doctrines and detailed demonstrations of their internal contradictions and illogicality. In these they often showed intimate understanding of the beliefs of Monophysites, Diophysites and Chalcedonians. But one feature that is perplexingly notable by its absence is any sustained discussion of the cross and its significance in Christian beliefs. Muslims were certainly aware of the centrality of the cross in Christian life and worship, for from the earliest times caliphs are reported granting protection to carvings of crosses on churches, and directing Christians when they processed in public with crosses to avoid the Muslim sectors of towns.[2] They also sometimes mocked the Christian custom of venerating the cross as worshipping a piece of wood. More substantially, some Muslim theologians were well acquainted with the account of the descent of the Son from heaven in order to rescue fallen humanity from the grip of Satan, and knew the formula that in Christ God had died 'for us'. Nevertheless, there is hardly any reference to the cross and its implications, apart from the odd passing mention, in any major refutation of Christianity that has survived from a Muslim hand.

The reason for this curious absence becomes apparent when the main topics of these Muslim works are examined. Taking the refutation of the ninth century Baghdad theologian Abu 'Isa Muhammad Ibn Harun al-Warraq as

[1] Finkel 1926: 18; Finkel 1927: 328-9

[2] 'Al-Salib' (the cross) (VIII) 1960

representative,[3] it can be seen from his exhaustive analysis, which was entitled The Refutation of the Three Christian Denominations (by which he meant the churches he calls Nestorian, Jacobite and Melkite), that his main concern lay with the two doctrines of the Trinity and the uniting of the divine and human natures in Christ. After an initial exposition of Christian beliefs, in which he includes among other items a full account of the differing views about the crucifixion and the death of Christ's divine nature with his human nature, this theologian then embarks on a protracted analysis of the versions of the doctrine of the Trinity that he knows, followed by an equally protracted analysis of the ways in which the uniting of the two natures in Christ was explained.

Needless to say, al-Warraq finds internal contradiction and irrationality in everything he examines. By implication, though never explicitly, he points his reader to the conclusion that any teaching which states that God is other than an absolute, undifferentiated unity, and that there could be proximity between him and a created human is inconceivable. In this way he effectively vindicates the Islamic belief in the oneness of God by showing that divergences from this norm are not viable in terms of both reason and consistency.

Al-Warraq's book, the main contents and concerns of which resemble a number of other early refutations of Christianity, emerges not so much as an examination of the doctrinal basis of the range of Christian doctrines as a scrutinisation of those Christian doctrines that directly contradict, and so could be taken to threaten, the central Muslim doctrine of tawhid, the oneness of God. Al-Warraq's interest is not so much Christianity in itself as those aspects of the faith that rival his own.

This and other examples like it from this period seem to be instances of Muslim theologians approaching Christianity for the purpose of showing how Islam is the only faith that can credibly be followed by people of sound mind. By showing the fallacies in this alternative depiction of Godhead, in its Trinitarian form and its propensity to mingle with humanity, they point to the ineluctable conclusion that only the Islamic version is correct. Here the examination of Christianity is in reality Islamic apologetic.

Of course, Muslims were supported in their ignoring of the cross by the teaching of the Qur'an that the crucifixion of Christ was not an historical event: 'And because of their [the Jews'] saying: We slew the Messiah Jesus son of Mary, Allah's messenger - They slew him not nor crucified, but it appeared so unto them' (Sura 4.157).

These words were universally taken to mean that Christ was not on the cross, with some commentators supplying the explanation that a substitute (variously identified as a disciple or even Judas) was crucified while Christ was raised up to God. But this denial alone cannot explain the wholesale lack of interest among Muslims who wrote about Christianity. Rather more plausibly, their main interest in discussing this other faith was to support the claims of

[3] D. Thomas, 1992; D. Thomas, 2002

their own by showing the defects in this rival form.

So it seems that Christians living under Islamic rule did not so much suffer persecution and threats to life and possessions - though this did happen on occasion - as suffer the frustration of being ignored as bearers of a truth about God's engagement with the world. They were rarely called on to live or die sacrificially, but equally rarely had opportunity to explain the sacrifice of Christ as the event of central significance they understood it to be. And predictably, they often reacted by judging Islam as a faith less ample and complete than their own.

Among the records of exchanges between Christians and Muslims in early times there are many which completely reject the other faith as worthless. On the Christian side it was, for example, customary to depict Islam as no more than a set of teachings borrowed by a self-seeking Meccan merchant from a heretical Christian monk.[4] But alongside such negative judgements, others were expressed that show more charity and consideration for what Islam actually teaches. Two in particular stand out.

One of these, found for the first time in the surviving works of the early ninth century Nestorian 'Ammar al-Basri, is that Islam is less developed in its perception of God than Christianity.[5] On the one hand, argues 'Ammar, the Muslim perception of God as a naked unity about whom nothing can be stated with certainty deprives him of the full character that the doctrine of the Trinity guarantees him by showing that life, knowledge and other necessary attributes are integral to his essential being. And on the other hand, the doctrine of the Incarnation takes further the Islamic doctrine of the sending of messengers and prophets. For, says 'Ammar, if God is generous enough to give his guidance to his creatures through verbal instructions, as Islam professes, then his full generosity is shown by his actual coming among his creatures to communicate with them directly. So if God is a God who really is concerned for what he has made, then it logically follows that he must come among his creatures without any barrier between in order to show his concern and love.

This early estimation of Islam presents it as a faith that contains some of the richness of Christianity, though only a portion of the whole. The other main positive judgement of Islam that can be perceived among Christians in these early centuries is related, though focusing more on the Prophet Muhammad. For Christians in all ages the status of Muhammad is, of course, problematic since he claimed to bring a teaching from God at a time after the coming of Christ. In consequence, many Christians have habitually dismissed him as a charlatan. But one judgement that is found in a succession of works through the early centuries is less uncharitable than this. It places Muhammad in the line of prophets who were sent from God, but restricts his ministry to the pagans of

---

[4] See Roggema, 2001

[5] For the Arabic text of his works and a French summary, see Hayek, 1977

Arabia alone.[6]

This judgement is found in a developed form in some letters written probably in the late twelfth century and early fourteenth century by the Chalcedonian bishop Paul of Antioch and by an anonymous Cypriot master who reworked what Paul had written.[7] These authors both concede that Muhammad was a messenger from God, and demonstrate by many judiciously chosen quotations and references that the Qur'an supports the truths of Christianity. But from the reported assertions in the Qur'an itself that it is an Arabic revelation they infer that it was not meant to be universal in scope, and they conclude that it was intended to bring the pagan Arabs of the desert away from their worship of many gods to the worship of a single God. So for these Christians Muhammad is a pre-evangelist, preparing his people for the full revelation but never delivering the truth of the Gospel to them.

The Christians who issued these estimations of Islam lived, of course, under Islamic rule. They could not, therefore, ignore the faith in practice, and because they witnessed the continuing military and political success of the empire they realised they could not dismiss it in principle. Hence they allowed that it was divine in origin, but contended that it lacked the character of the full revelation that had come in Jesus Christ. In developing these ideas they were, one might say, maintaining the potency of the cross as a climactic disclosure of God's real character, and the concern for humanity that lies at the depth of his being. Islam, they believed, lacked the full intensity of this disclosure, teaching no more than the transcendence of God and one aspect of his nature. It was only with the acceptance of God on earth and of the cross as sign of God's saving love that Muslims might be led into the fullest understanding and liberation.

In Christian eyes it made sense for Muslims to do this. It was God's intention that they should leave behind the partial revelation they had received in a book and embrace the full revelation that had come in the life and crucifixion of Christ. In this way, the curious absence of the cross in Islamic concerns would be made good.

---

[6] See Samir in D. Thomas, 2001

[7] See D. Thomas, 2001. A major part of the correspondence is edited and translated by Ebied and D. Thomas, 2005

Debating the Cross in Early Christian Dialogues with Muslims

Ivor Mark Beaumont

Dr Ivor Mark Beaumont is Vice-Principal of the Birmingham Christian College, UK

Introduction

With the arrival of Islamic rule in the nominally Christian Middle East during the seventh century came the rejection of the cross as basic to faith in God. Since the Qur'an clearly refuted the Christian claim that Jesus was put to death by crucifixion it was obvious that Muslims who encountered Christians would contend for the right way to understand the end of Jesus' life. Sura 4:157f. was interpreted by Muslims as a rebuff to a mistaken Christian teaching, for it contained the testimony of 'the people of the Book' that they 'killed the Messiah, Jesus, Mary's Son, God's messenger.' In the context, these are Jesus' own people the Jews who rejected the one sent to them by God. However, the Qur'an proceeded to refute their claim. 'But they did not kill him. They did not crucify him. Rather it seemed so to them…No, God raised Jesus to himself.' The true story was that these Jews sought for the death of Jesus but were denied the result they longed for. In fact Jesus was taken to be with God apparently without going through the natural process of death.[1] What were Christians to make of this repudiation of the New Testament accounts of the crucifixion? For them the historicity of the cross was central to their faith. Had not the Apostle Paul summarised Christian belief in 1 Corinthians 15:3f as 'Christ died for our sins, was buried, and was raised on the third day.' If Christ had not died on the cross for the sins of others then there could be no freedom from sin.

Documentary evidence of Christian dialogue about the cross with Muslims comes from the end of the eighth century, and any earlier discussion that may have taken place is not available in writing. Just after Timothy was consecrated Patriarch of the Nestorian churches in Baghdad in 780 he was invited by the Muslim Caliph al-Mahdi to give an account of a range of Christian beliefs that differed from Islamic teaching. Timothy subsequently produced a report of the discussions in Syriac and an Arabic translation came out probably in the 790's.[2]

---

[1] That Jesus escaped death altogether by being exalted to heaven has been the standard interpretation in the history of Islamic scholarship.

[2] Timothy describes his debate with the Caliph in a letter to a priest named Sergius in 782/3. See Epistle 59 in Bidawid (ed.), 1956: 42f. The Syriac text is edited and

While these written versions may not be transcriptions of the actual debate, it is hardly likely that the questions posed by the Caliph were put into his mouth unless he actually asked them. It would have been foolhardy to use the name of the Caliph as merely a literary device to cover for an invented Muslim personality. As it turned out al-Mahdi asked most of the questions only allowing Timothy the occasional counter-question. When the Caliph turned his attention to the cross he was concerned with three issues, the fact that the Qur'an denied it, the impossibility of God allowing his messenger to be humiliated by such a death, and the threat to the eternal character of God if a divine Jesus died on the cross. These became the three major themes in subsequent Muslim-Christian dialogue on the cross. We will investigate how each of these themes was discussed in the late eighth and early ninth century period of active debate between Christians and Muslims.

The Cross did not happen to Christ

It is hardly surprising that al-Mahdi quotes Sura 4:157, 'They did not crucify him' to Timothy and waits for the Christian response. For al-Mahdi, self-evident truths do not need to be defended or interpreted. Timothy declines to comment on the quoted text preferring to produce his own Qur'anic verse, Sura 19:33, where the young Jesus says, 'Peace be on me, the day I was born, the day I die, and the day I am raised alive.' He interprets this to mean, 'That Jesus died and was brought to life.' [3] It is significant that Timothy should be able to handle the Qur'an with facility, and this indicates that after a century of Islamic rule Christian theologians thought it necessary to be conversant with the Scriptures of Islam. Still, al-Mahdi does not agree with the chronological reading of the text, explaining, 'Jesus is not yet dead but he is going to die.' Here is early confirmation of the traditions about Jesus later collected in the Hadith that he will return from heaven at the end of the age, break the crosses of the churches, preach Islam and then die for the first time. [4] In other words, by the turn of the ninth century Muslims typically believed that Jesus had not died at the end of his earthly life but that he would appear again to lead humanity to the truth of Islam and ultimately die after a successful period of service. Far from the abject defeat of the cross Jesus would triumph in his role of God's messenger, and would confirm that role by breaking Christian crosses In the light of such traditions the cross must have seemed to Muslims as a symbol of a pathetic and distorted faith. Nevertheless, Timothy presses the chronological case for the priority of death over exaltation. 'If Jesus is not dead

translated into English by W.A. Mingana, 1928: 1-162. The Arabic text is edited by L. Cheikho, 1921: 359-374 and 408-418. This version is reproduced with a French translation by H. Putnam, 1975.

[3] Putnam, 1975: appendix, 45

[4] See the traditions for example in *Sahih Muslim* 1:72, 287-293

he would not have ascended to heaven. But it is affirmed by you that the ascension of Jesus to heaven and his resurrection took place a long time ago, as your book testifies.'[5] Timothy challenges, not the veracity of the Qur'an, but al-Mahdi's interpretation of it. The plain meaning of the text is surely that Jesus predicts his death before his being raised alive, so it strains the usual sense of language to reverse the normal stages of the end of a person's life. Al-Mahdi does not reply to the further questioning but proceeds to ask Timothy about the shame inflicted on Jesus if he was crucified.

The earliest Muslim writing on the cross is possibly by al-Qasim ibn Ibrahim al-Hasani al-Rassi [d 860] whose *Reply to the Christians* may have been written when he was living in Egypt between 815 and 826.[6] He knows that the belief in the cross is key to the veneration of Jesus by Christians, since his death solves the problem created by the sin of the first man Adam. The inheritance of Adam's sin by all of his descendents leaves them subject, not only to a tendency to sin, but also to the grip of Satan. Christians look to the death of Jesus as a solution to this problem through believing that 'he delivered them from the power of Satan by offering himself on the cross.'[7] Sadly, the Christians have been misled because the crucifixion never happened, as the Qur'an points out. Despite the story in the Christian gospels that the Jews succeeded in having him killed, the Jews themselves never accepted the accuracy of this claim, and so 'the Christians gave their interpretation from their own opinions.'[8] Ultimately for al-Qasim, the story in the gospels is an imaginative scenario that has kept generations of Christians in thrall to a false estimate of this messenger of God.

This outright denial of the historicity of the crucifixion and this portrayal of Christians as gullible people who cannot distinguish fact from fiction posed a serious problem for Christians who wanted to give an account of their faith to Muslims. One solution was to ignore the Qur'ānic denial and show that the death of Christ was essential in God's plan of salvation in the hope that Muslims might see the utter centrality of the cross in the mind of God. This was the method of Theodore Abu Qurra, Chalcedonian Bishop of Harran in Syria between 785 and 799 who had a reputation for debating with Christians, Jews and Muslims and who was said to have debated with the Caliph al-Ma'mun in 829. [9] In a treatise addressed to Muslims entitled, *There is no Forgiveness for Sin without the Suffering of the Messiah on behalf of Humanity*, he questions the Islamic belief that God forgives sin without the intervention of a mediator. God's mercy should not be greater than his justice and his law should not be set aside by his clemency. The role of Christ as fulfilling the law on behalf of those

---

[5] Putnam, 1975: appendix, 46

[6] See D. Thomas, 1996: 29-38

[7] Al-Qasim, 1921-2: 317

[8] Al-Qasim, 1921-2: 319

[9] See J.B. Chabot, 1899-1910: 32-4; and J.B. Chabot, 1937: 22f.

who have failed to do so is essential to the maintenance of a balance between law and forgiveness. According to 'the books of God' there is no forgiveness of sin 'without the shedding of Christ's blood on behalf of the living and the dead.' [10] Abu Qurra probably hopes to convince his Muslim audience that if the books of God, that the Qur'an claimed Moses and Jesus brought, testify to the necessity of the death of Christ for sin then it must follow that God revealed this plan and carried it out. In a frankly combative tone he concludes his treatise with this challenge. 'We in the Christian community receive forgiveness when we accept the sufferings of the Son for our sins. But non-Christians who do not accept the sufferings of the Messiah for their sins will die in their sins.' [11]

A diametrically opposite approach was to present the incarnation as the means of salvation and to play down the role of the crucifixion in that process. An anonymous apology in Arabic on the Trinity and incarnation was written by a Chalcedonian theologian probably from a Palestinian monastic milieu with copious allusions to the Qur'an in order to explain to a Muslim audience that the Christian faith in the Trinity and incarnation is consistent with Islamic beliefs. This apology closes with the words, 'If this religion was not truly from God, it would not have stood firm nor stood erect for seven hundred and forty six years.' If the writer was counting from the birth of Christ then the apology can be dated around 750 but if from the resurrection and beginning of the church then the date moves to around 785.[12] The apology may then be contemporaneous with the debate between Timothy and al-Mahdi and shows the diversity of Christian apologetics in the Muslim world of the time, both geographically and theologically. According to this writer God sent his Word to deal with the weakness of humans by putting on human flesh to make humans strong. Humans are weak in the face of Satan who continually succeeds in drawing people away from God into rebellion against him. Thus God decided to send his Word clothed in human nature to defeat Satan and set people free from his power in order to serve God. The Apology only refers to the cross once. 'He crucified sin by his crucifixion and put an end to death, which was inherited from Adam's disobedience, by his own death.' [13] However, it often refers to Christ defeating Satan by clothing himself with human nature, which suggests that the act of incarnation is key to the downfall of Satan rather than the cross. Indeed, the writer summarises his presentation of the salvation brought by Christ without mentioning his death at all. 'He came down from Heaven to save Adam's descendants from Satan and his evil, and then he ascended to Heaven where he had come from.' [14] It is probable that the

[10] Abu Qurra, 1904: 89

[11] Abu Qurra, 1904: 90

[12] Samir and Griffith support the earlier date but M. Swanson holds to the later date. See Samir, 1994: 61; Griffith, 1998: 21; and Swanson, 1993: 140

[13] Gibson, 1899: 84

[14] Gibson, 1899: 86

apologist is deliberately avoiding talk of the cross to maintain the interest of his Muslim audience. Christ came and was exalted to God as the Qur'an says. His intimate knowledge of the Qur'an used to support the Trinity and incarnation is a reason for his reluctance to challenge the denial of Christ's death found there. Accommodating Muslim sensitivities is the style and attitude of this writer, but his emphasis on the incarnation as salvific is also found in Athanasius of Alexandria [d. 373] in his work *On the Incarnation* so has Patristic support.[15] Although Athanasius was quite clear that the death of Christ defeated the power of death over humans, this apologist gives the impression that the embodiment of the Word accomplished this.

A third solution was to reinterpret the Qur'anic denial of Christ's death by crucifixion. This was the suggestion of Habib ibn Khidma Abu Ra'ita, a Jacobite theologian associated with Takrit to the north west of Baghdad, who claimed to have debated with Abu Qurra, and is named as a participant in a synod in 828.[16] In his *Letter on the Incarnation*, he deals with Sura 4:157f by arguing that the Jews claimed to have killed the Messiah but that this was not the complete truth. Indeed the Qur'an says that 'God is exalted far above what people do to slander him"[17] and this means that their claim was false. However, this Qur'anic denial of the death of Christ on the cross can be understood to agree with Christian teaching about the death of Christ.

> Since he is God incarnate he did not submit his divine essence to crucifixion and death at all, and so he was crucified and died in his incarnate state. But the Jews intended his crucifixion and death to affect his eternity, yet he is exalted far beyond that. May he be praised for raising his substance above being killed and put to death. This is an example of making lies against God, and he is greatly exalted above that.[18]

For Abu Ra'ita it was possible to read Sura 4:157f to say that the Jews claimed to have killed the Messiah but they did not kill or crucify him in his divine nature and that their claim only applied to the crucifixion of Christ's human body. This ingenious reading of the Qur'an might appear to soften the seemingly outright rejection of the cross in the Qur'an, but only at the expense of a proper regard for the context of the statement. The natural sense of 4:157f is to refute the claim of an actual crucifixion rather than allowing for a crucifixion in one sense rather than another. [19]

---

[15] See Athanasius 2006:54

[16] See his *Reply to the Melkites* in G. Graf (ed.), 1951: 65; and J.B. Chabot, 1899-1910: 50

[17] See Suras 17:43; and 4:50, 10:60, 69

[18] Abu Ra'ita, 'al-risala fi-l-tajassud' in Graf (ed.), 1951: 63

[19] This has been the almost universal interpretation among Muslims. Occasionally there have been attempts to accept that Christ was put on a cross but that somehow the truth he stood for was not put to death. In the tenth century the Brethren of Purity held such a

The Cross would be a humiliation of God's messenger

Caliph al-Mahdi suggests to Timothy that the cross dishonours Jesus and that it is inconceivable that God should 'deliver him into the hands of the Jews so that they could kill him.'[20] In reply, Timothy quotes the Gospel of John 10:17f, 'The Father loves me because I lay down my life of my own free will.' Therefore the death of Jesus did not demean him since he volunteered to die and willingly gave up the protection of God in order to give up his life to honour others. Timothy does not explain how this voluntary life-offering maintained the honour of God, but this is the central concern of the Caliph who concludes that the hideous defeat of one of his prophets would leave God looking shamefully weak. [21]

A generation later, another Nestorian theologian 'Ammar al-Basri dealt with the same accusation of the dishonour of the cross. Little is known about 'Ammar's life apart from the fact that he was treated to debate in 'a refutation of 'Ammar the Christian in his reply to the Christians,' by the Muslim scholar Abu l-Hudhayl al-'Allaf [d.c.840], which is unfortunately no longer extant. [22] In *The Book of the Proof* 'Ammar suggests that just as John the Baptist was put to death and yet was honoured as a prophet then so could Jesus be put to death and still be held in honour. [23] John's death is mentioned in the Qur'an but without the beheading story found in the gospels, and there is no suggestion in Sura 19:15 that Yahya was put to death by his enemies. [24] A Muslim would not necessarily think that John's death was dishonourable, so the problem of the alleged dishonourable death of Jesus still remains unresolved and the use of the John the Baptist parallel is not so obviously helpful. 'Ammar's second defence of Jesus' honour is the exaltation of Christ by God after death and resurrection. Christ's willingness to die for humanity enabled people to be rescued from sin, to overcome death, and to experience eternal life. As a result God gave him the highest honour, because Christ was willing to stoop so low out of love for others. [25] In a longer work, *The Book of Questions and Answers,* he offers two parables to uphold the honour of Christ's death. He asks his reader to imagine a prize-fighter who uses up all his strength to defeat an opponent, or a doctor who suffers from testing medicine before giving it to a patient. In both cases self-inflicted death leads to a positive result, and in the same way 'Christ chose to rescue humanity from wrong-doing and from slavery to Satan by submitting to

---

view. See Y. Marquet, 1982: 146. In the twentieth century Ayoub has allowed for the crucifixion of Christ but not the killing of his message. See M.M. Ayoub, 1980: 103

[20] Putnam, 1975: appendix, 48

[21] Putnam, 1975: appendix, 48

[22] See B. Dodge (ed.), 1970: 388

[23] See 'Ammar al-Basri, 'kitab al-burhan' in M. Hayek (ed.), 1977: 79

[24] See Sura 19:15, 'Peace on him (Yahya) the day he was born, the day he dies, and the day he is raised alive.'

[25] 'Ammar al-Basri, 'kitab al-burhan' in Hayek (ed.), 1977: 80f.

death in order to raise to life those subject to death.'[26] A Muslim might well ask why it was necessary for Jesus to go through death and resurrection to offer the resurrection to others. Could not the preaching of the resurrection suffice? For 'Ammar, Jesus' experience of death and resurrection proves the resurrection to humans and 'places firmly in their hearts the promise of their resurrection' [27] Therefore, Jesus honours others by accepting a degrading death on their behalf.

An alternative defence of the honour of Christ was provided by Abu Ra'ita when he argued that the death of God's Son is a demonstration of the lengths to which God was prepared to go to save lost humans. Here the focus is on the plan of God to save humanity and far from dishonouring God this proves that God chose freely to offer Christ as a gift of grace and kindness to humanity. [28] Now if a Muslim asks whether Christ died against his will merely to do the will of God a Christian should reply that Christ voluntarily laid down his life to submit to the will of God. In other words, the will of God is taken up exactly by Christ so that there is no discord between them. But if the Muslim reader of the gospels notices that Christ on the cross says in Matthew 27:46 'My God, my God, why have you forsaken me?' and then asks Christians how Christ can be said to accept his death as God's will, Abu Ra'ita suggests that rather than Christ refusing the will of God on the cross, he is merely expressing the fear of death that any human being might experience. But this all too human cry of despair should not cancel his submission to the will of God. Christ aligned his will with that of God even though he went through the pain of death. In fact the cry of dereliction proves that he was really human. 'This shows that his incarnate state was truly human just like our human natures that detest death.'[29]

A further problem is raised by Muslims who wonder how God's honour can be kept intact if the Jews succeeded in putting Christ to death. Surely this is the basic falsehood about the account of Christ's death in the Christian gospels which the Qur'an corrects? How could God allow evil people to triumph over his prophet? This was al-Mahdi's concern quoted above but not directly dealt with by Timothy. Abu Ra'ita refers to two sides to Christ's death. Firstly, in his human condition he consented to being put to death since this was the plan of God for the salvation of humanity. Thus God planned that evil people should have Christ crucified and these evil people had no power to dishonour God. Secondly, in his divine condition Christ did not consent to being put to death and humans had no power to kill his divinity and, therefore, they could not dishonour Christ. Either way, both God and Christ are exempt from any dishonour that humans thought they could bring against them. [30]

---

[26] 'Ammar al-Basri, 'kitab al-masa'il wa-l-ajwiba' Hayek (ed.), 1977: 229f.

[27] Hayek (ed.), 1977: 233

[28] Abu Raita, 'Al-risala fi-l-tajassud' in Graf (ed.), 1951: 41f.

[29] Graf (ed.), 1951: 59

[30] Graf (ed.), 1951: 60f.

The Cross would be the death of God

The third issue raised by the Caliph al-Mahdi was the damage done to the divine nature that Christians claimed Jesus possessed if he died on the cross. 'Is it possible that God died, supposing that [Christ] is [God]?' he asked the Patriarch Timothy, who replied 'in so far as he was God, Christ did not die: but in so far as he was human, in his human nature he died.'[31] The possibility of the divine nature of Christ dying on the cross was dealt with by 'Ammar in *The Book of Questions and Answers*, by accepting that only the human nature died. But his understanding of the divine and human union in Christ was that although only the human nature suffered and died, there was 'no separation or distance between them'[32] In practice this means that the eternity of God is not united with the human nature of Christ as a result of the incarnation and thus is unaffected by death. However, other attributes of God such as authority and power are united to the human nature but are temporarily reduced to impotence before the resurrection.

This separation of the divine and human natures of Christ is also found in the writing of Abu Qurra. 'The divinity abides in the Incarnate Word, not subject to any limitation, suffering or death, which belong to the human nature.'[33] 'Ammar the Nestorian and Abu Qurra the Chalcedonian were divided on the exact description of Christ's divine and human natures but they agreed that the death of Christ did not affect his eternal nature. [34] The Miaphysite Abu Ra'ita held to one divine nature animating Christ but he too agreed with his diophysite rivals that the death of Christ did not affect his eternal reality. In the argument already presented about the Jews claiming to have put the eternal nature of Christ to death but being completely mistaken, Abu Ra'ita makes the case that the Jews were mistaken precisely because they were wrong to believe that in killing Christ they could put the divine Word to death. Christ's divine nature was unconquerable. In his *Letter on the Incarnation* he directly answers Muslim objections to the death of God that appears to happen if Christ died by crucifixion. 'If God died how could he still rule the world?' [35] His reply is that God still rules the world when Christ dies since only Christ's body died. His divine nature lived on through the loss of the human body in which the divine nature had been clothed. He replies to the further Muslim question, 'why do you separate his divinity from his body and nullify the unity between them?' by arguing that the human body of the Word did not influence the Word and therefore, the loss of the body did not impact the Word.[36] This miaphysite

[31] Putnam, 1975: appendix, 44

[32] 'Ammar al-Basri, 'kitab al-masa'il' in Hayek (ed.), 1977: 224

[33] Abu Qurra, 'Confession of the Orthodox Faith' in Dick (ed.), 1959: 59

[34] See I.M. Beaumont, 2005: 28-112 for an analysis of the Christologies of Abu Qurra, Abu Ra'ita, and 'Ammar al-Basri.

[35] Abu Ra'ita, 'Al-risala fi-l-tajassud' in Graf (ed.), 1951: 39

[36] Graf (ed.), 1951: 40f.

conviction that the humanity of Christ was merely a body of flesh, and not a human body and mind working in harmony as the diophysites thought is more remote from a Muslim understanding of Christ than the Nestorian and Chalcedonian views. At least Abu Qurra and 'Ammar al-Basri held that Christ had a union of divine and human minds and that therefore Christ could really suffer and be put to death. Belief in a real suffering of Christ was much more difficult for Abu Ra'ita. [37]

Muslim reaction to this kind of argument is found in *The Refutation of the Uniting* by Abu 'Isa al-Warraq (d.861) who produced a thorough critique of the concept of a union of the divine and human in Christ. Christians who claim that the death of Christ did not affect his divine nature have to accept that at the point of death the union between the human and divine natures is broken. If that is so, Christ did not die because Christ is defined as a union of two natures. 'But the human alone was not the Messiah in your view. So then the one who was crucified, killed and buried was not the Messiah.'[38] If Christians separate the divine from suffering and death they end up losing a coherent Christ, and if they hold that the united Christ suffered and died then they must accept that the divine nature ceased to exist, which is intolerable. In other words they cannot come up with a sensible understanding of Christ and the Islamic corrective is all the more needed. Christ was a human being and a rational person would not be persuaded to add some kind of divine character to him.

Perhaps a more difficult Muslim challenge came from 'Ali ibn Rabban al-Tabari (d. 855), a Nestorian Christian who wrote a *Reply to the Christians* after becoming a Muslim at the age of seventy. His appeal to the Gospels to show that Christ was human and therefore not divine was possibly more effective than the logical arguments of al-Mahdi and al-Warraq. Among the multitude of Gospel texts he uses to show the humanity of Christ, al-Tabari refers to Matthew 27:46 where Christ calls out to God in his agony on the cross and argues that Christ can hardly be divine if he feels rejected by God. 'If you say that you call him God because that is what he claimed then you nullify what he did, since he confessed that he had a God in his saying when he was crucified, 'O my God, O my God, why have you forsaken me?'[39] al-Tabari is not claiming that Christ was actually crucified or actually said these words, but is simply reminding Christians that their Gospels show a Christ quite vulnerable and distant from the God he honoured. His thesis in the *Reply* is that the Nicene Creed has distorted the presentation of Christ found in the Gospels and that far from being the eternal creator as the creed teaches, Christ is a spiritual man who is abandoned by his God at the point of his greatest need. Therefore, the

[37] See S. Rissanen, 1993: 188f., for a comparative study of the death of Christ in the writing of Timothy I, Abu Qurra, and Abu Ra'iṯa.

[38] D. Thomas 2002: 119

[39] 'Ali ibn Rabban al-Tabari, 'al-radd 'ala al-nasara' in I-A. Khalifé and W. Kutsch (eds.), 1959: 144

suffering and the crucifixion and the horrible death of Christ in the Gospels only prove that he was a real human being and that the Church has mistakenly divinised him. If only Christians would study their books carefully they would, like him, reject the corrupt interpretation that many Christians have given of him. The gulf between this interpretation of Matthew 27:46 and that given by Abu Ra'ita above is wide. But it shows that Christians were forced to give an account for their traditional readings of the Gospels by this aggressive re-reading by Muslims. [40]

Conclusion

Muslims were confident that they had a truer understanding of Christ than Christians, because he was exalted to heaven without being put to death by his enemies and so was spared an utterly shameful ending to his life. If he had died on the cross as Christians allege then he could not be divine since God could not die in his crucifixion, and therefore the crucifixion story proves that he was only a man despite Christian belief that he was God. Christians were both guilty of a logical error in their thinking about the cross and of an inability to read their own Gospels correctly.

Christians were equally confident that the cross was historical, that God was not dishonoured by the hideous crucifixion of his Word, that God honoured Christ for submitting willingly to his plan to save humanity, and that Christ honoured humans by dying for them in a shameful way. They grappled with the testing challenge to the union of the divine and human in Christ posed by his death on the cross. While affirming that the divine and human in Christ were not separated by his crucifixion they all held that only the humanity of Christ died but his divine nature was not affected by death. They defended their interpretation of the Gospels in the face of Muslim appeals to the teaching and life of Christ to support his humanity and to question Christian belief in his divinity and his ability to die for the sin of others. They argued that beliefs in his divinity and atonement were not the creations of the early Christians as Muslims alleged but were taught by Christ himself.

[40] See Beaumont, 2005: 20-27

REFLECTIONS FROM CONTEXTS

Selected Regions

The Gospel in Afghan Pashto Poetry, Proverbs and Folklore

Leonard N. Bartlotti

Dr Leonard N. Bartlotti is Associate Professor of Intercultural Studies at Biola University, USA

Introduction

The blood feuds, treachery and violence usually associated with the jagged borderlands of Afghanistan are a surprising landscape in which to discover cultural gems that reflect the Gospel of Jesus Christ. The premise of this paper is that embedded within Muslim cultures - specifically, within the 'folk' literature and 'lore' of Muslim ethnic groups, there are significant resources for contextualizing and telling the story of the Cross, and for peace-making, inter-faith dialogue and reconciliation. These folk notions, narrative themes, oral forms, and localized traditions can provide conceptual, theological, cultural and aesthetic bridges to the hearts and minds of Muslim peoples, and an indigenous mechanism to contest more militant, chauvinistic and hegemonic religious understandings that may promote conflict.

Some approaches to Christian-Muslim relations foreground notions associated with religious and communal identity and inter-faith polemics. Inter-religious dialogue tends to involve, by definition, religious discourse and an implicit or explicit marking of communal boundaries. Conversations on faith issues are generally not only communal but textual, deriving from and based upon the authority of scriptures and written interpretative traditions. Yet, however globalised our faith discourse, inevitably authentic dialogue between believers and faith communities must be actualized in local dialogue in specific contexts, in relationships and faith conversations between a Self and Others in which the unique nuances of local language, identity and custom can be appreciated and affirmed, and the meaning of Jesus in that context can be explored.

Folklore is related to the worldview of a culture, and as Kraft affirms, 'one would look to fables, proverbs, riddles, songs, and other forms of folklore for overt and covert indications of the worldview.'[1] A folkloristic approach to Muslim cultures can help us understand the dynamics of local meaning systems and their expressions in and through oral literature and other traditional forms.

[1] Kraft, 1979: 55

An examination of the proverbs, poetry, and folklore of ethnic peoples can uncover an 'implicit theology…a grassroots or oral theology' as a resource for faith dialogue in local terms and for the indigenisation of Biblical faith.[2]

This paper argues for a reappraisal and re-emphasis on Islamic folklore in the context of a broader anthropological approach to Muslim peoples. Within ethnic folkloric traditions, followers of Jesus from any faith background may discern images of the Cross.[3] The paper presents a case study of a folkloristic approach to Islam and ethnic contextualization of the message of the Gospel. Instead of a 'reflection *on*' the Cross, I will look at 'reflections *of*' the Cross in a particular Islamic context, specifically, the way concepts associated with the Cross are reflected in the folklore of the Muslim Pashtun people of Afghanistan and north west Pakistan. I will focus on three interrelated themes - Separation and Reunion, Friendship and Reconciliation - as these are expressed in a selection of Pashto poetry and folklore.

Background

The Pashtun are the largest ethnic group in Afghanistan and are the traditional rulers of that land; Pashtuns also formed the ethnic core of the infamous Taliban movement which controlled the country until 2001. In neighbouring Pakistan, Pashtuns comprise a significant minority, particularly in the treacherous mountain borderlands of the North West Frontier Province and Baluchistan, and in the city of Karachi. The 27 million Pashtun have been called the largest Muslim tribal society in the world.[4]

Pashtun identity is distinguished by certain common attributes: patrilineal descent from a putative common ancestor, Islamic faith, and a set of understandings, customs and behaviours associated with the traditional code of honour and customary law called *pashtunwali* (or *pakhto*, the same name as the language).[5] Pashtuns speak of 'doing *pakhto*' and 'having *pakhto*.' This code of behaviour and value orientations emphasise male autonomy, and egality, self-expression and aggression, and practices like hospitality (*melmastia*), revenge (*badal*), refuge (*pana*) and asylum (*nanawati*).[6]

For many Pashtuns, the Pashto language also represents an important

---

[2] Bediako, 1995: 59-60

[3] Material for this article is drawn from research and personal conversations with Afghan and Pakistani Muslims over a period of fourteen years (1985-1999), when the author and his family lived and worked in the Pashtun city of Peshawar, Pakistan, and the author's doctoral research on Pashto proverbs, Islam and the construction of Pashtun identity. This article is based on lectures given in a variety of locations over the past five years, most recently in Kabul, Afghanistan, to an inter-agency gathering of NGO leaders and workers, November, 2004

[4] Anderson, 1988: 168 and Hart, 1985: 3

[5] Barth, 1981 [1969]: 103-106

[6] Bartlotti, 2000a: 67-74. See also Caroe, 1985 and Spain, 1962

symbol of identity and group membership, as well as functioning to transmit systems of meaning and patterns of thought and behaviour in a variety of domains central to Pashtun life.[7] Nevertheless, Pashtuns say, 'He is a Pathan (Pashtun) who *does* Pashto, not (merely) who *speaks* Pashto,'[8] a proverb that cajoles Pashto speakers toward honourable and manly *pakhto* action.

'Doing *pakhto*' also involves the skilful use of words. Pashtun identity is constructed and contested not only in and through social fora (the *hujra* or men's guest house; hospitality; *purdah* or the honorable maintenance of domestic life), but in the verbal arena. In this context, highly valued folkloric genres like proverbs and folk poetry are important cultural resources and rhetorical tools for the reconstruction and negotiation of meanings associated with Pashtunness and Pashtun identity (Bartlotti, 2000a).

Islam and Honour

In my conversations with Afghan and Pakistani Pashtun friends and acquaintances from urban and rural contexts over the last twenty years, I have had many opportunities, over extravagant meals and myriad cups of sweet *chai*, to talk about a variety of life issues. On many occasions have my Pashtun hosts respectfully raised questions about the nature of my personal faith. However inquisitive, they also relish the opportunity to explain - in their own terms - their Islamic faith. This sometimes includes cynical, humorous and anti-clerical comments, and less than 'orthodox' or 'fundamental' understandings of 'true Islam.' Pashtun 'quoting behaviour' in these settings may include proverbs, poetry and stories as much if not more than Qur'anic verses.

Islam and *pashtunwali*, faith and honour, constitute two distinct ideologies, moral authorities and discourses among the Pashtun. Islamic terms, idioms and understandings are reflected in folklore, and flavour conversations and interactions.[9] Nevertheless, the boundary between Muslimness and Pashtuness, Islamic identity and ethnic identity, is clearly marked in the content, discourse and usage of folklore.[10]

Pragmatically and inductively, I discovered that, instead of foregrounding our communal religious identities, it can be more helpful to discuss religion in Pashtun ethnic, folkloric and cultural terms, rather than exclusively religious (Islamic or Christian) terms. My most fruitful conversations have taken place on the grounds of our common identity as men who enjoy the Pashtun pastime of 'chatting' and 'gossiping' (*gup lugawel*) informally about anything under the sun. Rather than emphasizing the assumed and/or ascribed labels of 'Muslim'

---

[7] Bartlotti, 2000a: 74

[8] Cited by Barth, 1969b: 105

[9] Ahmed, 1984

[10] Bartlotti, 2000b

and 'Christian,'[11] we talk as 'believers' and people of faith, men who understand ourselves to be frail, weak human beings grateful for the mercies and blessings of a Holy God. In such settings, Pashto folk literature and poetry, especially proverbs, folk poetry (*landay*, also known as *tappas*), songs, and classical poetry, have provided forms, a common language, and a traditional, inoffensive, culturally accepted mechanism for the expression of personal views and sentiments, including religious sentiments.

Theology and Culture

Anthropologists have argued that anthropology must inform missions.[12] Theologically, the cultural and historical particularity of the Incarnation demonstrates that 'God has taken both humanity and culture seriously.' The Incarnation tells us that 'God is not afraid of using culture to communicate with us.'[13] Thus, the Incarnation is the supreme model for ministry and for communication.

Despite the acknowledgement of the value of proverbs, poetry and the verbal arts, there appear to be relatively few Christian practitioners who are actively researching and theologising using folklore in Islamic contexts. Yet in the world of Muslim folklore and oral literature, 'Islam' is often a softer, gentler reality, mellowed by local and/or Sufi understandings of God as Beloved Friend, and by blunt critiques of official religion, its institutional expressions and leaders.

Some writers[14] encourage a deeper understanding of 'Folk Islam.'[15] Nevertheless, these studies of 'folk Islam' tend to focus on local and 'occult' beliefs and practices, rather than the 'folk.' The full range of genres, local meanings and performances associated with the field of folklore studies and embraced by the concepts of 'folklore and folk life' have been overlooked.[15]

---

[11] In recent years, in several Asian contexts, new social movements have emerged comprised of Muslim followers of Jesus who reject these dichotomies; these 'insider movements' consider themselves Muslim (culturally and communally) but, having experienced the love of God in Christ, have chosen to follow Jesus. See John Travis and Anna Travis (2005)

[12] Kraft, 1979, Hiebert, 1985 and Whiteman, 2004

[13] Whiteman, 2004: 84

[14] See e.g., Love, 2000 and Parshall, 1983

[15] See e.g., proverbial stereotypes of the *mulla* in Pashto proverbs in Bartlotti, 2000a: 256-71

[16] 'Folk Islam' is generally contrasted with 'Formal Islam.' Though the term 'folk Islam' is now out of favour with most Islamicists and anthropologists, it has helped to focus attention on the spiritualistic orientation of what some have called 'popular Islam,' and the emotional and mystical beliefs and practices of everyday Muslims, including issues of spiritual power (power persons, objects, places, times and rituals) (see e.g. Love, 2000: 19-38)

Also unrecognized or not emphasized in discussions of 'folk Islam' are the unique ethnic understandings, practices, and views of the world, self and Other that together comprise local 'folk' identity. In most Christian explorations of 'folk Islam,' the emphasis is on 'Islam,' not the 'folk.'

For Christians, the 'anthropology of Islam' can lead toward a more appreciative and nuanced insight into Muslim diversity and ethnic identity. This approach also illumines the degree to which 'Islam' is grounded in local social realities and understandings. Anthropologically oriented studies of Muslim peoples tend to avoid questions of orthodoxy and orthopraxy, and focus on local meanings associated with Islamic symbols, the way in which Islam is understood and practised in local contexts.[17] The concern is with the 'shared local traditions' and 'particularistic interpretations' among Muslims in a given locale.[18]

In what follows, I have selected several texts that highlight themes in Pashto folklore that provide a language for dialogue about faith, and a means to contextualize and 'gift wrap' the Gospel more artfully into local Pashtun terms. Each of these texts is at once a conceptual, theological, cultural and aesthetic bridge to the minds and hearts of Pashtuns, and a means of theologizing in indigenous local terms. Though derived from a (Central and South Asian) Afghan and Pakistani context, the approach is suggestive of a more general approach to local theologies and contextualizing the Good News of Jesus in Islamic contexts, and of folk communication using traditional genres.

Biblically, this approach can be grounded in the 'Wisdom tradition' of Scripture, which includes the Book of Proverbs, Song of Solomon, Job and Ecclesiastes. More broadly, God's Word in the Bible comes to us through a variety of oral and written literary genres, including, in addition to proverbs, songs, poetry, letters, riddles, chants, blessings, curses, covenants, genealogies, stories, parables, etc., as well as a host of other historical-cultural and folkloric details. In the ancient Near East, there is also evidence of a category of person called a 'wise man,' for example, Daniel, who was trained in 'the language and literature" of the Babylonians, and to whom 'God gave knowledge and understanding of all kinds of literature and learning,' as well as supernatural insight (Daniel 1:4,17). Jesus Christ, the Master Teacher, communicated with common people using local images, idioms and genres.

The first examples below are in the form of *landay* (also called *tappas*), a unique form of folk poetry among the Pashtun.[19] *Landay* is considered the oldest and most popular genre of Pashto poetry. These brief, anonymous,highly structured folk poems tell a story in two unequally metered lines (9 + 13), and always end with the sound of the letter *he*. Equally popular among men and

---

[17] Eickelman, 1982

[18] Eickelman, 1995: 341, 339

[19] The largest collection of *tappas* is available in two volumes; Shaheen (ed.) 1984, 1994)

women, *landay* are sung at a variety of social occasions, e.g. weddings and times of grief, as well as in the context of daily life; though traditionally sung without instruments, they may be sung accompanied by instruments (a flute, or the lute-like *rebab* and *mangay*, a waterpot used as a drum), or merely quoted in conversations.[20] The themes of these poems vary widely, from romance to religion, happiness to grief, using images from the daily social and cultural life of the Pashtun. Also included below are sample proverbs and sayings.

Separation and Reunion

(1) In the school (*madrasah*) of separation (*beltun*)

I read the Book (*kitab*) of sorrows (*gham*), and weep.

The theme of 'separation' is common in Persian poetry and that of other Indo-Iranian languages. In Pashto, this notion is expressed by the terms *judai* and *beltun*.

The 'separation' referred to in the text above depends on the situational and linguistic context in which the words are spoken or sung, and may refer, for example, to the separation of the Lover from the Beloved, a man from his family (e.g. by the requirements of a job or exile due to a blood feud), or the ultimate separation of loved ones at death.

The anonymous poet uses a distinctly Islamic term, *madrasah*, a religious school, and metaphorically likens his experience of grief to one undergoing the strict discipline of the '*madrasah* of Separation.' In this school, the primary textbook is not the usual 'Book' (*kitab*, the Qur'an), but the 'Book of Sorrows.'

Here the poet employs another aesthetically powerful Pashto term, the concept expressing emotion, *gham*. The term, *gham*, can be glossed variously as 'sorrow,' 'grief,' 'mournng', 'burden,' 'suffering,' or 'troubles,' and is a common theme in Pashto poetry, music, drama, and proverbs.[21] Pashtuns commonly visit each other at *gham* events, for example, illnesses, deaths and times of loss. As Grima has shown, the construction of honour among Pashtun women is associated with the endurance of suffering, and expressions of the emotion of sorrow (*gham*) through stories told in the context of women's visits (*tapos*).[22]

In the above poem, the lessons learned are the fateful lessons of life, supremely the grief associated with separation from one you love. In the

[20] Aziz (2006) and 'Hujra.net' (2006) for a contemporary collection of transliterated untranslated *tappas*

[21] For proverbs using the term *gham*, see *Rohi Mataluna (Pashto Proverbs)*, Bartlotti and Shah Khattak (eds.) (2006, forthcoming)

[22] For a discussion of the concept expressing emotion, *gham*, in Pashtun society, particularly among women, see Grima, 1993

textbook of life's 'school of separation,' one learns the inevitability of tears.

The succinct narrative of this *tappa* is paralleled in the *Book of Genesis* (Chapters 1-3), where God's relationship with Adam and Eve is described in words filled with pathos and delicate anthropomorphism. 'They heard the sound of the LORD God walking in the garden at the time of the evening breeze, and the man and his wife hid themselves from the presence of the LORD God among the trees of the garden.'[23]

In the beginning, humankind enjoyed an intimate friendship with Almighty God. Tragically, Adam and Eve's wilful sin resulted not only in judicial condemnation, but separation from God and expulsion from the Garden. By siding with Satan and his rebellion, Adam and Eve condemned themselves and their progeny to separation from God, fractured relationships with each other, and a life of pain and tears. Their hearts and ours bear the inscribed memory of love's Garden lost. Since that time, humankind has suffered the disciplines of 'the school of separation;' we 'read the Book of sorrows, and weep.'

The concept of separation and its primacy in the emotional and poetic life of Pashtuns provides a way to speak of the concept and consequences of sin in relational, emotional, aesthetic and narrative (each *landey* tells a 2-line story) terms, in contrast with a more judicial, religious and conceptual discussion of sin, law, and judgment. This story line of 'separation' and 'love lost' sets the stage, for the larger Story of God's love, and for the New Testament concept of 'reconciliation.' The notion of 'reunion' is more clearly implied in the following *landay*.

(2) Separation (*judayi*) came, our paths became two;

I accept death, I do not accept separation!

In this poem, 'separation' is personified, an evil being whose arrival cruelly separates the Lover from the Beloved, friend from friend, a dear one from his family. When 'Separation came,' the Lover laments, I was torn away from the one I love: 'our paths became two.'

But there is a change of tone in the second line of the poem. The Pashtun experiences not only the pain and sorrow of separation, but defiance! The disjunction in emotion between the first and second line is best expressed by the Pashtun concept *ghairat*. The notion of *ghairat* is at the very heart of Pashtun culture, and captures the spirit of autonomy, pride, zeal, courage and manly self-assertion associated with being Pashtun and 'doing *pakhto*.' When insulted or challenged, *ghairat* wells up in the heart of a Pashtun. To be *be-ghairat* (without honour) is to be shamed, weak, impotent. It is *ghairat* that compels a Pashtun to defend his honour and that of his women, family and tribe, whatever the cost, as expressed in the Pashto proverb,

[23] Genesis 3:8 (NRSV 1996, c1989)

(3) A Pashtun will throw himself in the fire for the sake of his honour (*ghairat*).

Thus, despite Separation's power and intent to divide Lover and Beloved, the true *ghairati* Pashtun cannot and will not tolerate separation. He would rather embrace death than be separated from his Beloved: 'I accept death, I do not accept separation!'

In this simple, highly evocative couplet, we discover a reflection of the profound essence of the Gospel story. When God created mankind, God the Lover and man the Beloved lived in unity and happiness.[24] But through sin and Satan, 'separation came.' We were separated from God and ever since have walked a lonely path of disobedience, darkness and sorrow. All of the violence, revenge, selfishness, and corruption we see around us, not only in Afghanistan but in our own countries and in the world, can be traced to humankind's being cut off from a nourishing love-union and life-giving relationship with Almighty God. Because of sin and Satan, 'separation came' between us and God; instead of walking together on a path of righteousness and friendship, 'our paths became two.'

But the second line of the *landay* expresses a bold truth. Someone loves us so much that He refuses to tolerate separation. He pursues us as a Lover pursues the Beloved. He loves us so much that he is willing to die in order for us to be reunited. 'God's sovereign action is a manifestation of His own *ghayrat*. As one Pashtun says, 'God is *ghayratmand*.' A Pashtun's will to act (*ghayrat*) reflects the Divine.'[25] As *ghairat* wells up in the heart of God, it is expressed in holy, self-sacrificing Love.

The story of the Bible can be summed up in this *landay*, this 'Sacred Romance' on the Afghan frontier. The Redeemer (*nijatkawunkey*) courageously 'accepted death' on a Cross, and laid down His life as a voluntary blood sacrifice (*khunbaha*).

In that act of holy *ghairat* in defiance of Satan and in radical obedience 'unto death, even death on a cross,' Jesus 'becomes flesh' as an honourable Pashtun. 'I lay down my life - only to take it up again. No one takes it from me, but I lay it down of my own account' (John 10:17-18). His death was an act of assertive self-sacrifice, an act of love, and an act of honour (obedience to death for the glory of God). 'I accept death, I do not accept separation!'

As is apparent in the above, distinctly religious terms and understandings are not absent from these conversations. The point is, however, that religious terms and themes are used in the context of folk narrative motifs, discourse and genre that have conceptual, aesthetic and rhetorical power when used and performed

---

[24] Note that in Sufi poetry, man is the one pursuing God as a Lover pursues the Beloved. In the Bible, God is the One who takes the initiative in a mission to save and redeem and reconcile mankind to Himself. This is expressed in the concept of *missio dei*, 'the mission of God,' and is at the heart of the Christian concept of mission.

[25] Bartlotti, 2000b: 274

in a given local or ethnic context. The communication paradigms are more ethnic, than Islamic; similarly, it is ethnic, not Islamic, identity that is appealed to and foregrounded in the relationship. Jesus 'becomes flesh' as a Pashtun among Pashtuns, not as an imagined 'ideal Muslim' or 'Christian' figure.

This is apparent in the use of a manifestly poetic term in the following verse from the *Pashto New Testament* (Matthew 5:8):[26]

(4) Blessed are the pure in heart for they shall see (*didun*) God.

The opposite of 'separation' is another theme common in Pashto and Persian poetry, that of *didun* (Persian *didar*), which can be glossed as 'reunion,' 'meeting,' 'seeing,' 'visiting' (face to face).

The picture is not that of a casual meeting between two people, but of a dynamic encounter that restores the immediacy of a relationship lost due to separation. *Didun* is a folk and literary notion filled with conceptual and emotive power. For example, when a tribal Pashtun returns home after working for two years in the Persian Gulf to make money to support his family, and emerges from the airport to be greeted by a joyful, hugging, weeping throng - his wife and children, father and relatives, his mother wiping away tears with her *chador*, his brother placing a garland around his neck - that is *didun*. When a man has been separated from his Beloved, and then, finally, sees her walking toward him through the field, or meets her at the stream where she fills her water pot - that encounter is *didun*. In faces shining with tears of recognition, in joyful embrace, in the 'seeing' and 'meeting' and 'reunion' of family and friends, the world disappears and *didun* happens. Those who were separated are one again.

Astonishingly, in the verse above, the Lord Jesus promises to the 'pure in heart' a supreme reunion (*didun*) with God Himself.

In an older version of the Pashto New Testament, the same verse was translated much as we have it in English versions. 'Blessed are the pure in heart for they shall see God.' 'To see' (Pashto, *lidel*) conveys the visual and factual reality of 'seeing' someone, but in *lidel*, the 'seeing' is more black and white than in colour, and lacks emotional and relational depth. By using *didun* - 'they shall do or have *didun* with God' - the translators have captured (perhaps better than any English translation) the blessed exhilaration and inexpressible joy that shall be the lot of the 'pure in heart' who 'meet' God on the last Day. His eyes will gleam as He welcomes the pure in heart to their heavenly home. For the pure in heart, the joys of paradise (*jannat*) are not sensual pleasures (as in the common Muslim understanding), but the pleasure of reunion as the soul meets its Beloved - *didun* with God. In this life, while they await and long for that Day, followers of Jesus enjoy an intimate friendship with God in and through His Holy Spirit - the gift of His Presence and a foretaste of what is to come.

[26] Published in Lahore by Pakistan Bible Society, 1991

Through the Spirit of Jesus, the 'pure in heart' 'sees' - have *didun*, intimate prayerful communion with - Almighty God.

Friendship

(5) Some people seek refuge from sorrow;

As for me, I am happy to be submerged in the sorrows of my friend.

The 'folk' concept of 'friendship' provides a second reflection of the Cross in Afghanistan. In text #5, the poet touches on two literary and cultural themes, 'refuge' and 'friendship,' as well as the contrasting emotions of 'sorrow' and 'happiness.'

Friendship is a highly idealized conception in Pashtun culture.[27] The Pashtun world is a dangerous place. In the face of challenges and competition, honour must be validated consistently through physical and verbal behaviours and sentiments that are recognized as stereotypically 'Pashtun.' In this context, Pashtuns long to find a 'true friend.' Qualities and behaviours associated with understandings of true friendship include empathy and self-sacrifice, as encapsulated in the emotive *landay* above.

The concept of 'refuge' is common in Middle Eastern tribal societies, including traditionally pastoral-nomadic tribes like the Pashtun. Closely tied to 'hospitality' (*melmastia*), offering 'refuge' (*pana*) to strangers and anyone in need is a core aspect of the *pashtunwali* code of honour: a host is honour bound to defend a stranger or guest at the risk of his own life. Even notorious and unscrupulous characters have found sanctuary in the Pashtun borderlands of Afghanistan and Pakistan, to the frustration of central and provincial governments.

An interesting illustration of the vitality of the concept can be seen in an incident that occurred on June 28, 2005, when a team of four US Navy SEALS were ambushed by Taliban insurgents in northeastern Afghanistan. Three men were killed; the fourth commando, severely wounded, managed to crawl to safety. A few days later, he was discovered by an Afghan shepherd named Gulab, who brought the man to his Pashtun village. A village council met and offered the wounded commando sanctuary. That night, Taliban insurgents arrived and demanded that the 'infidel' be handed over to them. The reply by the village chief, Shinah, was classically Pashtun: 'The American is our guest, and we won't give him up as long as there's a man or a woman left alive in our village.'[28]

In the poem above, the picture is that of someone desperately 'seeking

[27] See Lindholm, 1982

[28] 'How the Shepherd Saved the SEAL' (2005)

refuge' from a powerful pursuer, 'sorrow' (*gham*). The first line is stated as a truism: 'People want refuge from sorrow,' that is, they try to hide, seek sanctuary from, and avoid pain, grief, trouble and sorrow.

But quite in contrast, the poet cries out in the second line, 'I am happy (*khoshala*)' - the reverse of the emotion *gham*) to be 'submerged,' literally 'drowned,' 'in the sorrows of my friend.' The term for friend (*ashna*) is an endearing word that can be used for one's 'darling,' so there is a hint here of romantic love. The dominant sentiment is that of empathetic, self-sacrificing love.

The notion of 'sacrifice' or self-sacrifice is implied or expressed explicitly in various Pashto proverbs, idioms and poetry. It is commonly understood that 'doing *pakhto'* - behaving with the ethos and manners associated with Pashtun concepts of manliness and honour - is costly. This includes, for example, the price of liberality and hospitality, as expressed in the following tongue-in-cheek proverbs:

(6) May I sacrifice my head for you, but don't ask me for a loan.

(7) May I sacrifice my home for you--but only up to the outside door.

Each of the texts above begins with an idiomatic phrase 'May I sacrifice my (self, head, home) for you' (more on this idiom below), and ends with a clever counterpoint or proviso 'but…'

More 'costly' for Pashtuns is the responsibility associated with blood feuds and revenge (*badal*) and the honour of women (*namus*). The price of protecting the honour and reputation of one's household and womenfolk is expressed in the following advice,

(8) Sacrifice everything for your life, sacrifice even your life for the honour of your women.

However, the 'sacrifice' of proverb texts #6 through #8 is different from the (self) 'sacrifice' of *landay* text #5: in the latter, one does not suffer for his own honour, so much as with and for the sorrows of another. This type of friend does not hide or flee suffering and grief; he is willing to embrace and endure happily the overwhelming sorrows faced by his friend. Who would not long for such a self-sacrificing friend?

The Gospels tell a similar story. Incredibly, Almighty God Himself is not aloof from our sufferings. The miracle of love is that God comes near to take on flesh in order to redeem us: 'God was reconciling the world to himself in Christ' (2 Corinthians 5:19). Christ did not 'seek refuge from sorrow.' He was called 'the friend of tax collectors and sinners' and 'wept' at the death of His friend Lazarus (Luke 7:34; John 11:35). The night before He died, so great was His anguish that His sweat was like great drops of blood (Luke 22:44).

Nevertheless, He chose to do the will of God. He drank for us and on our behalf 'the cup' of suffering, death and the wrath of God, that we his friends and followers might drink instead the 'cup of blessing' (Luke 22:42; 1 Corinthians 10:16). 'Greater love has no one than this, that he lay down his life for his friends' (John 15:13).

Jesus was 'familiar with suffering' (Isaiah 53:3), yet it was not his own suffering He endured, but ours: 'Surely he took up our infirmities and carried our sorrows.... He was pierced for our transgressions, he was crushed for our iniquities; the punishment that brought us peace was upon him, and by his wounds we are healed' (Isaiah 53:4-5). On the Cross, the 'Man of Sorrows' (Isaiah 53:3) was 'submerged' in our sorrows.

(9) May I sacrifice myself for you!

The phrase introducing proverbs #6 and #7 is also used as a stand-alone idiomatic phrase in other contexts, as in text #9 above. 'May I sacrifice (myself) for you!,' says a mother to comfort and reassure a crying child. 'May I sacrifice (myself) for you!,' says one friend to another to pledge his loyalty and devotion in the face of danger, threat, or death. Again, as in earlier expressions, behind the words is *ghairat*, the ethos and core value of *pashtunwalit* - autonomy, bravery, pride, self-assertion, and zeal.

In 1992, I put this text to music as the theme song of a two-hour Easter pageant, presented in Pashto and English with songs in four languages (Pashto, Urdu, Persian and English) performed before a mostly Muslim audience in a Pakistani city: *Qurban de shum* (1992). Beginning with Adam and Eve's sacrifices of praise in the Garden and their fall into sin, the pageant traced the theme of sacrifice through the Old Testament and Prophets, up to the sacrifice of Jesus, 'The Lamb of God who takes away the sin of the world!' (John 1:29). The Cross of Jesus Christ is the ultimate expression of self-sacrificing friendship, as He says, *Qurban de shum* - 'May I sacrifice myself for you!.'

(10) I am not going to heaven without my friend!

A final idiomatic phrase in this category captures the same spirit. The words are those of a Pashtun standing before Almighty God on the Day of Judgment. As the door to paradise opens to him, he proclaims, with the audacity and infamous pride of a true Pashtun and a true friend, 'I am not going to heaven without my friend!'

Several years ago, I was visiting an elderly Pakistani scholar. We had become friends, and used to sit together on his verandah, drink sweet *chai* and, in between his frequent visitors, chat about all kinds of subjects.

One day, our private conversation turned to the topic of heaven. He said, '*Inshallah* (if God wills) I will go to heaven.' 'But,' he said with resignation, 'I don't think I'm going to make it.' I said to him, 'Professor *sahib* (sir), with your permission, may I tell you how I know I am going to heaven?' (In Pashtun culture, requesting permission (*ijazat*) is an important sign of respect toward adults; a guest must even ask 'permission' from his host in order to leave.) I then shared briefly about Jesus' promise that everyone who believes in him has forgiveness of sins and eternal life. I assured him that God hears prayers spoken in the powerful name and mediation (*wasita*) of Jesus - they go straight to the Throne of God, as in the Pashto couplet,

> (11) In one leap I have seen them go to the Throne of God - the prayers of a holy man!

Not only will God hear our prayers in Jesus' Name, but at the time of death, his followers are assured that their souls, too, will go 'in one leap' to be 'with the Lord forever' in Paradise!

The old gentleman listened politely and respectfully. Then he shook his head sadly and said, 'I'd like to go (to paradise). But I don't think I'm going to make it.' In that moment, a few simple words in Pashto welled up in my heart. I looked into his eyes and said gently but firmly in Pashto, *zə janat ta nə zum be-mulgarey* - 'I am not going to heaven without my friend!' His eyes flooded with tears as he stood and embraced me, 'Mr. Len, you're a real friend, a real friend.'

Reconciliation

A final example of ethnic contextualization of the message for Muslims is another custom associated the Pashtun code of honour, a practice called *nanawati.*[29]

There is considerable variation in the meaning of *nanawati* and the practices associated with it across Pashtun areas.[30] While generally the term *pana* is used to refer to the seeking of 'asylum' or 'refuge', *nanawati* (often translated 'refuge', and thus confused with *pana*) includes notions of 'asking', 'begging' and 'apology', in particular, 'begging asylum', or 'begging favour or forgiveness', in the context of conflict.

Like most Middle Eastern and North African tribal societies, Pashtun society is riven by blood feuds. The law of revenge exacts an enormous price. Conflicts among Pashtun can be resolved in one of two ways. In the *jirga* (council) system, a solution can be negotiated or imposed by village elders. This involves the balancing of guilt and injuries between the parties, usually through the payment of land, money, weapons or women, leading to (a more or less fragile) peace between the adversaries. Among some tribes, this agreement may be

[29] The following material is based on the author's research into the custom of *nanawati*, as described in 'The Pashtun Peace Ritual' (2000, unpublished paper)
[30] Bartlotti, 2000a: 278, n.362; 347, n.416

marked by laying a stone marker (*tiga*). Another alternative to resolving blood feuds is the peace ritual of *nanawati*. By doing *nanawati*, the offending party (*zalim*) openly admits his guilt, 'apologizes' and 'begs forgiveness' from the offended party (*mazlum*).

Among some Afghan Pashtun tribes, the folk practices associated with doing *nanawati* constitute it as a kind of peace or reconciliation ritual. Atayee interprets the 'favour' being sought as forgiveness or 'pardon' and defines *nanawati* as 'the ceremony of pardon-begging.'[31] *Nanawati* as reconciliation ritual or 'ceremony of pardon-begging' restores relationships between blood enemies, and is thus 'a palliative to the harsh concepts of *badal* (revenge).'[32]

Certain customs and symbolic behaviours are associated with the performance of *nanawati*. Initially, family elders may visit the injured family to determine the latter's willingness to receive the penitent offender and forgive the offence. Given the ambiguities of meaning, intrigue and suspicion associated with 'doing *pakhto*', gauging sincerity is not an easy task for either party.

For petty offences, a mullah takes a sheep to the opponent's house. For more serious offences, *nanawati* consists of sending mullahs, village elders (*spingiri*), or 'people of sacred lineage' (*stana khel*), along with sheep and - in 'very grave' cases - women with a Qur'an on their heads.[33] In the case of murder, the killer is also taken and placed at the disposal of the relatives, to pardon or take revenge (usually the former) as they will. In one description, the killer has a rope around his neck and grass in his mouth, a self-humiliation that in effect says, 'I am like the cattle of your field - you may slaughter me if you will.'

Edwards' description notes that the side suing for peace will 'signal their intention' by 'sending a delegation of women carrying Qur'ans and accompanied by one or more mullahs to the compound of their enemy;' the women will lower their shawls in the domestic quarters, revealing their hair and faces as they would when visiting relatives, thus signalling their male kinsmen's desire to negotiate and enter into friendly relations (1996: 68). This picture of women holding holy Qur'ans and crossing the line of conflict is a moral representation of a sacred request, conjoining that which is of greatest value to a Pashtun, his honour, represented by his women (*namus*), and his faith, represented by his holy Book.

In some descriptions of *nanawati*, a slaughtered sheep is laid at the gate of the injured party; if the sacrifice is taken inside, it is assumed that pardon has been granted; if not, the gesture of apology was in vain. In the processional description above, the sheep will be slaughtered and eaten at a meal (though the guilty party himself does not attend), where the offended party announces his

---

[31] Atayee, 1979: 65

[32] Hanifi, 1976: 90

[33] Hanifi, 1976: 65-66

forgiveness of the offender.

The practice of *nanawati* provides another bridge to the hearts and minds of Muslim Pashtuns. One example of the power of the concept is illustrated by an encounter I had several years ago with a Afghan Pashtun tribal leader. Accompanied by half a dozen burly bodyguards, the distinguished Muslim leader had attended our International Easter Celebration in a Pakistani city. After viewing a film and hearing a message about Christ's suffering on the Cross, the chief asked for prayer. He was ill and in much pain. We prayed for him in Jesus' name, and he was healed immediately. It got his attention.

About two weeks later, I received a message, 'The *khan* wants to see you.' A colleague and I went to the chief's house and were escorted graciously to his private quarters. Sweet tea, cakes, and cookies were set before us in the generous hospitality characteristic of Pashtuns. But our conversation quickly turned to spiritual things.

The tribal leader had many sincere questions: 'Do Christians pray and fast? How do you worship? Do you believe in one God? What is heaven like?' As with many Muslims, he was not resistant to nor had he rejected the Gospel; this dear elderly man had never really understood what Christians believe or what it means to follow Jesus. He only knew what his own religious teachers had told him.

Near the end of our two hour conversation, I said, 'You have a custom called *nanawati*.' 'Yes!' His face brightened with recognition and appreciation. 'Khan *sahib*,' I continued, 'you must come to God in this same way, begging forgiveness for your sins. You must do *nanawati* with God. But you also need a sheep. One of the prophets you revere, John the Baptist, saw Jesus and told the people, 'Behold the Lamb of God who takes away the sin of the world.'

The Holy Spirit's presence filled the room as I continued. 'As God provided a lamb to be sacrificed in place of Abraham's son, so God has provided a Lamb to take away your sins - to die in your place so you can have peace and be reconciled to God.' We prayed together, and as I left he honored me by kissing my cheek.

Conclusion

The presupposition of this paper is that followers of Jesus can find conceptual, theological, cultural and aesthetic bridges to the hearts and minds of Muslims within the folklore and folk literature of Muslim ethnic peoples. In this brief survey, we have found conceptual, theological, cultural and aesthetic bridges to the hearts and minds of Muslim Pashtuns. We have seen how three interrelated themes of Separation and Reunion, Friendship, and Reconciliation are expressed in Pashto proverbs, poetry and folkloric practice. This missiological approach and communication challenge requires facility in linguistics, anthropology and theology, and an ability to interpret both Scripture and culture.

Methodologically, theological reflections on ethnic folklore must be based on ethnographic data and research. That is, 'new' meanings and applications cannot be divorced from, and must actually build upon, contextual meanings determined by interaction with 'insiders'. Practitioners seeking to use folklore to communicate Biblical and spiritual truths must first do their ethnographic homework. This includes understanding the connotations of terms and what texts 'mean' to insiders, as well as how they are used, performed and understood in various situational and cultural contexts. Anything less lacks integrity and amounts to 'using' folklore for one's own ends. Rather than a pragmatic appropriation and manipulation of culture, we need to aim for a humble, respectful and redemptive embrace of culture with an eye to common grace and the models provided by the Incarnation and the translatability of Scripture.

In articulating 'a theology of culture' Gailyn Van Rheenen concurs:[34]

> [T]he boundary between social or cultural anthropology and theology is artificial, constructed by modern thinking, and not founded upon biblical theology nor reality as a whole. The disciplines of theology and anthropology must merge, intermingle, and unify. If the dichotomies of modern thought are used, a missiologist must become both a Christian anthropologist and a culturally aware theologian. Anthropology cannot become Christian, nor be truly useful without the merging of these two disciplines.

The intersection between theology and anthropology can be seen, for example, in the account of the day of Pentecost (Acts 2), when the Spirit of God was poured out on the new-born church, issuing in proclamation of the Good News in the languages of the surrounding nations. Kwame Bediako comments:[35]

> The ability to hear in one's own language and to express in one's own language one's response to the message which one receives, must lie at the heart of all authentic religious encounter with the divine realm...(The) deeper significance...is that God speaks to men and women - always in the vernacular. Divine communication is never in a sacred, esoteric, hermetic language; rather it is such that 'all of us hear...in our own languages...the wonders of God.

While folkloric forms have been recognized as an aspect of an anthropological approach to mission, their importance in Islamic contexts has been undervalued in comparison with the Qur'an or specifically religious discourse and literature. While traditional proverbs and folk poetry do not arise from a Christian framework or perception, the challenge is to relate theological

---

[34] Van Rheenen, 1997: 33

[35] Bediako, 1995: 60

reflection to vernacular understandings. As Bediako affirms, 'Taking the vernacular seriously then, becomes not merely a cultural but also a theological necessity. For it is only through the vernacular that a genuine and lasting theological dialogue with culture can take place.'[36]

[36] Bediako, 1995: 73

AN ISLAMIC 'GOOD FRIDAY': CELEBRATING THE FEAST OF SACRIFICE IN INDONESIA

Jonathan E Culver

Dr Jonathan E Culver is Mission Professor at the Tiranus Bible Institute in Bandung, Indonesia

The Feast of Sacrifice

It was Friday, February 22, 2002. That morning I asked my Muslim neighbors in Bandung, West Java, if I could observe their Feast of Sacrifice (*id al-adha*) (sacrifice of sheep, goats or cattle) commemorating Abraham's sacrifice of his son, Ishmael. They readily agreed and one of them walked with me to a small open space filled with people and animals. Since it was Friday, I thought to myself, "This is like an Islamic 'Good Friday' service." Instead of communion wine representing blood, however, I saw real blood spurting out accompanied by shouts of '*allahu akbar! allahu akbar*! (God is great!).' In the space of about two hours I saw the local *imam* (leader) and his helpers dispatch three bulls and twenty-five sheep and goats. In one particularly riveting scene, the *imam* and his six assistants tied up the legs of a struggling bull and toppled it to the ground. Then the *imam* pulled out a long butcher's knife, recited a short prayer in Arabic, and slashed the jugular vein and wind pipe of the victim, allowing the blood to spurt into a hole dug in the ground. The struggles of the stricken beast and the massive outpouring of so much blood were almost more than I could bear.

When I asked a small group of Muslims why they were slaughtering these animals, they told me that they were commemorating Abraham's sacrifice of his first-born son, Ishmael—not Isaac as in Genesis 22.[1] But a lot more than remembrance and re-enactment was going on here as I will explain below.

As the multiple sacrifices proceeded, I noticed that each of the sheep and goats had a person's name hanging from their necks. Likewise, a white card graced the neck of each of the bulls, but with seven names inscribed on it. According to Islamic law, one person could gain merit through the purchase and sacrifice of a sheep, while up to seven could simultaneously gain merit by combining their funds and purchasing a sacrificial bull. On these cards were the

---

[1] The Qur'anic text on this subject (Sura 37:100-112) does not name the son whom God ordered Abraham to sacrifice. For the historic Islamic debate on the identity of the sacrificial son see R. Firestone, 1990: 135-159

names of those who had sacrificed by paying out $45-65 for a goat (a large sum by Indonesian standards) and about twice that per person for a bull. I then asked Pak Umar, one of the seven persons whose name was on a card, what merit he hoped to gain by paying out his share for a $600 bull? He replied: 'I do not hope for any merit. I am only obeying God's command with a sincere heart, following in the steps of Ibrahim and Isma'il. They each made a great sacrifice (Abraham sacrificed his most precious possession, his son; Ishmael likewise, sacrificed his most precious possession, his life). If God wants to bless me for making such a small sacrifice, *inshaallah*, it's up to Him.' Pak Umar's answer accords with mainstream Sunni Islam. He would have passed a doctrinal test with flying colours.

However, some of the other Muslims gave different explanations for their participation in this annual sacrifice, explanations that would have greatly displeased the Ulema, the guardians of orthodox Islamic law. Some expressed the hope that the moment they sacrificed their animal, angels would circle overhead and make intercession for their sins before Allah. But when asked where this teaching could be found in the Qur'an and Hadith, they did not know. I suspect the Ulema would have rebuked them for holding to such a belief. While this particular belief about mediation for sins is not in accord with mainstream Islam, the Qur'an does speak obliquely of angelic intercession by the permission of Allah.[2]

Another participant told me that he believed that on the Last Day Allah would resurrect the lamb that he purchased to ferry him across the *sirat al-mustakim* (the straight path).[3] In Islamic teaching this 'Straight Path' is a bridge that righteous Muslims cross to enter into Paradise on the Judgment Day. According to Islamic tradition, this bridge is said to be a seven-plaited cord that is thinner than a hair and sharper than a sword. For the unrighteous this path will be impeded by tortures and traps, causing them to slip and plunge into the dreaded fires below.[4] Apparently, many Muslims are afraid that they will not be counted among the righteous when the time comes to cross the bridge. Thus, they feel that there is no way they can cross this bridge unaided. In order to have greater certainty, many Muslims have seized upon one of the popular traditions in Islam which ascribes efficacious powers to the sacrificial ram or bull to carry them safely to Paradise. One of the great theologians of Islam, Abu Hamed Muhammad ibn Muhammad al-Ghazzali (d. 1111 A.D.),

[2] Yet an *imam* gave me the same explanation when I observed a sacrifice festival in 1997. He too could not tell me where this teaching came from. The Qur'an and Hadith literature do mention the intercession of angels, but the intercession seems to be related to the Day of Judgment and only provided for those who are acceptable to God (Sura 53:26). For the Hadith references see, A.J. Wensinck, 1927: 112

[3] See Sura 1.6

[4] For the Hadith references see Wensinck, 1927:40. For an authoritative description see T.P. Hughes, 1994: 595

refers disparagingly to this teaching by quoting what was for him an untrustworthy Hadith in which Muhammad was said to have taught: 'Seek the assistance of the animal that you have sacrificed, for he is your transport [across the *sirat*] on the Day of Judgment.'[5] Even though it is considered unorthodox, this teaching is held by a large number of folk Muslims throughout India and Southeast Asia.[6]

The orthodox Ulema may decry these popular ideas of the *id al-adha* animal sacrifice, but it is such a fundamental part of popular Islamic thinking in Indonesia that Yusuf Roni, a well-known Indonesian Christian convert from Islam, uses the concept to good effect in his witness to Muslims. When Muslims ask Yusuf, 'Why did you leave Islam to become a Christian?' Yusuf responds by explaining, "When I was a Muslim I was very concerned about going to Paradise after I died. I knew that there was no way that I could cross the bridge. But I read in the *injil* (Gospel) that *'isa al-masih* (Jesus the Messiah) said, 'I am the way, the truth and the life.' And it was at that point that I put my trust in 'Isa to take me across the bridge.'" Yusuf's words here not only address the 'folk' Muslim, but the orthodox Muslim as well because in Islamic teaching there appears to be no absolute certainty in this life of gaining Paradise. Thus, the question of salvation remains unanswered in spite of the repeated sacrifices.

It is also interesting to note that even in official Islam there is a concept of a covering for sin, but is it a potential gospel bridge? The Hebrew word in Leviticus to 'atone' (for sin) is *kapar*, which literally means to 'cover' or 'hide'. Thus, in Leviticus the blood of the sacrificial lamb provided a covering for sin. There is a parallel idea here in the Arabic word, *kafara* which also means 'cover'. I was surprised to read the comments of an Islamic scholar who uses this Arabic term in his discussion of a 'covering for sin' (*kiffarat dosa*). This scholar maintains a strictly Islamic slant by insisting that Muslims can avail themselves of this covering for sin, but only by performing meritorious deeds and prayers, which is a long way from the concept of a redemptive blood sacrifice.[7] I suspect that in pre-Islamic times this term was used for idolatrous sacrifices to appease the wrath of local deities.[8] In Leviticus, we are told that the Lord God said to Moses: 'For the life of the creature is in the blood, and *I have given it to you* to make atonement for yourselves on the altar,' (emphases mine).[9] But, somehow, the connection between a blood sacrifice and a covering for sin was superseded by the traditional teachings of Islam after the destruction of the idols in the Ka'bah which might have closed the door to the idea of God himself providing a blood sacrifice as a covering for sin.

[5] A.H. Ibriy (trans.): 136 (Part 1, Book 7 of the *Ihya Ulum al-Din*)

[6] T.P. Hughes, 1994 (reprint): 192-194; Bowen, 1993: 278

[7] Bowen, 1993: 259 and Shihab, 1999: 29-32

[8] T. Nöldeke, 1915: 665-666

[9] Leviticus 17:11

In conclusion, the purpose of the Feast of Sacrifice in Islam is to recall and commemorate Abraham's sacrifice of his son, Ishmael. Ishmael is also honored because of his willingness to become the sacrificial victim. But traditional Islamic teaching denies that the blood of lambs, goats and bulls can make any atonement for sin. The emphasis is placed on Muslims who 'obey and sacrifice', rather than on the animal being sacrificed. In short, in official Islam there is no place for blood atonement as in Christianity. Yet, in spite of Islam's official position on a redemptive blood sacrifice, we have seen that large numbers of Indonesian 'folk' Muslims yearn for something more than commemoration when they perform the annual Feast of Sacrifice or *id al-adha*. Many of these Muslims here in Indonesia are searching for forgiveness of sins and assurance of entry into Paradise. This yearning causes them to place their hopes on the sacrificial lambs. Indonesian Christians who understand the mind set of their Muslim neighbors speak of Jesus as *'isa al-masih,* the Lamb of God who takes away the sin of the world[10] and as the *sirat al-mustakim,* the straight path or the bridge into Paradise.

[10] See John 1:29

The Cross and Reconciliation in Palestine

Salim Munayer

Dr Salim Munayer is Dean of Bethlehem Bible College and Director of Musalaha Ministry of Reconciliation in Israel

The cross has a unique role in this land where 2,000 years ago, Jesus was crucified. Followers of Christ in Palestine and Israel are essentially a minority amidst the Jewish and Muslim majorities. As so much of this region is defined by the conflict between groups, believers in Jesus look to Him as a basis for reconciliation. While Muslims and Jews reject the cross, believers who pursue reconciliation are seeking to fulfil Christ's prayer for unity in John, so that their testimony of unity will reflect His work of reconciliation (John 17:21).

The conflict between Israelis and Palestinians is multi-faceted and appears intractable. The reality of the situation is that Israeli and Palestinians live in close proximity. There is no choice but to live side-by-side; therefore co-operation, reconciliation and relationships are essential. While peace accords have attempted to work out a solution, the political solutions have failed to mend inter-group relations, or to alter attitudes of hatred and prejudice that continuously undermine political agreements and fuel the cycle of violence. Both sides are emotionally charged by their pain and enmity. While hammering out a way for them to share the land, the political process has not induced the change of heart required to live alongside each other.

This is the context in which Palestinian Arab Christians and Messianic Israeli Jews find themselves. Believers live on both sides of the conflict, and are not immune to its impact. None are untouched by the tide of prejudice and hostility between groups, and the gap between people, including believers, continues to widen. While violent conflict, political ideologies and theological disparities cause divisions, followers of Jesus are compelled to address these issues in the context of the cross.

Through Christ's act on the cross, God extends his reconciliation to us; it compels us to reconcile ourselves to others. The Gospel provides a resource and a framework through which to approach the other, even the enemy. The cross brings together leaders and followers alike from the Messianic Israeli and Palestinian Christian communities to demonstrate the effectiveness of the divine mandate for reconciliation. Through organizations like Musalaha, a non-profit organization facilitating reconciliation programmes between Palestinians and Israelis, believers meet in desert encounters and conferences, in order to face the challenge of practicing Biblical principles in the midst of conflict.[1] In our experiences at Musalaha encounters, a variety of issues and obstacles to reconciliation continuously emerge, particularly regarding issues such as identity, power imbalance, justice, prejudice, hatred and revenge. This paper discusses these trends, and the manner in which the cross provides a model response to these challenges.

The Cross as Atonement for Sin

The cross is a central theme in reconciliation. I John describes the nature of God as love, a love made apparent through Christ's act on the cross (I John 4:7). He is love not only in his identity but also in his act of sending his son as atonement for our sin (I John 4:10). This basic principle is important as the foundation of Biblical reconciliation. God loves and embraces a world that rebels against him. All of humanity is sinful and in enmity with God, yet he declares through the cross that he wants a relationship with us that is intimate and eternal. God's act of embrace towards sinners enables us to have a relationship with him, which in turn provides a mandate for us to embrace others.

This act on the cross not only makes an impact on us personally and individually, but also informs our relationships and attitudes towards others. Each of us belongs to various communities, ethnic, cultural, religious backgrounds and are influenced by the attitudes that our group might hold towards other groups. In the case of Israelis and Palestinians, as their histories intertwine in often painful and complex ways, attitudes of hatred, prejudice, and separation are inherent. The cross has a bearing on these perceptions and understandings of the other side.

Attitudes towards the other reflect deep-seated dehumanization and demonization. Dehumanization disregards the humanity of the other side. Palestinians and Israelis often see one another as the enemy, and not as a people with lives and families. Each group demonizes the other side, relating to the enemy using religious language, portraying them as the instrument of the devil, as being beyond redemption.

The act of Christ on the cross rejects these attitudes. God's grace, just as it extends to us in our sinful state, extends to our enemies as well, for we were all once sinners and enemies of God. When he could reject the human race, he looks on us with love and redeems us. His act of atonement and embrace is our model and point of reference in reconciling with each other.

[1] For more information on *Musalaha,* see www.musalaha.org

The Cross as Deliverance

Solidarity with the human condition of suffering

Christ, through his life, death and resurrection, identifies with those who suffer and are oppressed. Jesus recalled, 'He has anointed me to preach the Gospel to the poor…to heal the broken-hearted. To proclaim liberation to the captives and recovery of sight to the blind. To set at liberty those who those who are oppressed' (Luke 4:18-19). Christ brings deliverance in several aspects of human life, including the spiritual, social, and physical life of the victim.

Jesus' experience of suffering and his teachings concerning the sufferer compel us to attitudes of compassion, even towards our enemies. His sympathy towards the victim is not only a comfort to those who suffer, but also a demand for the same from us. In a conflict where both sides see themselves as the victims, often groups are unable to see the suffering of the other side. A victimization mentality blinds one group to the suffering of the other. While also being a source of redemption and relief, the cross presents a challenge to look beyond our own situation and to attend to the suffering and pain of others. God is calling us to be like him, to have solidarity in suffering and bring freedom to the oppressed.

The Cross as liberation from the roles of victim and oppressor

The trends of victimization and oppression are major factors in the Israeli-Palestinian conflict. Both Israelis and Palestinian strongly perceive themselves as victims, and therefore have difficulty seeing themselves as a threat to the other. If we are the victims, then we cannot be the victimizers. This monopoly on victimization fails to acknowledge that each side has also played the role of perpetrator. Perceived victimization can become a justification and excuse for violent and sinful acts.

In addition, victimization can also lead to a fatalistic point of view. The parties believe that nothing can be done to change the enemy who is full of hatred and wants only to destroy. This justifies the use of power and pre-emptive violence for perceived self-preservation.

The cross addresses this dynamic by redefining the roles of victim and oppressor. In as much as Christ's death addresses the victim, it also deals with the oppressor. Just as God showed his love and liberated the oppressed, the oppressor is also set free on the cross.

Both oppressor and oppressed are liberated from the cycles of conflict. We are often caught in arguments and a vicious cycle of competing narratives and of diverging perceptions of truth and justice. This can lead to violence that ends in a cycle of more violence and revenge. After time the cycle becomes confused and people forget the origins and main issues of the conflict. The cross can help us to avoid entering into this cycle, because in him on the cross is all truth and justice.

In the cross we see the reality of our own injustice, shortcomings and contribution to the conflict. The cross opens the way to changing perceptions of others that divert us from the cycle of revenge and retaliation. 'Vengeance is mine,' says the Lord. He will administer punishment and justice. It is fundamental to recognize that God, who knows and sees all, takes upon himself the role of the judge. If we take on the task of judgment, we are assuming the role and authority of God. By taking upon himself the revenge and punishment of evil, God frees us from focusing our life on hatred and vengeance, from a life that is damaging to ourselves and others. This is an important aspect of breaking the cycle of retaliation, because we are set free from the bondage of thinking about the injustice we incur and also the justice we deserve. In Middle Eastern history, for the lack of a central authority, families took on the role of administering justice, thus making vengeance a strong element in the culture. The cross brings an alternative message of God as the instrument of justice. Through the cross, we are liberated from the feelings of injustice and the victim mentality, and come to recognize areas where we too deserve God's wrath and judgment.

In receiving freedom through the cross as either the victim or oppressor, we can be engaged with imitating what God did for us. After we are transformed, we can become a part of transformative relationships. Receiving what Christ did on the cross for each one of us, frees both sides to engage with the other in an act of love and embrace. Through forgiveness and confession, both the oppressor and the oppressed are released, and through this freedom we can be involved in developing relationships and restoring the community.

The Cross Transforms Identity

The issues of identity and belonging to a group are major aspects of the conflict. Identity greatly influences how parties relate to one another and behave towards each other. In our context, religion is a major factor in defining our identity, separating Christian, Jew and Muslim, and in playing an important role in the interaction between groups.

The cross not only sets us free from our identities as sinners and from the roles of victim or oppressor, but also brings security to our own identity, a freedom that liberates us to embrace and accept others. The perfect love that casts out fear protects us from guilt or fear of sin, protects us from fear of rejection and brings security (I John 4:18). This is significant in a conflict where there are major struggles and insecurities concerning identity and the rejection of the other.

Determining identity can also be a political statement and can be seen as affirming or denying one's existence. The dynamic between the weak and the powerful plays a role in determining identity. The weak may feel the need to define themselves in a certain way in order to appease the strong for reasons of survival, prosperity and access to power. As a result, they may deny elements of their background. This is a common struggle for the Palestinian Arab citizens of Israel. In the eyes of some, the word Palestinian is a political statement that might be threatening.

In contrast, the cross frees us to be who we are because it affirms God's love for creation and humanity. We have been created in God's image and likeness, as Arab, Jewish, Israeli or Palestinian. The Bible assures us of God's love for all, and says that, 'There is neither Jew nor Greek, slave nor free, male nor female, for you are all one in Christ Jesus.' (Galatians 3:28). However, these boundaries do not cease to exist and the characteristics of Jew and Greek or man and woman are not removed but rather transformed according to God's purposes.

We can acquire an understanding of our identity that is complementary and not contradictory to the behaviour and identity of others. The cross that gives us freedom to be ourselves also gives security and freedom to engage with others; and as we engage with others, just as when we encounter God, the encounter is transformative.

There are those aspects of our identity that require transformation. While parts of our identity are positive expressions of culture, tradition, and history, at the same time, our identification with a group can mean adopting certain negative attitudes towards the other. Social identity theory claims that when we categorize ourselves in one group, this often results in specific feelings or discrimination towards those outside the group. Thus, as we identify with a group, we take on certain attitudes that confirm our identity and self-esteem.

There is the tendency to distinguish between 'us' and 'them,' and to evaluate one's own group with sensitivity and favour. We are able to understand our own group, recognize its good qualities, and become attached to it. We overlook our own shortcomings because it is important to distinguish between us (who are right and good and merciful) and them (who are evil and wrong).

At the same time, we can fail to see plurality on the other side. We generalize and stereotype the other, saying things like, 'They all hate and want to kill us,' or 'They are the animals, they are the evil ones.' We are unable to see them as individuals with unique feelings and thoughts as God created them. While we understand and perhaps accept the variety of feeling and opinion within our own group, we do not recognize the debates and disagreements within the other group. Rather, we see them as one group united together against us.

Palestinians feel that all Israelis are the same and cannot be trusted. Israelis feel that all Palestinians are the same and cannot be trusted. *Suspicion* and mistrust run high. It is easy to develop a 'conspiracy complex,' anticipating that 'they' are conspiring to harm us.

The cross challenges these attitudes and provides a firm alternative to the division between us and them. It offers a new way of viewing identity. Firstly we see our own identity transformed as we are atoned and redeemed, and are given new eyes to understand the other, who is offered the same grace and the same transformed identity.

Ephesians 2 is a key passage relating to identity, inter-group attitudes and ethnic conflict. The cross created one new man from the two (Ephesians 2.14-16). He is not demanding that Israelis and Palestinians give up their identity. As a matter of fact, the two groups are needed to make a third identity, a new man, the new community of the people of God. So often in group relationships, there is a denial and rejection of the other's identity. One group puts demands on the other to submit or to conform their identity to the wishes of the other. Aspects of culture, heritage and history are suppressed because they are uncomfortable or different. Here in Ephesians, Paul is saying bring your identity with you to the cross because it is transformed in Jesus to create a new community of the people of God, where each person contributes from the richness of their identity. As a result, both groups will experience peace because both are reconciled to God in one body through the cross.

The Cross Transforms Attitudes toward the Other

In this act of reconciliation, Christ put to death our hostility and enmity, and he does so by bringing people together. Interdependency exists in our reconciliation to God. We are dependent on each other to end the hostility that is between our groups and within ourselves. There is a solidarity in sinfulness and a solidarity in redemption. Our identities are transformed in relationship and not in separation. When coming to the foot of the cross, we require each other in order to deal with the hostility within our own hearts and to establish peace.

Ephesians confronts the hostility that exists in inter-group relationships. While it addresses enmity at the individual or personal level, this passage also deals with enmity between groups; in our case, the hatred that exists between two nations in a violent struggle over land (Ephesians 2.11-13). In verse 11, Paul talks about relationships between Jews and non-Jews in the early church. In the days before the early church, Jews did not look on non-Jews favourably, calling them names and viewing them as outsiders, i.e. them and us. Between the communities there was alienation, rejection, and lack of belonging. Paul's declaration that what brought the two peoples together was not a change that happened among them, but the act of Jesus on the cross. By the sacrificial act of Christ, those 'who once were *far off* have been brought near by the blood of Christ' (v. 13). People who did not experience God's actions and blessing in history are now brought together.

The Cross Creates a New Community

Peace comes not as a new ideology or politics, but is the result of the identity and action of Jesus. One aspect of peace in Ephesians is the peace that humanity has with God as a result of His forgiveness (Ephesians 2). Another aspect of peace is the end of separation or strife between groups. This peace comes as a result of people uniting through the spirit of God that cleanses us from sin, and brings us both to the Father. Peace in humanity is integrally related to humanity's peace with God.

For Israeli and Palestinian believers, this means an end to hostility toward each other. We are no longer strangers, and cannot desire to destroy the other group. Now we are equals, on the same level and part of the same family, all together under the judgment and grace of God. This unity diffuses the tension by adding a new aspect to our identity as Palestinians or Israelis. Our new identity as the people of God brings us together as a community that embraces rather than rejects one another. We are fellow citizens (Ephesians 2.19). Our unity has the purpose of building a dwelling place of God in the Spirit. We are all given different roles, in order to meet that purpose. In essence the cross, by removing the dividing wall of hostility, enables groups to move forward toward co-operation.

Our transformed identity, our belonging to a new kingdom, is liberating. Our identity is secure because we are the beloved and forgiven of God. We can be engaged, because of the freedom and security received in the cross, in self-giving, that is an imitation of Christ. It removes us from the cycle of revenge because we now view the oppressed and oppressors from a new perspective. There will always be different views, historical narratives will clash, and theological understandings will not concur. What will change are the ways in which understanding the other and our attitudes towards them. No longer will we maintain the selfish, victimized identity, but we are liberated and secure to interact with the other. Without this interaction, there will not be transformation or an end to the hostility within each of us. Relationships with the crucified Lord and with each other are the foundations for ending hatred and bringing healing and unity.

In our Middle Eastern context, as Paul said, we continue to 'preach Christ crucified: a stumbling block to Jews and foolishness to Gentiles' (I Corinthian 1:23). Although the majority groups of Muslims and Jews both reject the cross, through our ability to reconcile believers we will continue to demonstrate His act of embrace by coming together and embracing one another in reconciliation.

THE CROSS AND 'OUTREACH' LITERATURE IN EAST AFRICA

John Chesworth

John Chesworth was Programme Director of Post-Graduate Courses in Islam and Christian-Muslim Relations at St Paul's University, Limurur, Kenya. He is on the staff of the Oxford Centre for Mission Studies, UK

Introduction

In 2002 in the course of presenting a paper on Christian-Muslim Relations in Uganda a colleague referred to an incident that had taken place that year in the town where he was working. A Muslim organisation had come and run an outreach campaign, which seems to have been a full-blown affair, very similar in pattern to Evangelistic rallies run by Christians throughout East Africa. What was intriguing was the fact that this outreach rally run by Muslims was billed as a 'Crusade'. After the presentation, I queried whether the term 'crusade' had been the term the Muslim organisers had used. This was confirmed.

Having spent many years working on Christian-Muslim relations and teaching students on the importance of being sensitive to Muslims by not calling evangelistic rallies 'Big November Crusade' and the like, to find that Muslims had appropriated the word because of its contemporary meaning and were ignoring the value-laden meaning of the past, has caused me to become aware of the shifts in understanding amongst the younger generation of both Muslims and Christians.

The tradition of using pamphlets for the propagation of beliefs is a long one and they have been used in East Africa since the coming of the modern missionary era in the 19th Century. In fact L. Krapf, on his arrival on Zanzibar in 1844, remarked that the American Consul, R.P. Waters, distributed Bible Tracts. This was before any mission agency arrived in the region!

The purpose of this paper is to reflect on the understanding of the cross itself and its appearance in 'outreach' literature. Both Christians and Muslims in their writings use scriptures in order to refute the faith of the 'other' and to influence them to change their allegiance. As a part of on-going research a number of pamphlets have been surveyed. The following examples show how references to the cross are used.

Examples from Muslim and Christian Writing on the Cross[1]

Firstly, the following example shows how a passage from the Qur'an is used by both Muslim and Christian writers (Sura 4: 157):

> That they said (in boast) 'We killed Christ Jesus the son of Mary the Apostle of Allah;' but they killed him not nor crucified him but so it was made to appear to them and those who differ therein are full of doubts with no (certain) knowledge but only conjecture to follow for of a surety they killed him not .[2]

Use of the verse in the Tracts

Five different Muslim tracts surveyed use this verse:

1. Muhammad Samiullah Imran, *mafundisho ya yesu kwa nuru ya qur'ani* (The teachings of Jesus in light of the Qur'an).[3]
2. Said Musa, *maisha ya nabii 'isa (alahais salam)* (The Life of the Prophet Jesus (Peace be upon Him).[4]

Three different Christian tracts:

3. K.K. Alavi, *kutafuta uhakika* (In Search of Assurance).[5]
4. S. Masudi, *nuru ing'ayo Gizani: ushuhuda wa kijana mwislamu aliyetafuta njia ya Kweli* (Light breaks into the darkness: the witness of a Muslim youth who searched for the way of Truth).[6]
5. I. Jadeed, *hapana! dini ya kristo haijabatalishwa* (No! The religion of Christ has not been abrogated).[7]

Imran, Musa and Alavi quote the verse in its entirety whilst Masudi and Jadeed only use a small part of it. Imran and Musa closely follow the standard Swahili version of the Qur'an by al-Farsy, with only variations in spelling. Musa also includes the inserts in parenthesis, whilst Imran does not. Masudi and Jadeed follow al-Farsy for the small sections they quote.

---

[1] All the examples come from Tracts published in Swahili in East Africa; the translations into English are by the author

[2] Quoted from 'Ali (trans.), 2001

[3] Imran, n.d. Purchased from Victory Bookshop, Dodoma, January 2000; originally printed in India and contains 40 pages

[4] Musa, n.d.. Foreword is dated October 1970. 40 pages in Swahili, with Qur'anic verses in Arabic, printed in India; purchased on the street in Dar es Salaam, February 2000

[5] Alavi, n.d. contains 35 pages in Swahili. Purchased in Nairobi, May 2000

[6] Masudi, 1991 contains 102 pages in Swahili. Purchased from the Diocesan Bookshop (Anglican) Morogoro, January 2000

[7] Jadeed, n.d.. contains 24 pages in Swahili. Purchased in Nairobi, May 1990

Interpretations of the verse in these Tracts

[1] Imran introduces this passage with:

Did Jesus die on the Cross?

Initially in his service, Jesus began to condemn the religion of Judaism as was followed at that time. He preached many times against hypocrisy of the bad character and principles of Judaism. This is why the Jews became enemies of Jesus and they announced that he is a criminal; concerning the belief of Christians, he was judged and crucified by the Romans.

The Qur'an explains clearly that Jesus himself was not crucified. It is certain that at the time when the soldiers entered to seize Jesus Christ in his home, he was inside. A certain person entered the house before anybody else. It so happened that the soldiers seized the one who entered first, as he was made to resemble Jesus Christ. … Now read what the Qur'an has to say about this: 'And certainly they say: 'We killed the Messiah, Isa, [Jesus], Son of Mary messenger of Almighty God - they did not kill him nor did they crucify him, rather it seemed so to them; and for certain! There are those who differ on this matter, they have doubts, therefore, they have no experience in this matter, except that they have been persuaded by [their] beliefs; for certain they did not kill him, rather Almighty God raised him to himself. Always Almighty God is Strong, Wise.'

Concerning the verse of the Qur'an above it clearly explains that Jesus was raised to heaven whilst he was alive, without meeting with the Jews who nailed him to the cross or by any other means whatsoever (Sura 3: 23-24).

This explains why it appeared to the Jews that they had crucified Jesus. This explanation largely follows that of Chapter 216 of the *Gospel of Barnabas* and that of orthodox Islam in denying Jesus' death and that he was raised directly to heaven.

[2] Musa sets the passage in its context by writing:

The prophet 'Isa was saved by strange actions of those who wanted to kill him.

The Prophet Jesus received news that the Jews were conspiring to kill him. This was because they hated him as his teachings were good and he had a following. They knew that if he lived longer their status would decrease and he would rule over them. In their delegations to the Roman rulers they argued that Jesus was disrespectful of the rulers and their laws and that he pretended to be (God).

The Almighty God wanted to save his Servant [*lit.* Slave] from the unusual actions of the Traitors. He changed the face of the leader of those rebels so that it was that of Jesus. Therefore the soldiers seized him and in this great uproar rushed him to the place of punishment. And there they nailed him to a tree so that the traitor was indeed given his reward and Jesus was saved. The Prophet Jesus hid and separated himself from this mix up, and these traitors say that: 'We killed Jesus, the Messiah, the Son of Mary, the Servant/apostle of God.' Well, they neither killed him nor crucified him rather they confused him with another person. And certainly those who differ from each other about the certainty (of killing) the Prophet Jesus, are in doubt. They have no certainty concerning this (that they truly killed the Prophet Jesus as they claim) except that they search for an idea only. And certainly they did not kill him. Rather Almighty God raised him up to himself, and Almighty God is victorious and wise.[8]

Musa uses Chapter 216 of the *Gospel of Barnabas* to explain the reason why the Jews believed they had killed Jesus.

[3] Alavi:

And they say, 'We killed the Messiah, Jesus, son of Mary, Apostle of God;' they neither killed him nor crucified him, rather they were confused. And, certainly, those who are confused in this are together in doubt. They have no certainty about this, except they think so. And, for certain, they did not kill him.[9]

Alavi uses the passage to show that Muslims deny the death and crucifixion of Jesus, 'Certainly, following Sura An-Nisaa, Muslims deny the truth of the Bible concerning the death of Jesus, his resurrection and ascension.'(26) However, he makes no attempt to comment or to refute this view in any detail.

[4] In interpreting the verse in question, Masudi attempts to address both the Ahmadiyya and the 'orthodox' Islam's positions:

We killed Jesus who was the Messiah, son of Mary, messenger of God. They did not kill him even if it appeared that they did this.

Masudi comments:

The teachings of Ahmadiyya are often contradictory. They do not often agree (among themselves) on the various positions and this led me to despise their teaching.[10]

(Both Ahmadiyya and 'Orthodox' Islam have traditionally rejected the cross) but, the verse 155 clearly shows how the Jews killed their prophets. So I asked myself,

[8] Musa, n.d.: 38-39

[9] Alavi, n.d.: 26

[10] Masudi, 1991: 92

how can it be that a prophet is not a prophet because he has been killed? To me, it would seem that it is a matter of honour to be killed as a prophet.[11]

Here, Masudi is using the passage to further his argument that Jesus was a prophet and one who was indeed killed.

[5] Jadeed uses the verse in question to challenge the excessive attention of Muslim writers on this verse. He speaks of other verses which are often ignored by the same scholars:

Certainly, there are some verses in the Qur'an that agree with the question as to whether Christ died, even if other interpreters have held on to the meaning of these words, 'Certainly they neither killed him nor crucified him.'[12]

Jadeed refers to Sura 5: 116-117 and encourages readers to learn more about the death of Jesus by contacting the organisation and obtaining a booklet called: *msalaba katika injili na kurani* (The Cross in the Gospels and the Qur'an).

Examples of Passages Concerning the Cross in the Bible

The first example comes from a pamphlet[13] circulated anonymously by post in Tanzania in 1990. In this five page tract, 250 Bible passages have been cited to argue the case for the truth of Islam. This is what the tract says about the Crucifixion:

FOR ANYONE that is able to read and understand the Bible well it is necessary that he should abandon the perverse faith of following the teaching of Paul. He should abandon the faith that is concerned with the humiliation of the cross and falsely charging that Jesus was killed on the cross for the following reasons:

i. It is not possible for the Apostle Jesus to be cursed as Paul claimed. (Deuteronomy 21:22-23).

ii. Jesus himself did not want to be killed on the cross as he asked the Almighty God that he should take this trouble away from him (Matt. 26:39; Mark 14:36; Luke 22:42).

iii. The supplication of Jesus was accepted by God and so, Jesus could not have been crucified (Psalms 43:5, 42:6-10, 6:3-10, 31:5-8, 13-15, 18:1-9; Matt. 26:36-39; John 1:5, 12:27-28; Hebrews 5:7; Luke 23:44).

---

[11] Masudi, 1991: 93

[12] Jadeed, n.d.: 5-6

[13] Chesworth, 1999

iv. Those who claim that Jesus was crucified only follow a notion and they do not have any proof of this:[14]

John 19:14-18: Jesus was crucified at six o'clock.
Mark 15:25: Jesus was crucified at three 'clock.
Matthew 27:46: Jesus was crucified at nine o'clock.
Who is the Jesus that was crucified at three different times?
Galatians 3:1 Jesus was not crucified.

Christian Tracts

The two Christian Tracts used here were produced by Tanzania Evangelical Literature Ministry are as follows:

(1) *Isa (yesu kristo) ndani ya kurani na biblia* ('Isa [Jesus Christ] in the Qur'an and the Bible).[15]
(2) *Neno la mungu ndani ya torati, injili na kurani* (The Word of God within the Torah, Gospel and Qur'an).[16]

They both refer to the death of Jesus, however in both cases they give no commentary on the Bible passages used. All they do is to set a Bible passage against passage(s) from the Qur'an.

[1] The death of Jesus

'He humbled himself and became obedient to the point of death-- even death on a cross.' (Philippians 2:8)

(Remember) Almighty God said: 'O Jesus! I will take thee and raise thee to Myself and clear thee (of the falsehoods) of those who blaspheme; then shall ye all return unto Me and I will judge between you of the matters wherein ye dispute' (Sura 3:55).

[2] He came for the purpose of dying

By a perversion of justice he was taken away. Who could have imagined his future? For he was cut off from the land of the living, stricken for the transgression of my people. They made his grave with the wicked and his tomb with the rich, although he had done no violence, and there was no deceit in his mouth' (Isaiah 53:8-9)

---

[14] Times in Swahili start from dawn. The times mentioned are *saa sita* (6 o'clock) = 12.00 midday, *saa tatu* (3 o'clock) = 9.00 a.m., *saa tisa* (9 o'clock) = 3.00 p.m.

[15] *'Isa* n.d. Contains 8 pages in Swahili. Obtained from the Christian Council of Tanzania (CCT) Literature Unit, at Morogoro, March 1993

[16] *Neno* n.d.. Contains 20 pages in Swahili. Obtained from Ngara, Kagera Region, Tanzania, April 2001

> 'He humbled himself and became obedient to the point of death - even death on a cross' (Philippians 2:8)
>
> Jesus at the time of his babyhood talked about his death: 'So Peace is on me the day I was born the day that I die and the Day that I shall be raised up to life (again)!' (Sura 19:33)
>
> (Remember) Almighty God said: 'O Jesus! I will take thee and raise thee to Myself…then shall ye return unto Me.' (Sura 3:55)

Concluding Remarks

These examples illustrate that the death of Jesus on the Cross, its importance for Christians and its denial by Muslims, remain an area of misunderstanding and contention between the two faiths. The Cross is central to the faith of Christians and is still an offence for Muslims. The very centrality of the Cross is a stumbling block. But if the message of the Cross is removed from the centre of Christianity, its faith becomes meaningless. Muslims are aware of this and will continue to challenge Christians. Christians who waver and put the cross to one side when in dialogue or discussion with Muslims will lose more than the argument.

A Girardian Reading and Response to Communal Violence in India

Jose Abraham

Jose Abraham is a faculty member of the United Theological College in Bangalore and is currently researching at McGill University, Canada

Introduction

Violence is generally understood to be a universal phenomenon. But, contemporary manifestations of violence appear unprecedented in human history. It has literally wiped out millions of people, communities, cultures, ideologies and worldviews. In ancient languages there are no words to describe the violence as we have it today. And yet, violence remains one of the least understood fields of human social life. Rene Girard is one of the most significant theorists of violence in recent years and his works enjoy a large international following. He locates the origins of violence within the anthropological and religious framework. He believes that human culture is founded upon the principle of the 'scapegoat mechanism' resulting from the 'mimetic desire and rivalry', which is rooted deep in our biology.[1] The scapegoat mechanism unites individuals and groups who were, otherwise, in mutual conflict. So he concludes that collective violence upon an innocent victim is the driving energy that creates and sustains a social system.[2] Girard claims that no contemporary human society is entirely free from this tendency. Every social system is founded on an actual cult of sacrifice.[3] Biblical revelation put an end to the scapegoat mechanism that dominated human cultures. Scholars from a number of different disciplines such as theology, psychology and economics use his theory to understand their respective fields of enquiry.

In this paper, I will not attempt a comprehensive critical study of Girard's theories; instead I hope to read certain aspects of communal violence in India through the Girardian lens. As far as I know this is one of the first attempts to use the Girardian framework to understand communal violence in India.[4] To

---

[1] Girard, 1996: 268, 262

[2] Hamerton-Kelly 1992: 21

[3] Kearney, 1995: 4

[4] Singh, 2004a discusses several aspects of Girard's theories on violence. See also Singh, 2003b: 206-216

accomplish this I shall give a brief overview of Girard's basic theoretical framework. The remainder of the essay will then be devoted to read and respond to communal violence in India from a Girardian perspective.

The Girardian Framework

Mimetic Desire and Rivalry.

Girard locates the roots of violence in a psychological process, which he calls 'mimetic' or 'triangular desire', the fundamental concept of his theoretical framework.[5] He argues that a 'feeling of existential lack' drives us to imitate others, who represent for us greater fullness of being that we feel ourselves lacking.[6] These become our 'models' or 'mediators'. They are our models because they mediate to us the 'true reality' about the world, experience, specific assumptions about life-settings, etc.[7] We become fascinated by the objects, which, we think, are instrumental in conferring on these models 'a heightening of the superior reality and self-sufficiency we feel they must enjoy.'[8] So Girard argues that the deepest goal of desire is not the objects but to be the model itself.[9] But when our desire converges with that of the model on a common object, the model becomes our rival and a potential enemy who prevents our access to the object.[10] Competing desires for the same object leads to envy, rivalry and eventually to violence. Girard calls this a situation of 'mimetic crisis.'

Thus, rivalry is built into the very nature of mimetic desire. But if the rivalry is allowed to continue unchecked, it will lead to endless cycles of conflict, hostility, and destruction. The rivalry itself becomes more important than the object of desire, when the model turns into being a rival.

The Scapegoating Mechanism

In order to break the cycle of violence generated by mimetic rivalry, violence should be channelled into a single victim who becomes a substitute for everyone.[11] Girard uses the term surrogate victim or scapegoat to refer this figure, whose death will put an end to the mimetic crisis.[12] Non-conscious

[5] Livingston, 1992: xii. Girard develops this theory in his work [Y. Freccero (trans.)], 1965). Almost all the elements of Girard's framework of analysis are present in this work.

[6] Bellinger, 2001: 74. See also Webb 1988: 185

[7] Girard (Williams ed.), 1996: 291

[8] Webb, 1998: 185

[9] Girard (Williams ed.), 1996: 290

[10] Williams, 1988: 320

[11] Girard, 1977: 161

[12] Fredricks, 1998: 154

convergence upon a victim enables a group of mutually hostile individuals to control their aggression. It will transform them into a community, which is 'united in the mutual hatred of a single victim.'[13] Thus, the victimization of the scapegoat serves to engender a greater social cohesion. [14] In Girardian understanding, therefore, culture stems from the social order resulting from a victimization mechanism and maintained by a system that differentiates the victim from rest of the community.[15] Since the community may be ignorant of this, in order to understand the cause of this newly found social cohesion, it looks for a cause outside the community.[16] It is believed that the killing and expulsion of the surrogate victim resulted in the newly found communal peace and harmony. It implies that the source of the original rivalry and conflict was also the victim. So the victim 'will seem to them both the source of ultimate evil, reciprocal violence, and the source of its antidote, mutual love.'[17]

Girard argues that this human tendency eventually paved the way for the culture of sacrifice. The sacrifice of a ritual victim will re-enact the killing of the original scapegoat that enabled the community to regulate the profane violence, which was destructive, retributive, and self-sustaining, into 'proper' channels.[18] Sacrifice further strengthens the already established social bond. But once the social order is established, communities often forget their deep hatred for the scapegoat. Rather they divinise the initial victim and regard it as their saviour. The scapegoat thus becomes a founding symbol for the community.[19] Eventually, the scapegoating mechanism generates myths that justify the guilt and resultant killing of the surrogate victim. Myths are 'the embodiment of mimetic rivalry and accusation.'[20] So, contrary to the claims of structuralist and neo-positivist schools of ethnology, Girard argues that 'all myths are rooted … in *actual* persecutions of *actual* scapegoats.'[21]

The Anti-sacrificial Nature of Biblical Revelation

Girard believes that Biblical revelation stands radically contrary to 'mythology'. The Bible acknowledges the innocence of victims that myths would regard as justly immolated.[22] The Bible sides with the victim and tells the story of violence from the victim's standpoint. Thus, the message of the cross sensitized the world to the plight of victims and the non-violent means of

---

[13] Webb, 1998: 196. See also Lefebure, 1998: 372
[14] Fredricks, 1998: 154
[15] Girard (Williams ed.), 1996: 293
[16] Girard (Williams ed.), 1996: 269
[17] Webb, 1998: 196
[18] Fredricks, 1998: 155
[19] Kearney, 1995:1
[20] Girard (Williams ed.), 1996: 279
[21] Kearney, 1995:4
[22] Girard (Williams ed.), 1996: 272

solving conflicts:[23] 'If violence is the subject of every mythical and cultural structure, then Christ himself is the one subject who escapes from that structure in order to liberate us from its grip.'[24] In Jesus, the 'supreme scapegoat', God entered the world as a powerless victim. But Jesus never yielded to mimetic pressure.[25] He is a real person and a perfect model who can be imitated.[26]

Girard believes that the passion and crucifixion of Jesus, unmasked the scapegoat mechanism. Thus, Biblical revelation 'exposes the scapegoat mechanism as contrary to the will of God.'[27] The death of Jesus 'marks the beginning of a new dispensation in which it is no longer possible to obscure the innocence of victims of violence with the mystifications of religious and social notions of hierarchy, purity, and moral rectitude.'[28] Since the cross renounced the culture of violence, it has been a 'world shattering and socially destabilizing force in Christian tradition.'[29] Through non-violent love, the cross liberates cultures.[30] Girard argues for the necessity of a non-sacrificial reading of the Bible. Human beings who are under the power of mimetic desire and rivalry can achieve true freedom only when this non-violent love of God becomes the source of their actions. True freedom will enable them to take the position of victims and to choose a course of action that is free from the power of mimetic desire.[31]

A Girardian Reading of Communal Violence in India

Communalism in India is a complex phenomenon. It is integrally related to the socio-political, religio-economic context of India. Caste and religious identities are particularly significant in shaping communalism. It is also shaped by macro/micro-level issues. Macro-level issues are more 'ideologically oriented' but micro-level issues tend to be more 'local-issue oriented'.[32] According to Nandy urban and industrial areas are the centres of communal violence in India.[33] Even though two-thirds of Indians live in rural areas, between 1950 and 1995, villages accounted for only less than 4 percent of the total deaths in communal violence.[34] Large scale urban migration results in the separation of

[23] Lefebure, 1998: 372
[24] Girard, 1978/1987: 318-319
[25] Girard (Williams ed.), 1996: 280
[26] Girard (Williams ed.), 1996: 269, 279
[27] Lefebure, 1998: 372
[28] Fredricks, 1998: 164
[29] Fredricks, 1998: 164
[30] Williams, 1988: 321
[31] Webb, 1998: 218-219
[32] Engineer, 1989: 2
[33] Nandy, 2002: 91-92
[34] Varshney, 2002: 6

families, the disintegration of traditional group solidarities, the loss of ancestral values and the encounter with 'strangers'. In this situation the 'cultural group, which brings the 'primordiality' related to shared myths, memories, values and symbols to the fore, thus assumes a vital healing function.'[35] Exploitation of this situation by the cultural groups for political gains makes cities vulnerable to communal riots. Nandy also observes that in contemporary India money, politics and organised interests play a major role rather than religious passions in contributing to communal violence.[36]

In order to understand the complexity of communalism, we require a multi-dimensional approach and perspective. Rene Girard has devoted his scholarly career to locate the origins of violence. He has mainly used insights from western literary and anthropological sources in order to develop his theories. Since his theory is not specific to any geographical context it may not be fully applicable to explain various aspects of violence in particular contexts. Girard's theory may not, for instance, help us to understand the communal violence in India in all its complexity. But Girard's anthropological and religious framework may clarify many aspects of communal violence that are hidden from a sociological or political framework.

'Communalism is the consciousness which is prompted by one's belonging to a distinctive religious community.'[37] In this sense, communalism in itself is not negative or destructive. But, in India, the notion of the 'other' plays a significant role in shaping one's communal consciousness. Identity of the 'other' is generally created from the 'partial projection of events, selective presentation of facts, and skewed assertion about the norms and customs of the 'other' community.'[38] The identity thus created is designed to demonise the 'other'. Society is thus made to believe that the 'other' deserves to be hated and humiliated. Myth-making provides a covert sanction to use violence upon the 'other'. Even though the 'other' is always the victim of communal violence, myths suggest that the 'victim is the culprit.'[39] These myths are propagated effectively through 'hate literature'[40] and all other possible means including 'rewritten' history text books. Thus, the 'communal violence is an articulation of the deep-set rot within society.'[41]

According to Sudhir Kakar many social scientists and political analysts have an 'instrumentalist' view about identity formation of Hindu and Muslim communities in India.[42] This view holds that elites are primarily responsible for

---

[35] Kakar, 1996: 206-210. The quotation is from page 210
[36] Nandy 2002: 116
[37] Mandav, 2000: 1
[38] Puniyani, 2003: 27
[39] Puniyani, 2003: 13
[40] See for details Peddiny, 1999
[41] Peddiny, 1999: 17
[42] Kakar, 1996: 211

communal identity-formation through myths, memories, symbols, rituals and ideals. Religion becomes a powerful instrument in their hands and they exploit their religious sentiments.[43] Elites simply 'instigate' communal violence in order to 'protect' their political and socio-economic interests. Thus, communalism in India results from the communal politics of these elite politicians. But, contrary to the 'instrumentalist' notion of the role of elites in identity-formation, Kakar holds a 'primodialist' view. According to this view, the images, metaphors and mythological allusions used by the elites are not entirely their own 'creation' but are taken from a traditional stock.[44] The values and forms that the elites 'endorse have a recognizable ancestry.' So along with Durkheim he affirms that 'every society displays and even requires a sense of continuity with its past.'[45] Thus, Kakar recognizes the role of communities in their own identity formation.

Girard's single most important contribution, in my understanding, is his notion that victims of violence are nothing but innocent scapegoats. He firmly believes that the crowd wrongly accuses the victims of being guilty and, therefore, liable to be killed. This notion affirms Kakar's 'primodialist' view that elites only 'revive' what is already 'given'.[46] They 'construct' from what already exists in common mythologies. According to Girard, we usually believe that victimization is a plot of leaders and rulers. But in fact, it is a collective activity by the entire community. The scapegoat is a mechanism that works unconsciously in cultures and societies:[47] 'leaders can manipulate it, but there must be something to manipulate, which is the belief of the crowd, our own belief.'[48]

The Girardian notion of the scapegoat mechanism promises interesting insights into the communal conflicts between Hindus and Muslims in India. As we have already seen, the scapegoat primarily unites individuals and communities who were otherwise in mutual conflict. This insight seems to be true with regard to the serious attempts made by the Hindutva[49] movement to forge a unity among all Hindus against the Muslims in India.[50] Historically

---

[43] Mandav, 2000: 17

[44] Kakar, 1996: 216

[45] Kakar, 1996: 234

[46] Kakar, 1996: 234

[47] Girard (Williams ed.), 1996: 266

[48] Girard (Williams ed.), 1996: 266

[49] Hindutva is not identical with Hindu religious traditions. It should not be understood as Hindu orthodoxy but as Hindu fundamentalism. Rashtriya Swayamsevak Sangh (RSS) is the driving force behind the Hindutva ideology and the Bharatiya Janata Party (BJP) is its political wing. There are more than fifty major frontal organisations which promote the cultural, political, social and religious dimension of Hinduva ideology. These organizations work together as different members of the same family called the *sangh parivar*.

[50] See Shah, 2002: 1391-1393

Hindus were not a united community as Hindu nationalism would have us believe. There was no social structure that united all Hindus irrespective of their caste differences. But, today, Hindu nationalists claim that the Dalits, and Other Backward Castes and Tribes are all part of one Hindu community. Sarvarkar, the first ideologue of Hindutva, proposed a much wider unity to create a 'Hindu nation'. In his understanding, a Hindu is one who follows a religious tradition that has emerged from within India such as Hinduism, Buddhism, Sikhism and Jainism.[51] Similarly, even though indigenous Hindu traditions are not 'religions' in the sense of 'Semitic' traditions, the Hindutva movement attempts to restructure them on the model of these traditions. Rama is redefined as the God and Gita as the book of this new 'Syndicated Hinduism'.[52] From a Girardian perspective these attempts of the Hindutva movement reflect the basic human tendency to imitate others - others' structural patterns of religion and nation.

As we have already seen, Girard believes that it is the system of differentiation that sustains a cultural unity. The Hindutva movement always maintained a system of differentiation that categorises people into 'us' and 'them'. It is held that 'us', the Hindus, are different from 'them', the Muslims or Christians. This differentiation is maintained through anti-Muslim, anti-minority myth-making. Myth-making consolidates Hindu unity and intensifies the politics of hate. In the recent past, the Hindutva movement has politicised the Mandal commission's recommendations, the Babri Masjid issue, the dialogue on religious conversions and the Godhra massacre in order to magnify this system of differentiation. But a system of differentiation is only an artificial mechanism created in order to sustain rivalry rather than to solve contentious issues.

A Girardian Response to Communal Violence in India

A Girardian response to communal violence in India demands a restructuring of the present social order. As we have already seen, the Girardian framework affirms that the social order is created and sustained by means of a victimization mechanism and myth-making. The present social order is founded upon those myths, which affirms that the 'victim is the culprit'. But the Gospels confirm the innocence of victims and reject the scapegoat mechanism that dominates cultures unconsciously. Myth-making reflects a false consciousness of the crowd that distorts the truth. Myths make people collaborate on the basis of a misunderstanding.[53] In order to see the truth from a victim's perspective a Girardian response demands the demytholgization of the present social structure. 'A genuinely peaceful society for Girard is one which has exposed

[51] See for details, Abraham, 251-261

[52] This is a word coined by R. Thaper; see for details, Puniyani, 2005

[53] Girard, 2005

the sacrificial mechanism of social conformity and opened itself to the possibility of true fraternity - a fraternity without scapegoats, without illusions, without myths: a fraternity which surmounts the perverted social imaginary of 'mimetic rivalry', with its recurring cycles of blood-letting.'[54]

A Girardian response will also demand a radical change or conversion of individuals from the crowd mentality. The new social order based on truth and non-violence requires a new set of ethical principles. For Girard, the Gospels provide these ethical principles.[55] The radical change will enable one to take the victim's position and understand violence from the victim's perspective. According to Girard, pure acts of violence do not exist rather violence is a relationship. It is the same principle that causes love and hostility in human relationships.[56] Human relationships are capable of reciprocating both violence and love. Just like bad mimesis leads human beings to violence and hostility, 'good contagion and 'non-violent imitation' enables them to engage with others in loving relationships.[57] A good mimesis helps one to transcend rivalries which give rise to the scapegoat. The end of mimetic rivalry creates a social order characterised by love and non-violence.

These two responses imply that renouncing violence is an active phenomenon. Any response to communal violence in India requires restructuring of the social order and demythologization of the communal consciousness. A social order based on an unjust socio-economic structure is the breeding ground for rivalries, communal politics and communal violence. Neither the minority appeasement of 'secular' political parties nor the majority appeasement of 'communal' parties will help us to respond to communalism. The urgent need is a social structure based on equality and justice.

Girard believes in the inherent tendency of modern democratic and economic principles to create rivalry and unjust social orders.[58] It is generally the scarcity of basic resources that force people to desire what others own and engage in myth-making to appropriate it. Just like myth-making, demythologization is also a collective phenomenon. In India, it includes unravelling the truth behind dominant anti-minority myths[59], the rewriting of history text books from a scientific historical perspective, depoliticizing education and culture etc. Just as Girard and Girardian scholars perform the non-sacrificial reading of the Bible, the religious and non-religious literatures of India need to be re-read from the victim's standpoint. This will bring out and revive India's long tradition of non-violence and its anti-victimization mechanism.

---

[54] Kearney, 1995:2

[55] Girard (Williams ed.), 1996: 278-279

[56] Girard, http://theol.uibk.ac.at/cover/girard_oxford_video.html

[57] Girard (Williams ed.), 1996: 290-291

[58] Girard, http://theol.uibk.ac.at/cover/girard_oxford_video.html

[59] Puniyani, 2003

Conclusion

Communal violence in India is rooted in the socio-religious, politico-economic structure. The complexity of communal violence requires a multi-dimensional approach for any attempt to understand and respond to it. Since no theory is comprehensive enough to explain all aspects of communal violence, every attempt to study it from the perspective of various disciplines is welcomed.

Rene Girard is one of the most important theorists of violence in recent years. He offers us a comprehensive system to understand the origins of violence and how it operates in human societies. He started his career as a literary critic focusing on western anthropological and religious literature. He believed that violence was the end-product of the human tendency to be like others and the human desire to appropriate what others own. His most important contribution to the study of violence was his notion that the victims of violence are nothing but scapegoats who are wrongly accused by the crowd of being guilty. He believed that even though historical Christianity failed to understand the innocence of victims, the Gospels fully recognized it.

The message of the cross, in this context, stands in radical contrast to that of mythology, the embodiment of the scapegoat mechanism. In his opinion, this necessitated a non-sacrificial reading of the Bible, especially the Gospels. Girard's theory of violence sensitizes us to the plight of victims even as violence escalates at all levels. In order to understand the truth of violence, he challenges us to understand violence from the victim's standpoint. His most significant challenge to contemporary Indian society is the need for a non-sacrificial reading of religious scriptures and non-religious literature.

A PAKISTANI CHRISTIAN'S PERSPECTIVE ON THE CROSS

Pervaiz Sultan

Dr Pervaiz Sultan is Principal of St Thomas' Theological College in Karachi, Pakistan

General Comments

Christians in Pakistan revere the cross of Jesus Christ not only because it is central to the fabric of Christianity but because they live in the majority Islamic context. Pakistani Christians think of the cross as central to their faith and practice. The three hour long service of remembrance of the events leading up to the cross and reflections on the words of Jesus from the cross are central features of Pakistani Christianity. 1 Corinthians 1:18 is often used as encouragement: 'For the message of the cross is foolishness to those who are perishing, but to us who are being saved it is the power of God'. Fundamentally, the cross symbolizes the atoning death of Christ which is made effective by faith and is the way to the eternal salvation of humanity.

However, the surrounding culture of popular Islam affects the different ways in which beleivers see the cross in Pakistan. Faith in the cross is often taken by beleivers to extremes (reflecting the broader popular Islamic spiritualities where charms and amulets play a central role) as when a wooden or metal cross is seen as something infused by power against the dark forces of demons and malevolent spirits. This is prevalent in both urban and rural areas where relatively less educated Christians live in concentrated groups.

The use of the cross as a simple ornament is also prevalent among all Christians. Christian men and women outdo each other in sporting golden crosses around their necks both as a sign of their faith and simply as a fashion statement. Homes are often decorated with wooden or metal crosses on the walls or shelves where none of the objects may be necessarily seen as having any special power but are simply seen as objects that remind them and their visitors of their identity and give comfort in a world where they are a minority.

The cross is also known to be used by some in occult practices although, this is limited to some areas and is often very secretive because it is not generally accepted among Christians as the right use of the cross.

Pakistani Christians' understanding of the cross is pragmatic. This is to do with the daily work situation where they encounter their Muslim friends who, despite believing many things about Jesus, do not believe in his death. Pakistani Islam generally holds to the traditional belief that when his enemies tried to kill him Jesus was taken to heaven alive. God saved Jesus, and his enemies hanged someone similar to him. While answering Muslim enquiries about the Christian belief in the death of Christ, Christians are confident about defending their faith in the death of Christ. This is the point at which Muslims and Christians in Pakistan part ways.

Interfaith dialogue is a recent development in Pakistan. It is seens as a way of engagement with the people of other faiths. The main aim of dialogue is social harmony which is a great need in Pakistan where Christians, churches and other institutions are often attacked. These attacks have increased since 11th September 2001. But since the subject of the cross is a point at which Christians and Muslims part ways, there is very little discussion in a dialogue context. The media often cover events where discussions between Christians and Muslims take place, especially on occasions of religious festivals. The cross does feature in some of these discussions but it is difficult to speculate about the impact of these on the audience. One thing is certain, however, that these dialogues on Christian and Muslim Christologies remind those listening or watching that Christ lived on the earth with a purposeful obedience to God. This is the point about Christology which all seem to accept.

Christology in Context

Christians in Pakistan are fully aware of the meaning of Christology. They meaningfully sing Messianic Psalms in worship. The Psalms were translated into the Punjabi language during the early 1900s. These Psalms are sung by Christians regularly. Messianic Psalms which proclaim Christ's death and suffering receive much more attention in worship than do the other Psalms.

Most Pakistani Christians are from poor backgrounds. Only a handful of them are from the upper social classes. The majority have had a first-hand experience of poverty, persecution and alienation. They know suffering from close quarters. They understand and appreciate the dignity in both Jesus' life and his death. The cross is a powerful symbol of their experiences. For this reason, the meditations on Jesus' words on cross are extremely popular. These give them comfort, hope and guidance for a life lived with humility and obedience even when they feel alone and abandoned by rulers and even by God. Poverty leads to extreme debt which most find it impossible to clear. They see and appreciate the promises of God who cancels the debt of human sin in Christ. God pays the full price of human sin from his own resources and by offering his own son as a ransom.

The cross for Christians is not a symbol of defeat but of victory over death, sin and suffering. It is the symbol of the defeat of the Evil One. Christians in Pakistan reflect on the cross with the same faith. They are waiting for the return of Christ but in the meantime they are confident that all that appears to be against them is going to be taken care of by the power of the Spirit of God and that they will overcome the prevailing injustices and sufferings. In some traditional churches the processional hymn is sung with a cross-bearer in front of the procession. The hope in God being the judge and the final arbiter of justice accepts delay and takes the pressure off from churches as the means of overcoming injustice and evil from society.

The cross is also the substance of Christian mission and evangelism. It motivates sinners to repent of their sins. It invites them to have faith in Christ who died and Christ who came back to life by the power of God. This Christ is to them the source of confidence about life after death. Christians bear the cross as a symbol of witness to the death of Christ. They are not ashamed of it but rather, they bear witness to it in all circumstances. Within church circles, Pakistani Christians cherish their belonging to this Jesus who died and rose again. The suffering servant is not a theme of the past for Pakistani Christians but a contemporary concern. The naming of the chapel of St. Thomas' Theological College was, therefore not incidental, but arose out of the deep affinity Pakistani Christians feel with the suffering Jesus, and is called 'the Chapel of the Suffering Servant.'

The Episcopal churches including the Church of Pakistan adhere to a high church practice of the Holy Communion. In many churches Holy Communion services are held on all occasions for meetings. On Christmas Eve, Christmas Day, New Year Eve and New Year's Day, Holy Communion services are held at many large and small parish churches. This is a reminder to believers of the suffering and death of Jesus which is the focal point of all worship. The death of Jesus is the pivotal point of Christian reflection and experience in Pakistan.

The Cross of Jesus is also considered to be a means of blessing among Pakistani Christians. The sign of the cross is made by priests after the benedictions and on the forehead of children at baptism. This is a sign of blessing which is taken extremely seriously by Christians.

Many Pakistani Christians live in situations of conflict. They understand the need of a mediator to help them reconcile with those with whom they are in conflict. They also understand the value of peace. They appreciate the role Jesus Christ plays as the mediator and reconciler of humanity to God.

Some Elements of Islamic Christology in Pakistan

The word, Pakistan, literal means, 'holy land'. This land is unique in many ways. It has been in existence since 1947 and has been attempting to balance modern democracy with an underlying religious base. The Muslims of Pakistan are confident that its creation was for their socio-economic and religious betterment, something which they believe was impossible to achieve in India where the majority are Hindus. Like the Muslims of Pakistan, Christians and other religious minorities have been living in this land for ages and have equal rights to profess and practice their religious faiths. Christian political leaders played a central role in the Pakistan Movement. The white colour on the national flag of Pakistan is a public recognition of the fact that Pakistan is not exclusively a country for Muslims. Christians in Pakistan, a religious minority of about 2 per cent of the total population of 140 million, believe they have a unique role in this country with a Muslim majority.

Describing the spirit of Islam, Muslim scholars point out that acceptance of the various prophets is an essential part of Islamic teaching. Jesus is accepted as one among the major prophets who came with a book of revelation. However, a distinctive view of Islam is projected onto all of these prophets. Islam's primary concern is with the belief in one God and His righteousness rather than with dogma and formal religious observances.[1]

The ideas of mediation between God and man, priesthood, atonement, a saviour, sacraments, and dogmatic theology are rejected by Islam. Individuals relate directly with God. Salvation is linked to faith in the one God and His prophet, Muhammad and the righteous conduct of the believer. There is no need of a mediator between the believer and God. Moral behaviour can lead to salvation.[2] Good deeds are pleasing to God and make His mercy available to the believer on their way to paradise. Also, God forgives the sins of the people because He is merciful. The role of the true religion is to make people worthy of receiving God's mercy: 'Religion needs to be presented, not in terms of antiquated dogma, but in its essential spirit as a positively moralising force. The religious mission is to establish the kingdom of God on earth that justice and righteousness may prevail.'[3]

This understanding appears to be in line with the Old Testament and the Ecumenical Christian theology of religion. When Christology is discussed, Muslim scholars are defensive about their views on Jesus. Jesus to them is only one among the major prophets like Adam, Moses, David and the prophet Muhammad. They accept that Jesus was a 'means' of salvation but this was not necessarily distinctive from the salvation procured through other prophets. According to them, all prophets were saviours of their people in different contexts. They created the conditions for their peoples' salvation by engendering faith and belief in the hearts of people. Jesus was exceptional only in that he was especially endowed with the power of God to heal. He was not unique in being miraculously conceived. Adam too had a miraculous birth.[4]

Islam is optimistic about the human potential for doing good. Emphasis is laid on good works. Original sin has not corrupted human nature as sin is seen more in the context of practice than a condition of human nature. Also, since God is the great forgiver, Muslims do not believe that atonement for human sin is necessary for salvation. Therefore, the death of Jesus on the cross and the idea of the propitiation for human sin is out of place in the Islamic theology of

---

[1] Ali, 1978

[2] Ali, 1978: 50

[3] Ali, 1978: 58

[4] A discussion on these issues appeared on a private TV channel over Christmas of 2005 in Karachi.

salvation. Islam is also critical of the cross because it is a sign of defeat and humiliation. Jesus was a major prophet and was totally innocent. Therefore, it was not appropriate that God should allow this beloved prophet of His to die such a humiliating and pointless death. Notwithstanding this mainstream position, in the Urdu literature of Pakistan, the cross is widely used as a symbol of suffering. A reader of Urdu poetry and prose understands the Cross as a symbol of suffering and pain to those most vulnerable. This creates a background for meaningful reflections on the cross.

The cross of Jesus is the most essential doctrine of Christian faith about which there can be no compromise with mainstream Islam. The Christian experience of suffering and poverty gives them a unique insight into the meaning of the cross which they can share with others as part of their witness to Jesus. It can and has been a powerful motivation for their engagement in peace and reconciliation work. Where results have been slow in coming, the same cross has given Christians hope for something better to come when the kingdom of God will be fully established.

THE CROSS IN THE EGYPTIAN 'CHURCH OF THE MARTYRS'

Arne Fjeldstad

Rev Dr Arne H Fjeldstad has lived for several years in Egypt and is currently the Director of the Media Project, Oxford Centre for Religion and Public Life

You may have visited Egypt without even being aware of a little dark blue cross tattooed on the inside of someone's wrist (sometimes even on the hand close to the thumb). This tiny cross is a symbol of identity used by millions of Coptic Christians in Egypt. It is a very old tradition, and many children are given the tattoo of the cross when they are barely 2-3 year old, often during Christian holidays or festivals (*mulid*). It appears that a large majority (approximately 90%) of both Egyptian Christian men and women bear this tattoo.

As with any other tradition there are several possible explanations. One theory is that the custom started when Arab rulers allowed Christian children to be abducted from their families. Tattooing the inside of their wrist ensured that their true identity could not be hidden. Another legendary explanation is that the blue colour of the tattoo reminds Christians of the scars received when they were forced to carry heavy chains with a large iron cross during the rule of the very eccentric Fatimid Caliph Al-Hakim ibn Amr Allah (996-1021 CE). He inflicted all sorts of sufferings on Christians including the wearing of heavy chains with a cross at the end around their neck, thus leaving a bluish mark on the skin.

The Coptic Church is often referred to as 'The Church of the Martyrs' due to the persecution they were subjected to for nearly 2000 years. According to the tradition their founder and patron, St. Mark, was slain on Easter Monday of May 8, 68 CE. He was dragged by his feet by Roman soldiers all over Alexandria's streets and alleys before being killed. The Copts have been persecuted by almost every ruler of Egypt. Their clergymen have been tortured and exiled even by Christian brothers since the schism of Chalcedon in 451 CE which continued until the Arab conquest of Egypt in 641 CE. For this reason the Copts have a special affinity with the Cross. The Copts demonstrate this also by their adoption of the Calendar of the Martyrs, which begins each year around September 11 and commemorates those who died for their faith during the rule of the Roman Emperor, Diocletian (284 CE). The calendar is still used all over Egypt by farmers to keep track of the various agricultural seasons and the church year consisting of 265 days of fasting and prayer.

For the four centuries following the Arab conquest of Egypt, the Coptic Church generally flourished and Egypt remained basically Christian. Despite certain restrictive laws imposed on them in 750-868 CE and 905-935 CE under the Abbasid Dynasties, Coptic culture prospered and their church enjoyed one of its most peaceful periods. By the beginning of the second millennium of the Common Era, conditions worsened. The Copts, in addition to the *zizya* (protection) tax, suffered from numerous serious restrictions in their everyday life and religious practices based on the infamous 'Codes of Umar' (*shurut al-umariyya*). For example, there were restrictions on repairing old churches and building new ones, testifying in court, public behaviour, adoption, inheritance, public religious activities, and clothes. Slowly but steadily, by the end of the 12th century, the face of Egypt changed from a predominantly Christian to a predominantly Muslim country. The Coptic community was actively suppressed as it existed in an environment of constant fear of Muslim hostility and violence. The Copts suffered most during those periods when the Arab dynasties were politically at their lowest.

However, travelling around in Egypt one cannot avoid noticing the Coptic Orthodox churches with their distinct crosses stretching out to all the four corners of the world. They are yet another sign of a vibrant Christian presence in a 'Land of the Bible'. The crosses have survived centuries of varying degrees of oppression and persecution and witness to the resilience of the Christian faith in a hostile Muslim majority state. No one really knows the real numbers of Christians in Egypt for estimates vary between 4-15 million of a total of an estimated 77 million in 2005. It is however safe to assume that Christians form about 10 % or more of the population of Egypt today despite decades of their migration to the West.

Several different artistic expressions of the cross have their roots in Coptic Christian culture. Most notably from a history of religion perspective is the *ankh* cross with roots even further back in ancient pharaonic culture and religion. The Ancient Egyptians used the *ankh* to express life. It is also called *crux ansata*, i.e. 'cross-with-a-handle.' For the Coptic Church, the circle represents the eternal and everlasting love of God, as shown through Christ's crucifixion. Another cross that plays an important role in devotional life in the Coptic Church is the *iota* cross. This cross is inserted with lines and material in different colors, creating an intricate and beautiful pattern. Each colour represents a Biblical truth. It is used as an aid for contemplation and prayer.

The Coptic Christians have historically been a majority in Upper Egypt but their numbers have declined over the past 50 years for various reasons. Despite being a religious minority for centuries, the Copts have played an important role in Egyptian history. When the Egyptian nationalist movement began to organise itself more effectively in early 1900, the Copts joined forces with the nationalist Wafd Party. This party was so popular among the Copts and their influence so great on the party that the Cross in the Crescent became the symbol of Egyptian nationalist resistance to British imperialism. The coming together of the Cross and the crescent symbolised the unity of all Egyptians irrespective of their religion.

The Codes of Umar banned the exhibition of the cross on churches and homes (one among many restrictions). These codes, however, have been exercised variously under different Muslim rulers and from area to area. Nearly every Christian home in rural Egypt would have had a cross either carved or hanging on the door or outside the house itself. It was a demonstration of their Christian identity, an identity they were not ashamed of and it was also a sign of the Christian expectation of God's blessings and protection on all those who believe. It has been a general rule that the cross displayed on the top of churches should not be higher than the minaret of the mosques. In practice however, this rule has not been rigidly followed.

In the recent presidential decree (late 2005) the power to permit the building or repair of churches was delegated to the regional governors. However, the decree also required the governors to consult with the responsible authorities (the Internal Security offices). These authorities have their own list of questions and requirements, including an entirely new question about how high the highest cross should stand above ground. The corrupt bureaucracy ensures that there is little hope that the new presidential decree will ease the burdens of Christians. It appears that the largely Islamist-dominated lower and middle government bureaucracy are finding new ways of restricting the freedom of churches.

Yet the Christians in Egypt are no strangers to suffering and oppression meted out to them by rulers and administrators. There is a clear tendency in the Coptic Orthodox tradition to embrace suffering and submit to it. The Islamic core concept of submission may have further strengthened this attitude but it was also very much present during the Roman and Byzantine periods. When the Arabs conquered Egypt, the Melkite Patriarch asked the Pope of Alexandria to submit and carry this new 'cross'. During the initially very successful Bashmony (Delta area) revolution around a hundred years later, the Syrian Orthodox Patriarch was used as a hostage walking in front of the troops of the Caliph Al-Ma'mun in order to persuade the rebel army to surrender.

The cross is very much a focal point of Coptic Christian piety and everyday church life. It carries a variety of different meanings, from an outward sign of identity and cultural adherence to an inner faith centred on spiritual life and practices. As a spiritual concept, the cross symbolizes the pain and suffering the Egyptian Christians know so well and feel obliged to accept as their fate. Yet for many it turns out to be a choice based on love and a voluntary surrender to conditions allowed by God. Then it becomes a pain and a burden that is accepted with joy because it gives the Christian an opportunity to suffer with their Lord Jesus Christ. This suffering becomes a promise for the rule of Christ in eternity.

The Coptic Orthodox priest Youssef Assad in a privately printed booklet focuses on the positive understanding of the cross and the hardship a Christian has to endure.[1] His teaching is widely popular among Coptic believers. Assad outlines several aspects of the role of the cross in the life of a believer. Firstly, the cross leads to positive actions. Its bearing fulfils God's will in the believer's life and glorifies Jesus. The believer is 'an instrument in His hand'.[2] Secondly, the cross is not a burden that believers have to endure but it is rather a gift from God. Believers are obliged to thank Him for it.[3] Thirdly, when one bears the cross they do not wait for or rely on compassion from people. Jesus accompanies the believers in their suffering.[4]

The cross is also understood in a wider folk religious context as containing the *baraka* (blessing which generates its own intrinsic power). It enables the believer to defeat the Devil because the cross possesses real power. Making the sign of the cross many times during the mass is deemed to be efficacious in releasing this power. Kissing the fingers that have made the sign of the cross is an expression of love and veneration for Jesus, the quintescence of suffering. I have also often witnessed many Coptic priests holding a small leather or wooden cross and offering the people this cross to kiss. It is also common to kiss the hands of the clergy. Assad emphasizes, above all, that the cross is a redemptive symbol of Christ's atonement for sin.The cross opens the doors of Jesus' love and forgiveness for humanity.[5]

In the liturgy of matrimony the cross is used with great significance. When the priest places the cross on the heads of the bride and the groom, it signifies that both of them accept the living cross in their lives. They accept also that suffering in life is normal. There is no life without pain and, therefore, they ought to expect joy with sadness. This is what following Jesus means.

The Christians in Egypt are likely to continue to endure hardships in the years ahead. However, one must note that changes are happening and attempts to improve the life of the different groups of people in society are being made. The cross still provokes anger and hostility. During the recent invasion of Iraq, Coptic Christian girls and women were permitted to take off their cross pendants in order not to give any excuse for aggression. In October 2003, 11 converts from Islam to Christianity were arrested and imprisoned in Alexandria because they had changed their identity. One of them, Mariam Girgis Makar, experienced great pressure for her to return to Islam and to have the tattoo of of cross on her arm removed. She is reported as having said: 'You may remove the sign of the cross from my wrist, but you cannot remove Jesus from my heart!'

---

[1] Assad, 1996

[2] Assad, 1996: 41

[3] Assad, 1996: 49

[4] Assad, 1996: 41

[5] Assad, 1996: 52

PROPHETHOOD AND THE CROSS

Hwa Yung

Rt Rev Dr Hwa Yung is Bishop of the Methodist Church in Petaling Jaya, Malaysia and Chairman of the Board of the Oxford Centre for Mission Studies, UK

Living in a majority Muslim region of South-East Asia, Malaysia, I realize that at the heart of any serious engagement between Christians and Muslims is the question of role models, Jesus and Muhammad. Most Muslims generally believe that the prophetic revelations found in the Bible have been distorted by Jews and Christians. Muhammad is the last of the prophets sent by God (including Jesus) whose testimony to the truth confirms and corrects distortions of truth in previous revelations. Jesus was a prophet without the unique sacrificial role ascribed to him by Christians. To Christians, Jesus is the fulfilment of Old Testament prophecies about the Messiah and the one who comes to reveal God fully and to bring salvation to all through his death and resurrection (Hebrews 1:1-3; John 3:16).

Christians in desiring dialogue with their Muslim neighbours must ask whether there is a way around these antithetical positions. Here I seek to suggest just such a possibility. I do not pretend to begin from a totally unbiased point of view - something which, in the nature of the case, is impossible. I begin with certain deep Christian convictions about who Jesus is, and I am concerned with putting to our Muslim neighbours the question of whether their assessment of him is adequate. I attempt, at the same time, to be open to the Muslim position without necessarily compromising Christian convictions. This requires 'a will to relate and not to antagonize, to hold claims in abeyance in order to be open to meanings. It means being truly ready for the questions and not being too ready with the answers as if they were all foreordained.'[1]

Prophethood in Islam

Kateregga gives us an outline of Islamic teachings about prophets. I can do no better than present his outline here:[2] 1. A messenger/apostle (*rasul*) is sent with

[1] Cragg, 1984: 11

[2] Kateregga and Shenk, 1981: 34-47; See this summarized by Chapman in Woodberry (ed.) 1989: 127-148. For further details on Islamic teaching on the prophets, see Bell, 1970: 17-30, 156-158 and Watt, 1983b: 55-61

a divine Scripture to guide and reform humans. The four most important are those through whom Scriptures were revealed: Moses, David, Jesus and Muhammad. A prophet (*nabi*) carries information or proclaims God's message, but is not given Books like the messengers. Thus all messengers are prophets, but not all prophets are messengers. 2. Both prophets and messengers were given a message by God through revelation (*wahy*) for the guidance of a group or nation. They all brought essentially the same message - the message of Islam. Almost every nation has had its messenger or prophet. Twenty-five are mentioned in the Qur'an (e.g. Suras16:36 and 2:136) and 124,000 in Traditions. 3. All God's prophets were trustworthy, knowledgeable, and obedient to God. They were the best examples of moral trust. They were all human beings, but protected by God from serious sin and bad diseases. They set very good examples with their own lives, although (according to strictly Orthodox teaching) they were not sinless. 4. We must accept all God's prophets and messengers, and denying any one of them constitutes unbelief (Sura 4:150-151). Some prophets were more highly endowed than others (especially Moses and Jesus, Sura 2:253), but it is sinful to elevate any one prophet and put him on a higher level than others. 5. Many prophets were mocked and rejected (Sura 15:11; 17:94). Some prophets were delivered by God, for example, Noah (Sura 21:76; 26:118; 29:15, 24; 37:76), Lot (21:71, 74; 26:170), and Moses (Sura 28:20-22; 26:65). It is worth noting that in several of these passages the word used is *najjainahu* (we delivered him), where the verb is the same as that used in the Arabic Lord's Prayer for 'deliver us.' It seems to be understood that God is in some way *obliged* to rescue his prophets; he must intervene to save them from the hands of people. For example: 'Then shall we save Our Messenger and the believers, in like manner (as of old). It is incumbent upon Us to save believers' (Sura 10:103); 'Allah delivereth those who ward off (evil), because of their deserts. Evil toucheth them not, nor do they grieve' (Sura 39:61); and 'In Allah we trust... of Thy mercy save us from the folk that disbelieve' (Sura 10:85). 6. Some of the prophets, however, were killed 'wrongfully' (e.g. Abel, Zecharias and Yahya; Suras 2:61, 87, 91; 3:21, 112; 4:155, 183; 5:70). Those who were responsible for killing the prophets were later punished by God (Sura 2:61; 3:21). 7. Muhammad is 'the seal of the prophets' (Sura 33:40). In receiving what was revealed to him, he was to recite the stories of the previous prophets, partly as a warning to unbelievers (Sura 46:30-34), and partly as an encouragement to himself to persevere with patience in the face of opposition (Sura 46:35).

Muhammad's task was to invite his people back to the 'original' religion to which previous prophets had borne witness. He was a radical monotheist like Abraham, a lawgiver and warrior like Moses and a servant of God like Jesus. As 'the seal of the prophets,' the revelation brought through him represented perfection and finality. He was like his predecessors in the following ways:[3] 1.

---

[3] Waldman in Eliade (ed.), 1987: 11.2

He was chosen by God from among his own people, neither seeking to be chosen nor showing enthusiasm for the task; he was guided by God, whose guidance is given as needed; he was distinct from the angels, who are neither human nor divine; these qualities call attention to his immortality, just as his humanity emphasizes God's power. 2. He polarized his audience: he was believed by some and opposed by many, including Satan, partly because he rejected polytheistic ancestral customs in favor of *tawhid* (declaring God's oneness). Those who opposed him called him a liar and intended to harm him and finally succeeded in expelling him from Mecca. 3. He had two major functions related to the Day of Judgment: to bring good tidings of the possibility of salvation and to warn of punishment for wrong-doers. These objectives he fulfilled by bringing a book that comprises God's messages to humankind. 4. He possessed a constellation of exemplary personal characteristics: patience, unswerving devotion, compassion, trust in God, and a pure faith that is the absolute opposite of *shirk* (letting anything share in God's power). 5. Obeying him is not separate from the need to obey God and belief in the Qur'an, the angels, and the Last Day; the obedience of those who accept him as God's messenger enables him to establish an *umma*, a community based on God's revelation, and to transmit to it the rules necessary for its survival and salvation.

An Assessment

In the early years of the Islamic epoch it appears that Arab Christians reacted by defining prophets in terms of all that they argued Muhammad was not. Genuine prophets were supposedly without earthly motives - non-materialistic, miracle-working and 'non-violent'. It is obvious that this definition of prophethood can at best find partial support from the Old Testament. Nevertheless, it found its way into Western Christian anti-Islamic polemic. This sort of dismissive approach still characterizes many Christians' attitude to Muhammad. An example of this is found in an anonymous evangelical tract, entitled 'Who is a True Prophet?' The tract begins by setting out four supposedly Biblical criteria for true prophethood: he must be born of the prophetic race; he must speak in the Name of God, Yahweh; his message must conform to the revelation which has gone before; and his prediction must be verifiable. On the basis of these, Muhammad is found wanting on every count. Hence, the tract's conclusion is clear: Muhammad was a false prophet.

The problem with this approach is plain. The criteria do not take into consideration the Muslims' concerns. Muslims can easily argue Muhammad was from 'the prophetic race' going back to Abraham. Muhammad does indeed speak in the Name of God. His message does claim to bring together all the previous revelations. The requirement of predictive prophecy is an unwarranted Christian imposition on Islam. Clearly, this sort of approach is doomed to fail. Some have, partly in reaction to traditional Christian anti-Islamic polemic, moved to the other extreme of an uncritical acceptance of the Islamic position.

Watt writes:

> Muhammad claimed to receive messages from God and conveyed these to his contemporaries. On the basis of these messages a religious community developed, claiming to serve God, numbering some thousands in Muhammad's lifetime, and now having several hundred million members. The quality of life in this community has been on the whole satisfactory for the members. Many men and women in this community have attained to saintliness of life, and countless ordinary people have been enabled to live decent and moderately happy lives in difficult circumstances. These points lead to the conclusion that the view of reality presented in the Qur'an is true and from God, and that therefore Muhammad is a genuine prophet.[4]

For all the positive assessments of Muhammad, there remain fundamental differences between Christianity and Islam which cannot be ignored. Watt's position can only be fully sustained through relativising Christianity made possible by the 'plausibility structure' of the Enlightenment which exalts doubt over faith.[5] It is not based on an epistemological position that the Islamic community respects. In the end it will only be seen as a capitulation by Christians in the face of Islam's superiority. In response to Watt's confession of Muhammad being a genuine prophet, some Muslims might rightly ask, 'Why don't you then believe in him and what he teaches in the Qur'an?' Both dismissive and over-accommodative approaches are undesirable. One wonders if there is might be a mediating position which takes seriously Islam's claims without forgetting Christian convictions.

Interestingly, Cragg points out that the Qur'an itself calls on Christians to make a careful appraisal of Muhammad's message on the basis of the *injil*, the Gospel (Sura 5:47).[6] But since the *injil* is believed to have been corrupted, this task of judging becomes more complicated. Christians, as 'the people of the Book,' in the words of Cragg, 'believe themselves in trust with a Gospel which is not teaching alone... but the good news of a whole personality, in Messianic fulfilment, achieving the salvation of the world in the grace of the love that suffers. *Injil*, so understood, is much more than verbal guidance; it is 'the power of God unto salvation.''[7] In taking up the call of the Qur'an in Sura 5:47, Christians will therefore want to bring this understanding of the Gospel to bear upon the message of Muhammad. No thinking Muslim will deny that to them. In the Gospel is revealed the truth of *immanuel*, God-with-us, through a self-denying and self-giving Incarnation which culminates on the Cross and the Resurrection. Although, this lies at the heart of the Christian *injil*, it appears to

[4] Watt, 1983b: 60f.
[5] Newbegin, 1989
[6] Cragg, 1984: 120-122
[7] Cragg, 1984: 122

have been denied.[8]

It is against this background that we can appreciate the wisdom of the replies of the Nestorian Patriarch, Timothy I (A.D. 779-823), to the Abbasid Caliph, 'What do you say about Muhammad?' The Patriarch said:

> Muhammad is worthy of all praise, by all reasonable people, O my Sovereign. He walked in the path of the prophets and trod in the track of the lovers of God. All the prophets taught the doctrine of the one God, and since Muhammad taught the doctrine of the unity of God, he walked, therefore, in the path of the prophets. Further, all the prophets drove men away from bad works, and brought them nearer to good works, and since Muhammad drove his people away from bad works and brought them nearer to good ones, he walked, therefore in the path of the prophets. Again, all prophets separated men from idolatry and polytheism, and attached them to God and his cult, and since Muhammad separated his people from idolatry and polytheism, and attached them to the cult and knowledge of one God, beside whom there is no other God, it is obvious that he walked in the path of the prophets. Finally Muhammad taught about God, His Word and His Spirit, and since all the prophets had prophesied about God, His Word and His Spirit, Muhammad walked, therefore, in the path of all the prophets.[9]

It is important for us to recognize that what the Patriarch affirmed about Muhammad was true within the latter's historical context. At no point did he compromise his Christian convictions. Note that he never did say that Muhammad is a prophet, only that he 'walked in the path of the prophets.' When challenged further by the Caliph, 'You should, therefore, accept the word of the Prophet (Muhammad),' 'that God is one and there is no other,' the Patriarch expressed his agreement to this and went on to say, 'This belief in one God, I learned from the Torah, from the Prophets and from the Gospel. I stand by it and shall die in it....I believe in one God in three, and three in one, but not in three different Godheads, however, but in the persons of God's Word and His Spirit.'[10] The call to 'the people of the Gospel' to 'decide/judge' in the Qur'an's Sura 5:47 appears to have been answered with wisdom and measured circumspection by the Nestorian Patriarch!

Relating to Muslims

Chapman looks afresh at how the Bible describes the relationship between God and his prophets.[11] He uses Jeremiah as a case study and compares him with the Qur'an's account of Muhammad where necessary to draw out any salient

---

[8] See more examples in Chapman in Woodberry (ed.) 1989 and Woodberry in Woodberry (ed.) 1989:149-160; and Cragg, 1984:121-139

[9] Quoted in Moffet, 1992: 351

[10] Moffet, 1992: 351

[11] Chapman, in Woodberry (ed.), 1989

features. What follows is an adapted version of Chapman work along with a comparison with Jesus which I have added.[12]

God's Relationship with his Prophets

The Biblical depiction of Jeremiah and Jesus are interesting: 1.The prophet has a clear call from God at the beginning of his ministry (Jeremiah 1:1-19), in which he feels that God has laid his hand on him (v.5), promises to give him the words to speak (v.7), and to rescue him from enemies (v.8). Jesus also was distinctly called and sent forth at his commissioning after his baptism (Mark 1:11ff).[13] 2. Jeremiah declares the judgment of God which will fall on a stiff-necked, stubborn and disobedient people (e.g. Jeremiah 11:9-17; 19:15). Judgment was also an important theme in Jesus' preaching (Luke 13:3; Matthew 12:36).[14] 3. Jeremiah calls for repentance (e.g. Jeremiah 1:1-8).[15] Jeremiah also recalls his people to obedience to a law revealed centuries before through Moses.[16] Jesus' call to repentance (e.g. Mark 1:15) was similarly rooted like Jeremiah's to the law revealed by Moses. Jesus went further in fulfilling the requirements of the Mosaic law (Matthew 5:17). 4. Jeremiah is identified with his people and, because of his identification with them, confesses their sins and prays for them (Jeremiah 8:18-9:1; 14:7-9). Jesus similarly identified with his people in baptism (Matthew 3:15). 5. At the same time, Jeremiah is identified with God, sharing the anguish of God over his sinful people (Jeremiah 6:9-12; 14:17-18). Jesus also anguishes in identification with God over the unrepentant Israel (Matthew 23:37).[17] 6. Jeremiah has to wrestle with the distinction between true and false prophets, and is given several tests to determine the difference (Jeremiah 23:9-40). Jesus too warns against false teachers (Matthew 23:1-36), and false prophets (Matthew 24:24). 7. Jeremiah receives God's message in different ways, and there is considerable variety in the kind of language used to describe the process of revelation Sometimes he is said to recite the words that are given to him by God (Jeremiah 1:7). Elsewhere the reception of the message is compared to drinking (23:9). In another place he listens to the words he is to convey (23:18).[18] With Jesus, the

---

[12] Many of the statements come from Chapman's study unchanged but they will not be in quotation marks so as not to make the whole section look clumsy and untidy.

[13] The call of Muhammad seems similar to that of Jeremiah.

[14] Similarly, Muhammad speaks of the imminent judgment of God.

[15] Muhammad has a similar message.

[16] Muhammad claimed to bring together the revelation received by all the previous prophets.

[17] The Qur'an does not use language of this kind to describe God's response to evil. It is far too human an emotion to be ascribed to God manifested by a human prophet.

[18] This language is of special interest when we appreciate how Muslims think of the process of revelation and inspiration: Muhammad is simply the human vehicle through which an eternal message is delivered to humans.

overall impression given by the Gospel narratives is one where he communicates with God through an intimate personal relationship, 'face to face' like Moses of old (Exodus 33:11). 8. Jeremiah's message is rejected, and he also is rejected (11:18-23; 12:6). The focus is clearly on not just the message but also the messenger. The same applies to Jesus (John 7:52; 11:49-51).9. Jeremiah suffers great indignities and is treated cruelly (e.g. Jeremiah 20:2; 23:2; 38:1-13; Chapters 36 and 40). Jesus went through similar indignities and suffering at his trial and crucifixion (e.g. Luke 22:47-23:49). 10. Whereas Jeremiah is called to take the cup of the wrath of God and make all the nations drink it (Jeremiah 25:15-31), Jesus in the Garden of Gethsemane finds that he himself is being called to drink the cup of wrath. What makes the prospect of his coming death so much more intolerable, therefore, is that he knows that those who should drink the cup are 'all the wicked of the earth' (Psalm 75:8). 11. In his agony Jeremiah pours out his complaint to God (especially Jeremiah 15:10-18 and 20:7-18), asking for judgment and vengeance on his enemies (20:12; cf. Lamentations 3:58). In contrast, Jesus prays for forgiveness on his persecutors (Luke. 23:34).[19] 12. Jeremiah has a message of hope - but only after judgment (Jeremiah 30-33, especially 30:3, 18; 31:2, 16-17). Jesus has a message of hope also - lies beyond the Cross (John 11:25f.; 12:23-26).[20] 13. Jeremiah's life ends in misery and shame as he is taken down to Egypt (Jeremiah 43:1-13). At the end of the book we are left asking the question: did God keep his original promise to deliver Jeremiah? The story of Jesus did not end with the Cross, but continues to the resurrection and beyond.

Finding a Bridge

How do God's dealings with His prophets, Jeremiah and Jesus, provide us with clues to approach Muslims? Several lines may be pursued here.[21]

One must recognize the depth of the perversity of humankind. The Islamic understanding of humans as being 'weak' and 'forgetful' does not square with the constant theme found both in the Qur'an and the Bible of people rejecting and persecuting the prophets of God. It is not just that they do not believe, but that the preaching of God's Word by the prophets draws out the worst in humankind, leading some of them to malign, persecute, and eventually, even kill (or attempt to kill) the prophets. This of course raises the question of the proper diagnosis of the human condition.

One needs to question the view that the concern for truth must always be linked with the necessity of a 'victory' over the 'enemy'. We see this in the

---

[19] When Muhammad is persecuted, he is given in the Qur'an examples of prophets who have suffered before him, and have been patient in their sufferings.

[20] Hope is founded on obedience to the law and prophetic guidance. Sacrifice of the prophet and its emulation have no special benefit for the believers.

[21] See Chapman in Woodberry (ed.), 1989: 131f. for an outline of some suggested lines to pursue.

concept of *Jihad* as understood by some today. As Cragg puts it, 'The whole logic of Muhammad's career is that the verbal deliverance of prophetic truth fails of satisfaction and must therefore pass to the post-Hijrah invocation of power.'[22] But what if the prophets are rejected and face apparent failure and suffering? This is what we find in the lives of Jeremiah and Jesus. Is there a place for us to think of suffering as being a necessary part of the prophetic experience? Could one be God's prophet and yet not be successful in the eyes of the world? Furthermore, when a prophet suffers willingly in submission to God, does it say something about how God deals ultimately with evil? Does the prophet's suffering then become a pointer to God's own suffering as he bears with his people and forgives them?

Our Muslim friends cannot simply ignore these concerns. Suffering and martyrdom are found not only in Christianity but also in Islamic traditions. Furthermore, within Islam itself, the deep divide between Sunni and Shi'i occurred precisely because the latter lost out in the struggle for temporal-religious power in the early years of the Islamic era. Sunnis won the battle and express this 'victory' in their theology of power; whereas Shi'is, having failed politically, resorted to 'a theology of suffering which developed the theme of the 'immaculate' *ahl al-bayt* (the people of the house) (Sura 33:33), the righteous ones whose innocent suffering possessed a merit which could avail for the redemption of the unworthy and for a deep emotional release and compensation.'[23] Can this serve as a bridge to some Muslims? Can the Biblical witness to prophetic suffering point to the possibility that suffering is indeed meaningful from the divine point of view?

This brings us to one of the central differences between Christianity and Islam - the Cross. Kateregga writes, 'It would seem most inappropriate for the Messiah to die through shameful crucifixion. God, who is just, would not permit the righteous Messiah to suffer in that manner. Muslims believe that Allah saved the Messiah from the ignominy of crucifixion much as Allah saved the Seal of the Prophets from ignominy following the Hijra.'[24] Huffard quotes an Iranian student, 'We honour him (Jesus) more than you do....Do we not honour him more than you do when we refuse to believe that God would permit him to suffer death on the cross? Rather we believe that God took him to heaven.'[25] Huffard, however, goes on to make an interesting point. Quite apart from the fact that there is only one verse (Sura 4:157) in the Qur'an which appears to lend support to the Islamic position, he suggests that the main reason for the rejection of the Cross may be cultural. In Arab culture, honour is an important concept and the greatest fear is shame.[26]

---

[22] Cragg, 1984: 155

[23] Cragg, 1984: 143

[24] Kateregga and Shenk, 1981:140

[25] Huffard in Woodberry (ed.), 1989: 164

[26] Huffard in Woodberry (ed.), 1989: 165f.

The place to begin communicating is probably 'The Parable of the Waiting Father' (Luke 15:11-32). This story is often wrongly called 'The Parable of the Prodigal Son' presupposing a Western reading of the Bible which often emphasizes guilt, rather than shame. To read it from the perspective of sin and guilt draws attention to the twin themes of repentance and forgiveness. Nevertheless it misses something crucial. The son's act brings enormous shame to the family. The father loses 'his face' in the eyes of the whole community. In this context, the father's decision to embrace his erring son and celebrate his return was truly great and costly. This is the story of God who embraces humanity by a costly means. Our acceptance by God is by no means cheap from God's point of view for it involves Him absorbing all our shame. This is the means He chooses to express His great love. This God is generous with His love and grace even when it costs Him 'his face'. Culturally, such a generous gesture demands an honorable response. Thus, 'To deny the Cross is a refusal to accept the generosity of God; it is to dishonor the giver.'[27] The theme of the suffering prophet is therefore not a source of shame and dishonour to God; rather, it is a means by which God's love is expressed and His grace and generosity are made available. Furthermore, it is a theme that demands a cultural obligation on the receiver to make an honourable response.

[27] Huffard in Woodberry (ed.), 1989: 171

PART THREE

THEOLOGICAL REFLECTIONS

CROSS-REFERENCE THEOLOGY: SPEAKING, THINKING AND LIVING THE CROSS IN THE CONTEXT OF ISLAM

Ida Glaser

Dr Ida Glaser is Senior Teaching and Research Fellow based in Oxford, UK

> If we mean to live in this world, it has to be said that cross-reference theology is the only one that there is.[1]

Witness and theology are intrinsically linked, since witness includes communication of the faith, and theology is articulation of the faith. In any context, therefore, relevant theology takes account of the people amongst whom witness is being given. That is, it is done in what Cragg calls 'cross-reference' to the beliefs and lives of others. It is my belief that such cross-reference theology will always refer to the Cross. Compared to all other worldviews, it is above all the Cross that makes Christianity distinctive. Theological reflection in the context of any other system is likely to take us again and again to the Cross at the heart of our faith.

This is, perhaps, nowhere more evident than in Islamic contexts, where the denial of the crucixifion indicates a worldview that has no need for the Cross. As Swanson demonstrates, Islamic denials of the Cross have provoked the development of apologetic and, therefore, of theological reflection on the Cross almost since the inception of Islam. Indeed, he argues that the doctrine of substitutionary atonement has a forerunner in the attempts of Abu Qurra to explain the Cross in his 9th century CE Islamic context.[2]

Both Islamic and Christian thinking have developed since Abu Qurra: in particular, Muslims have developed such a lively polemic against the ideas associated with substitutionary atonement that they are no longer an appropriate starting point in most situations. 21st century Christians continue to seek ways of explaining their beliefs to Muslims. What follows is a paper written to help such Christians in witnessing to the Cross. It originally appeared in the 'mission' section of a volume prepared for the National Evangelical Anglican Conference in Britain in 2003[3] and is, therefore, addressed to people who may have little knowledge of Islam.

---

[1] Cragg, 1986a: 13

[2] Swanson, 1995

[3] See 'Cross-reference Theology', chapter 13 in Gardner, Green and Wright (eds), 2003

It was my initial intention to prepare an edited version of this chapter for the present volume. However, I soon realised how contextualised the paper itself is, and how difficult it would be to re-contextualise it. It deliberately addresses its Anglican evangelical readers, with their interests in mission, and their desire to communicate the Gospel in terms of personal salvation through the death and resurrection of Christ. That chapter ends with a call to live by the Cross in relation to Muslims. This indicates my own context and interests. I believe that the 21st century world desperately needs what one of my students[4] called 'a missiology of grace': an embodied theology of love. I also believe that this is how the New Testament's own theology works. Jesus' first disciples were called to 'take up' their own crosses long before they understood what His Cross might mean. As observed above, theology and witness are intrinsically linked.

I have decided, then, to present the original paper, but to append to it a reflection on an alternative way of embodying a theology of the Cross in relation to Islam. It is a way which I had hoped was buried in the sands of history, but which, I fear, is being resurrected in new forms today. Here is a sobering 11th century Islamic account of a Christian witness to the Cross in Damascus:

> There was with the Franks a tall priest with a long beard who gave them guidance... He mounted his donkey and hung a cross round his neck and put two crosses in his hands and hung a cross round the neck of the donkey. He placed in front of him the Gospels and (more) crosses (and the Holy Scriptures). He then said (to the army) 'The Messiah has promised me that I will be victorious today.' When the Muslims saw him they displayed zeal for Islam and they all attacked him and killed him and the donkey. They took the crosses and burned them.[5]

One of the most urgent questions today is, 'What kind of theology of the Cross can prevent a repeat of this 11th century scenario?'

Cross-Reference Theology

> See the ignorance of the Christian appealing for protection to the Lord who was suspended (on a cross).[6]

Denial

Self: What does the Cross mean to you, as a Muslim?

Friend: It was the punishment they had in those days. But it didn't happen to

[4] Agwal, 2001

[5] Ibn al-Jawzi (d. 1200), quoted by Hillenbrand, 1999: 305-6

[6] Rumi, *Mathnawi*, III:2581, quoted by Ridgeon, 2001: 111

Jesus. There was a swap. Probably the king who condemned him swapped bodies with him, and was the one who was crucified.

Self: How do you think that differs from the way that Christians see the Cross?

Friend: They see it as almost synonymous with Jesus Christ. It's the centre for them. All about their sins being forgiven and that sort of thing.

Pause.

Friend: Of course, Christianity and Islam teach very much the same thing. All the religions do. It's just common sense.

I was asked to write a paper on how the theology of the Bible and the Cross develops in an Islamic context. To write about the Bible would have been easy. I and others have often reflected on how the contrast with a dictated text gives a new appreciation of the human dimension of the Bible. The contrast with a text that uses stories to illustrate laws and principles underlines that, in the Bible, it is the story of God's involvement with human beings that matters. The contrast with an eternal Word that became a Book makes us realise that the primary locus of revelation is not the Bible itself but Christ. The Islamic apologetic that insists on the corruption of the Bible sends us back to examine its human as well as divine origins, and to rethink the way we talk about inspiration and authority. I could have written a paper like that quite comfortably.

But I decided instead to focus on the Cross, and I have been anything but comfortable. I have realised anew that, after many years of dialogue with Muslims, I still struggle to find ways of drawing them to the Cross. It remains, for them, the foolishness and the stumbling block (1 Corinthians 1.23) that it ever has been. It is easy to talk to Muslims about God, about creation and judgement and sin and godly living. It is even easy to talk about Jesus' birth, life and teachings. But, when it comes to His death, even young children will say, 'He did not die.' This bare denial means that, as far as the Muslim is concerned, there is nothing to talk about.

Perhaps the most interesting thing about the above (real) conversation is that my Muslim friend did not realise, until I pointed it out, an inconsistency that any Christian would have noticed. How could it be that Islam and Christianity are basically the same when Islam denies the event at the heart of the Christian faith? The question is: what is basically the same? What is 'religion' about? My friend's answer: it's about what God wants you to do. As one *imam* began a lecture: 'What is the purpose of a religion? To regulate the whole of life.'[7]

It was the regulations that, my friend thought, were, in principle, the same. I want to suggest that these similar principles are what we would know without any special revelation - the existence of God, our answerability to Him, and

---

[7] This was a talk given to a group of Christian theological students in Oxford.

enough about what is good to leave us without excuse at the judgement (Romans 1.18-20). Islam adds to this many of the Biblical laws and stories, but they are in a different framework than in the Bible. It is this rather than historical consciousness and even, I think, the evidence of the Qur'an, that underlies the denial of the crucifixion.

The Qur'an refers to the death of Jesus in several places. In only one is the death denied: the much quoted Sura 4:157:

> (The Jews) said (in boast), 'We killed Jesus the son of Mary, the Messenger of Allah' - but they killed him not, nor crucified him, but so it was made to appear to them. And those who differ therein are full of doubts, with no (certain) knowledge, but only a conjecture to follow, for of a surety they killed him not.'

In Sura 19:33, Jesus speaks of God's blessing on him on the days of His birth, death and resurrection. In 5:119-20 and 3:55 Jesus speaks of God 'taking Him to Himself' - a word that usually refers to death. The most common[8] current interpretation of this is that, as my friend suggested, someone[9] was made to look like Jesus and crucified, while Jesus Himself ascended straight to heaven. His death is yet to come - at the end of time when He comes to bring Christians to Islam and to kill the Antichrist. It is after this that He will die and then the end of the world will come.

This is not the only interpretation that is possible of these passages. Moucarry[10] discusses the various interpretations that Muslims have offered for Sura 4:157, and adds his own suggestion that the verse denies the Jews' boast rather than the fact of Jesus' death. Christians would agree that it was not really the Jews who were responsible - it was God's own initiative, and anyway the people who crucified Jesus were the Romans. Some Muslims find this an interesting idea, and some see the Cross as a powerful symbol, but, in my experience, most persist in the belief with which they were brought up: Jesus did not die. One well-known Muslim polemicist entitles a booklet, Crucifixion or Cruci-fiction?' The story of our redemption is, he says, fiction. [11]

If the Qur'an has several places that refer most naturally to Jesus' death and only one verse that seems to deny it; and if other interpretations are possible, why does the emphasis on denial continue? It is not that Muslims have been unaware of the difficulties. Moucarry cites a classical commentator's exploration of six different objections to the idea that God should have

---

[8] Another interpretation, popularised by the Ahmadiyya, is that Jesus was put on the cross, but that He did not die there. He swooned, and later revived and went to preach in Kashmir, where His grave can still be seen.

[9] The most popular candidate is Judas, although some, like my friend, think it was Pilate.

[10] Moucarry, 2001: chapter 10

[11] Deedat, 2005

deceived people by having someone crucified in Jesus' likeness.[12] It is not the text of the Qur'an that requires the circumvention of the Cross, but the framework of thought in which Jesus should not have died on the Cross, when there is no need for Jesus to die on the Cross, and the Christian understanding of the Cross is immoral.[13]

Why should it not have happened? Because the ministry of God's Messenger should not finish in failure and disgrace. It would be dishonouring to God as well as the Messenger. Why is it immoral? Because each person should be punished for his own sin. It would not be fair of God to punish someone else on our behalf. The whole idea of God putting His Son to death like this is revolting. Why was there no need? Because, according to Islamic thinking, human beings are not fallen. They are only weak and ignorant, listening to Satan rather than to God. God is all-powerful, and can forgive us if He so chooses. What we need is guidance, and that is just what God has given us, through His prophets and books.

The Qur'anic Adam story has just this pattern: Adam and Eve are led astray by Satan, repent as soon as God reminds them of His command, and are simply forgiven. They are then sent down to earth, and told to be careful to follow God's guidance when it comes. A Muslim colleague[14] summarised the differences between Islam and Christianity during a lecture on the Adam stories in the Bible and the Qur'an thus:

Qur'an	**Bible**
Adam and wife tempted 'Fell' Repentance Forgiveness Promise of guidance Islam	Adam and wife tempted 'Fell' All have sinned Redemption needed Saviour needed Jesus Christ

Conversation

It is tempting for Christians to respond to all this by argument. The denial of the cross is a historical error, and we can seek to prove it so. We can present our arguments for Jesus being God's Son and for God's love and justice culminating on the Cross. Of course, history needs to be put straight, and reason is an important part of the discussion; but, this does not take us to the

[12] Moucarry, 2001: 34-7

[13] See Cragg's analysis in Cragg, 1999: chapter 6

[14] Jabal Buaben is at the centre for the study of Islam and Christian-Muslim Relations, Selly Oak. The main Qur'anic stories can be found in Suras 2:30-39 and 7:11-25

heart of the problem.

The denial of Christ's death has been one of the common Muslim criticisms of Christianity since the time of Muhammad. It stands alongside criticisms of the divinity of Christ, the doctrine of the Trinity and the reliability of the Bible. All have their roots in the Qur'an itself, and presumably, therefore, in Muhammad's interactions with the Christians of his time. Regrettably, Christian responses have often been centred around these same topics.

Why regrettably, when these things go to the heart of the Christian faith? Because, I want to suggest, such discussions open us to three dangers. Firstly, the danger of starting from differences rather than similarities. Any communication requires some common ground - at least a common language. Christians and Muslims can use the same words with different meanings, resulting in both sides convinced that they have won the argument, and no-one the wiser about the other's faith. Secondly, the corollary of neglecting to deal with deeper differences. The danger of apologetics is that we can focus on the arguments, and not take into account the underlying differences which make sense or otherwise of the incarnation and crucifixion. We can demonstrate the historical death of Christ on the cross to our entire satisfaction, but the Muslim is unlikely to accept it if it will not fit into his worldview. Thirdly, the danger takes us nearer to the heart of the matter: focusing on these issues keeps us on Islamic ground, and can, therefore, make us lose sight of the uniqueness of the Gospel.[15] For example, the Islamic question about the divinity of Christ is how a human being can logically be divine, since God and humans are quite different. We believe that Jesus is God and man not because this makes logical sense, but because we have found that we can interpret the person of Jesus in no other way than by accepting the wonder that God has come to be with us This is the uniqueness of the Gospel.

The Islamic question about the Bible is whether we have the books that God originally gave the prophets, or whether they have been lost. We do not believe that God gave books in the Islamic sense of word by word dictation. We believe that people wrote, under the guidance of the Holy Spirit, so that Scripture can be fully inspired and at the same time have a human form and history. This link between the human and the divine is one key to our Gospel in an Islamic context.

How, then, do we 'get to the root of the problem'? Effective communication needs to start from common ideas, to take account of differences in worldview, and to lead to the Gospel. It may be that, like Paul at Lystra where the worldview was very different to his (Acts 14:8-20), we can only take one step at a time. The Cross came at the end of Jesus' earthly ministry, and His disciples, even with their Jewish education and Jesus' own teaching, did not understand it until after the resurrection. Communication about the Cross requires a context.

---

[15] I am indebted to David Thomas for giving me the seed of this idea.

We examine here some ways of trying to communicate, and then go on to see how the Cross can take us to the heart of the issues at stake between Muslims and Christians.

Beyond the Orthodox

Muslims and their contexts are very varied. Most of this chapter is written in the context of orthodox Sunni Islam, but the Muslims we meet may think in many different ways, that suggest different ways of communicating the Cross.

Some Muslims find the very idea of the cross offensive. They may refuse to meet in a room in which there is a cross, and some have even asked to be excused from wearing a school badge which incorporates a cross. Experience suggests that there are people who will not listen to any explanation, so vehement is their denial. In general, the Cross is not the place to start talking with such people. It may take many years of friendship and introduction to Biblical ideas before they will be ready to recognise that Christian beliefs at least make sense on the basis of Christian assumptions.

Amongst 21st century British Muslims, the situation may be different. Many have learnt about basic Christian beliefs at school, and may be curious to learn more. Some parents have heard the story of the cross and resurrection from their children, and may be ready for an explanation. The 'post-modern' climate enables young people to accept the possibility that someone else's faith is valid, even if it is in categorical opposition to their own. In such situations, a simple explanation, like the 'bridge' model, can make sense, provided that the ground has already been laid in teaching about sin that separates us from God, and about God coming to us in Christ.

There are also practices within Islam that can act as a 'way in' to explaining the idea of atonement. For example: Muslims across the globe offer their animal sacrifices on the occasion of the 'Id. It commemorates Abraham's symbolic sacrifice his son. According to Orthodox teaching this is an obedient act of thanksgiving and remembrance, and is in no way a sacrifice of atonement. However, some popular thinking conveys the idea of transferring sin onto the animal. The *aqiqa* sacrifice - on the seventh day after birth, many Muslims shave the baby's head and sacrifice a sheep or a goat. The animal is said to be offered in substitution 'blood for blood, flesh for flesh, bones for bones, skin for skin and hair for hair'[16] for the child. In popular Shi'ism the idea of redemptive suffering can be seen in the tragic figures of Fatima and Ali, Hassan and Husayn.[17] In particular, the martyrdom of the latter gives rise to stories of his blood having healing efficacy, and weeping over his sufferings is a door to Paradise. Regarding honour and shame, Muslim societies usually see shame as more important than guilt. There are occasions when the shedding of

[16] See Thanvi, 1990: 284. Two animals are offered for a boy, one for a girl.

[17] See Ayoub, 1978

blood is seen as the only way of cleansing shame and restoring family honour.[18] Some Christians have traced ideas of honour and shame in the Bible, and point to God's honouring Christ and dealing with our shame on the Cross.[19]

Such ideas may help us to explain our understanding of the Cross to particular Muslims, but in practice many will still see no need for it. Muslims may have ideas of atonement, but they see it as available through their religious practices. They may even have ideas of mediation, but see Muhammad as the mediator approved by God. There remains the task of showing them why Jesus is needed.

Telling the Story

The Cross in the abstract may make little sense: the story of Jesus captures interest and moves hearts. The suffering of the Messiah seems a tragedy taken by itself: but as the disciples on the road to Emmaus found, and as the reading of the Old Testament shows it is a necessity.

It has often been noted[20] that the disciples after the crucifixion were very like present day Muslims. They believed strongly in one God. They hoped to see a visible kingdom for His people. They expected God to save His Messiah. They saw the crucifixion as a terrible tragedy. They knew nothing of the resurrection. They could only understand when Jesus took them right back through the Scriptures and the story of Israel, and when they realised that Christ was risen.

Many Christians working amongst Muslims have found it necessary to spend much time in telling the whole Bible story. We cannot expect Muslims to understand the atonement as a detached idea. I suspect that this is because it does not make sense as a detached idea: it only makes sense in the light of the God of Israel.

It also only makes sense because of the one who died on the Cross. Muslims are quite right when they suggest that one person being punished for another's sins is unjust. Ezekiel 18 recognises this. It is different if a person chooses to pay someone else's penalty, and different again if someone chooses to bear an assault and not to fight back. Christians believe that both these choices are implicit in the Cross. In Christ, God chooses to bear sin and its consequences rather than to punish us. In Christ, God also finds an acceptable sacrifice for our sins.

Neither of these makes sense if God was not in Christ. If Jesus is, as Muslims believe, simply a prophet, the first is simply impossible. No human being can bear the consequences of sin against all other human beings, let alone against God. The second is unthinkable. How could one person be sufficient sacrifice for everyone else's sins, even if this were just? And how do we

---

[18] This idea is behind the so-called 'honour killings' of women whose chastity has been broken in some Muslim communities.

[19] For example, Musk, 1995: chapter 4 and Huffard, 1989: 161-74

[20] See, for example, the introduction to Woodberry (ed), 1989: ix-xv

understand that God was in Christ? The New Testament tells us the Gospel stories. The epistles assume it - they never try to argue it. It is the Gospel story that shows us who Jesus is. It is only at the end of that story, at the foot of the cross, that the centurion of old said, 'Surely, this is the Son of God' (Matthew 27.54, Mark 15.39). Communication of the Cross to Muslims, as to others, needs to be in the context of the whole story of Jesus.

Muslims who watch the Jesus video often accept the death of Christ it portrays. This is not surprising. It is unthinkable that the Christ portrayed in the Gospels should avoid the Cross. It is also, I think, unthinkable that the Father portrayed in the Gospels would stop Him from taking His determined road. It was the Devil who tried to keep Him from the Cross - specifically at the temptations, and through Peter. In Gethsemane, the Father does not try to deflect His Son, but sends an angel to strengthen Him for His trials.

Moucarry's careful scholarly presentation of Christ in an Islamic context gives us an example of the centrality of the story.[21] He starts with an overview of Jesus in the Qur'an, and then explores Muslim interpretations of the denial of the crucifixion in some depth (see above). He focuses on the idea that the Cross should not have happened: Muslims cannot see how Jesus could both be from God and be crucified. He then deals with Jesus' historical context by noting that the first century Jews had the same problem. They concluded that, since He was crucified, He could not have been God's messenger. Muslims resolve the problem in the opposite way. Since He was God's messenger, they say, He could not have been crucified.

Moucarry moves from here to the Gospel story, which, he suggests, offers a third possibility: that Jesus was both sent by God and crucified. 'Indeed,' he says, 'the Gospels teach us that it was precisely through Jesus' death on the cross that he fulfilled His mission as Messiah.'[22] He then tells the story of Jesus through Peter's encounters with Him, showing how Peter moved from a denial of the possibility of Jesus' suffering to focus on the Cross in his epistles. It is only then that he proceeds to the historical evidence for Jesus' death and resurrection, through the idea of the servant King and titles for Jesus in the Qur'an and the Bible, to the question of Jesus' relation to God.

Whether exploring Qur'anic interpretation in the academy or watching the Jesus video in the home, the Cross is not an abstract idea but part of the history of God's life amongst His people.

Sentness and Suffering

Cragg has reflected on the Cross in the context of Islam for many years. He has focussed on the sin and suffering seen there, on Christ's obedience and self-giving in going there, and on what it means that God sent Christ to hang there.

---

[21] Moucarry, 2001: part 3

[22] Moucarry, 2001: 141

His 1956 book, *The Call of the Minaret,*[23]explores these three levels, and observes that Muslims can accompany us in the first two, but not the last:

Firstly, the Cross is a human act: it has to do with ungodly opposition to the Servant of God. It is on the Cross that we see the extent of human sin and rebellion, and the results of distorted religious understanding. Islam accepts the intent of the Jewish and Roman authorities to crucify Jesus. 'The Cross,' argues Cragg, 'is the prototype of all. The Cross bore a superscription in Hebrew, in Greek and in Latin. The human forces that made it what it was, as a human deed, are common to all humanity.'[24] We can, he suggests, point to the 'representative character of the Cross' in showing us the human response to God. Such an analysis challenges the Muslim to move beyond ideas of human beings as weak and ignorant towards seeing our fallen human nature.

Secondly, the Cross is not only something that people did to Jesus: it is something that Jesus chose to do. His own message required Him to suffer the consequences of peoples' hostility. He taught that we should not return evil for evil, but respond to hatred with love. Both to be loyal to His calling and to eschew violence in the face of expected opposition necessitated the Cross. The Cross, says Cragg, 'is what happens when a love like Christ's encounters a world like Jerusalem.'[25] Muslims accept Christ's willingness to obey God to the point of death. We want to tell them that God permitted Him this obedience: a death in forgiveness rather than hatred. This is a death that accepts and deals with the evil that causes it.

Thirdly, the Cross is an act of God. This is where we part company with most Muslims. That people wanted to crucify Jesus, and that He was willing to be crucified, they agree. That God could also have wanted it seems senseless to them. It only makes sense if this is not only God choosing this death for His prophet, but 'God was in Christ, reconciling the world to Himself' (2 Corinthians 5.19). It is not that the sacrifice of someone else 'somehow placates a propitiating God from without',[26] but that Christ Himself 'expresses the divine love already active towards sinful humanity.'[27] We can only make sense of the Cross in the context of the incarnation.

Cragg has developed such themes into an explanation of the incarnation and the Cross starting from Qur'anic ideas. In chapters 2-4 of *The Christ and the Faiths*, he starts from the idea of the greatness of God, as expressed in Mary's Magnificat and the *Allahu akbar* cry of Islam, focussing on Mary's 'His mercy is on them that fear Him' (Luke 1.50) and the parallel Muslim ideas of *rahmah* (mercy) and *taqwa* (piety or godly fear) in the context of an unbelieving world. In this way, he lays a firm foundation of common ground between Muslim and

[23] Cragg, 1986b: sections IX and X/chapter 10. See also Cragg, 1985a

[24] Cragg, 1986: 270

[25] Cragg, 1986: 270

[26] Cragg, 1986: 272

[27] Cragg, 1986: 272

Christian, while signalling differences in the way that we interpret these ideas.

He goes on to reflect on the shared idea that God speaks through prophets. Must these prophets not have some 'capacity for revelation', he asks? Muslims say that the Qur'anic words are given without the participation of the prophet: it is only after their receipt that he transmits and interprets them. Cragg argues that he must have a capacity to receive. 'God and His Messenger' frequently go together in the Qur'an. That is, the human recipient of revelation matters. Human and divine cannot be quite so incompatible as some Muslims suggest.

He then reflects on the Bible's telling of the messages of Christ and of Jeremiah, and argues that the message cannot be separated from the messenger. Neither can the rejection of the message be separated from the rejection of the messenger. We find that Jeremiah's sorrow at this rejection can scarcely be distinguished from God's sorrow (e.g. 12.5-11).

All this implies, suggests Cragg, that God as Sender is not only associated with the message that is sent, but also with the messenger. And this 'association' is in the context of the sufferings of the messenger. He recognises that this has taken him into ideas that are anathema to Islam - 'association' of anything with God (*shirk*) being the unforgivable sin. His exploration of the idea of 'sentness' leads him towards the idea that God became so associated with His Messenger that He not only sent, but came and suffered. It leads him to the Cross.

What do We See on the Cross?

What bearings do such attempts at communication with Muslims have on our theology of the Cross? They not only drive us towards different expressions of our faith, but also lead us to appreciate different aspects of it and develop new insights into it. I have found that the Islamic emphasis on revelation has led me to see the Cross in terms of revelation as well as atonement. This is not, of course, an either/or. The revelation is in the atonement. What is revealed is not a doctrine or an idea of atonement, but God in Christ reconciling the world to Himself.

Muslims see the Qur'an as the prime locus of revelation, as the eternal Word of God coming to us in a Book. Biblically, Christ is the eternal Word of God, coming to us as one of us. If God was in Christ, and if the Cross is the focus and climax of His ministry, what do we see when we look at Him there? Because the Cross is both the heart of Christianity and is missing from Islam, we see some of our crucial differences there.

We See OURSELVES

Muslims may deny the 'fall' but, on the Cross, we see the full extent and effects of sin. This is what human beings will do when confronted with the absolute goodness of God Himself. This is what God has to do to deal with human wickedness. It is not Christ's sin but ours that we see exposed on the Cross; and this focus on what we see takes us to another concept that is particularly relevant in many Islamic contexts - shame. Shame is about our sin being seen by ourselves and by others.

Muslims agree about the wickedness in wanting to kill Jesus. The main point of Sura 4:157 in its context is not denying Christ's death but putting the Jews to shame for their persistent rejection of God's message. This is right. The New Testament also puts them to shame for their treatment of Christ, but for an opposite reason. The Qur'an says, 'You killed Him not.' The apostles frequently tell their Jewish audience, 'You killed Him.' (Acts 2:23 and 36; 3:13-15: 4:10; 5:30) This comes to a climax in Stephen's sermon in Acts 7, with its relentless exposure of the goodness of God and the rejection of His prophet that culminates in the rejection of Christ.

Those sermons were addressed to Jews, but the New Testament addresses humanity more widely, and is clear that we are all implicated in Christ's death. The Cross shows us as nothing else does that we are fallen, and that guidance is never enough. Here is the best of messengers bringing the best of guidance. Not only do the religious people send Him to the Cross: His most faithful disciples deny Him and forsake Him. I can see the wickedness of the world and of myself in the light of the Cross.

'God was in Christ, reconciling the world to Himself.' (2 Corinthians 5.19) On the Cross, we do not just see God - we see Him doing something. He does not conquer sin and Satan just to show Himself as Lord, but to rescue us. How can that be?

For Muslims, the idea that someone should die for our sins seems unfair. But there is another way of looking at this. Paul also says, 'If anyone is in Christ, he is a new creation.' (2 Corinthians 5.17) Most Muslims come from cultures that function collectively, in ways that are incomprehensible to many western individualist Christians. Muslims know that, if you are a member of a family, you are implicated in all that happens to that family. In particular, one person can shame the whole family; and the honour of a family is shared by every member of it. Paul is telling us that, if we are members of Christ, we are implicated in all that happens to Him.

Paul can even say that those who are in Christ have died with Him (Romans 6:3ff, 2 Corinthians 5:14). We can see ourselves in Christ on the Cross. We see our sin that put Him there, but we also see the shame and the penalty for our sin nailed there. And, if we are implicated in Christ's death, we are also implicated in His resurrection. We have brought shame on Him, but He has borne it. Now, we can share in His honour and triumph.

We See GOD

'God was in Christ...' (2 Corithians 5:19). For the Muslim, this is an impossibility, because the human and the divine are totally different. For the Christian, accepting the compatibility between divine and human implied by the 'image of God', it is a wonder. God who can come to be with us does come to be with us. And, when He comes, He becomes totally involved in our lives, to the extent of entering our pains and our death.

This is God who is holy and just and righteous and loving; but the comparison with Islam brings out other aspects of Him.

This is God who does not overlook sin. Muslims believe that God can forgive by sovereign mercy: since He is not affected by human actions, He can simply wipe away the penalty for sin. In Christian terms, this is not really forgiveness, since it does not deal with the pain and the offence that sin causes. In the Cross, we see how sin affects God. We see a God who is not aloof from the world, but can be deeply wounded by it.

This is God who allows evil its full extent. When sin corrupted God's good creation, He limited its effects for the sake of His creation (Genesis 3:22-4; 4:13-16; 6:3; 11:6-9). He could have put an end to the wickedness at the Cross by destroying the perpetrators[28], or by rescuing the victim; but He did not. On the Cross, we see God allowing evil to have its full effect - not on us, but on Himself.

This is God who is not ashamed of His shameful creatures. According to custom, as in most Muslim cultures, the prodigal son's father should never have welcomed him back, and should never have gone to seek the elder brother. Both sons were shaming him by their actions, and the only way he could have kept face would have been to cast them off completely. But the father's love overcomes his shame - he honours them both by going out to them. On the Cross we see our completely honourable Messiah exposed to shame for us.

This is God triumphant. In Islamic thinking, God's honour and triumph are reasons for denying the Cross. It is dishonouring to God's prophet and, therefore, to God. 'We honour Jesus more than you do' is a common criticism. In Christian thinking, it is not Christ whose dishonour we see on the Cross, but our own. We see Christ's honour in His obedience to the father. We see His triumph in fighting sin and Satan to the very end.

And, of course, we see God honouring Christ and triumphing over all His enemies in the resurrection. In denying the crucifixion, Muslims seldom think about the Christian teaching about the resurrection. We, who see that 'God was in Christ', realise that it is a greater triumph to go through death to resurrection than to escape death. This is not only a triumph over the people who wanted to kill Him, but over sin and Satan for all time.

Embodying a Theology of the Cross

> If we mean to live in this world, it has to be said that cross-reference theology is the only one that there is.[29]

---

[28] Qura'nic prophets are often rescued by God's judgement on their opponents. See for example Sura 7:59-93

[29] Cragg, 1986: 13

Theology is always done in a context, whether recognised or not. The task of Christian theologians is to understand and express afresh the 'old, old story' for the current generation. We look to the Scriptures and their context, but also to the Church and to the world. If our theology is to be a help rather than a hindrance to our mission, it must be done in 'cross-reference' to the world to which we are called.

It is my belief that such cross-reference theology will always refer to the Cross. Compared to all other worldviews, it is, above all, the Cross that makes Christianity distinctive. It continues to be foolish and the stumbling block that it ever was, because it simply does not fit into any scheme other than that of the Biblical salvation story. Theological reflection in the context of any other system is likely to take us again and again to the Cross at the heart of our faith.

Christians called to minister amongst Muslims frequently testify to this. People consulted during the writing of this paper told me:

> The Cross has become so much more precious to me. I have grown in appreciation of the Creator God who is almighty, yet humbled Himself on our behalf. I keep seeing the significance of grace, and that's what the Cross is all about, isn't it? I began to think more of God's love being sacrificial, embracing suffering. This leads me to marvel at His grace and to love Him more.

This is no new phenomenon. S. Zwemer, one of the best known missionaries in the Arabian penisular, wrote a whole book on 'The Glory of the Cross'[30] towards the end of his life. He writes with a rare passion, and here is its origin: 'The following chapters are the result of meditation on the passion of our Lord and His Death on the Cross in the midst of men who deny the historicity of the crucifixion and the necessity of the atonement.'[31]

Islam's very denial of the Cross can make us realise afresh its significance. I trust that this short chapter has helped readers to do just that. But this is not only a theological significance. We cannot appreciate the Cross in our thinking without it impacting our lives. And this is, perhaps, the most important aspect of cross-reference theology. Muhammad chose the temporal victory of the *hijra*: Jesus chose the very different victory of the Cross. Which will we choose? Interaction with Muslims brings this challenge into sharp relief. Constance Padwick wrote in 1938: 'It is no easy achievement to meet the *hauteur* of Islam without answering *hauteur* but with penitent love.' And she quotes Temple Gairdner of Cairo (1837-1928):

> We are claiming the right to have it said to us, 'Ye are they which have continued with me in my temptations.' . . (Christ) too knew what it was to fall back on the Spirit, to realize and to confess that only by what seemed like weakness must all

[30] Zwemer, 1954

[31] Zwemer, 1954: 5

> that strength be met, *only* by the foolishness of the Message, *only* by the scandal of the Cross.[32]

Our times are no different. There are still social and political tensions between Muslims and Christians world-wide. There are still millions of Muslims who struggle with oppression and sin every day. The calls to mission, to peacemaking, to being salt and light in the world are no less urgent. Responding to the calls is no less costly.

The Cross is not only part of the Bible story and the Gospel story: if we are to communicate with Muslims, it must also be part of OUR story. We must allow our sin - communal and national as well as personal - to be exposed and dealt with. We must follow the obedience and meekness that led Christ to it. We must show in our lives the God who is involved in human affairs; who does not overlook sin; who accepts the effects of sin, but does it with forgiveness; who is not ashamed to be associated with sinful people; and who triumphs through death.

Muller's research on what makes an effective missionary amongst Muslims yields a startling result. What his subjects had in common, apart for love for Jesus, for the Bible and for Muslims, was that they had all suffered deeply, either in their personal lives or as the result of their ministry.

> Suddenly, I realised that Muslims weren't attracted to evangelists, they were attracted to God... They may not know it, and might not express it in those words, but when they see God in His beauty, lived out in the lives of his people, they are attracted to Him. In order for Jesus to truly shine through a life, the hard exterior has to be broken and removed.[33]

In Gethsemane, Jesus begged His Father, 'If it is possible, may this cup be taken from me.' (Matthew 26:39) If there had been any other way, we can be sure that the Father would have spared the Son. There was no other way for Him if we were to be saved. There is no other way for us if our Muslim friends are to see Him.

Reflection: Taking up the Cross

> Be Thou my consolation, my shield when I must die; Remind me of Thy passion when my last hour draws nigh. Mine eyes shall then behold Thee, upon Thy cross shall dwell, My heart by faith enfolds Thee. Who dieth thus dies well.

So ends 'O sacred head, sore wounded', the hymn attributed to Bernard of Clairvaux (1090-1153). Such moving lyrics on the suffering Christ, together

---

[32] Padwick, 1938: 341-54

[33] Muller, 2000: 24

with his passionate writings about loving God,[34] might lead a 21st century reader to expect a concept of 'taking up the cross' similar to that envisaged by Cragg, Padwick and Gairdner. But Bernard was a 12th century writer: his preaching mobilised thousands of soldiers for the second Crusade. 'Jesus, the very thought of Thee with sweetness filled the breast, but sweeter far Thy face to see and in Thy presence rest'[35] takes on a new dimension when we imagine it sung by knights seeking martyrdom in war against Muslims.

Bernard of Clairvaux was not alone in this sort of preaching, for joining the Crusades was seen as, quite literally, taking up the Cross; and taking up the Cross was the imitation of Christ and the sharing of His passion. As Christopher Maier's collection of sermons and sermon exemplars from the time of the first Crusade[36] indicate, calls to join the Crusade were seen as preaching the Cross.

> *If anyone wants to come after me, let him renounce himself and take up his cross and follow me.* Those who take the cross renounce, that is, adjure, themselves by exposing themselves to mortal danger, leaving behind their loved ones, using up their belongings, carrying their cross, so that afterwards they may be carried up to heaven by the cross... Eudes of Chateauroux.[37]

> May you have this cross of Christ on your heart and carry his stigmata on our body so that, offering the sacrifice of a burnt-offering inside, you may have his skin on the outside. He who claims to remain in Christ through internal love must walk as he walked by the open imitation of his deeds and passion. Gilbert of Tournai[38]

Such 'taking up the cross' and 'carrying the cross on your heart' were meant quite literally. The Cross was carried into battle, and sewn over the heart. Crusaders were often called *crucesignatus* - signed with the Cross - and there were rites for taking up the Cross at which they received an actual cloth cross, accompanied by prayers like the following:

> We beseech thee, Lord, holy Father, almighty eternal God, to vouchsafe to bless this sign of thy cross. So that it may be to this thy servant - an especial means of assistance, a support of faith, the consummation of his works, the redemption of his soul and a protection and safeguard against the fierce darts of all his enemies... Receive for the remission of thy sins the sign of the holy cross in the name of Jesus Christ who suffered on the cross for our redemption, with the help of the

---

[34] Bernard 2006
[35] This is the English translation of part of Bernard of Clairvaux's *Jesu dulce memoriam.*
[36] Meier, 2000
[37] Meier, 2000: 171
[38] Meier, 2000: 186-7

> same Our Lord Jesus Christ who with the Father and the Holy Spirit liveth and reigneth God.[39]

The Cross, says Cragg, 'is what happens when a love like Christ's encounters a world like Jerusalem.' How is it that this love of Christ could have become the motivation and the banner for attacking and killing Muslims[40] in a battle over that same Jerusalem? In particular, what theology of the Cross could have allowed this to happen?

In his study of crusade preaching, Maier[41] identifies two major meanings of the Cross. It symbolises not only redemption and salvation, but also the power and glory of God. With these, the twenty-first century Christian could, perhaps, agree, until one realises that the salvation is assured by the indulgences gained from fighting the Saracens, and that a major implication of the power and the glory is that the cross on the Crusader's shield protects its wearer in war. Here are two clues as to what went wrong:

Firstly, despite powerful theologies of Christ's passion and the forgiveness won on the Cross, there was a belief that something needed to be done in order for people to be sure of benefiting from that forgiveness. From the first crusade sermon of Urban II, the crusade was described as a pilgrimage that would provide complete forgiveness of sins - a plenary indulgence.[42] Taking up the Cross in the crusade, especially if martyrdom ensued, would enable a sharing in Christ's passion that would offer a guarantee of benefiting from its salvific effects that was otherwise seen as available only to members of religious orders.

Secondly, the power of God was seen in temporal terms. This is obvious. The Cross was taken up as part of a physical attempt to win a physical war. The physical crosses worn and carried by the crusading armies were considered as protection against physical enemies. Linked with this was the expectation of a miracle. There are many accounts of, for example, the miraculous appearances of crosses and of appearances of martyrs after their deaths. Jonathan Riley-Smith summarises the crusaders' conclusions from such miracles:

> It really was a holy war fought by soldiers of Christ to further the intentions of God; and God desired above all that Jerusalem be liberated. God's messengers, even God himself in the person of Christ, winged to and fro between heaven and the crusade, bringing messages of comfort and admonition.[43]

This leads to a third clue: the battle was focussed on the Holy Land. Part of

---

[39] The rite for taking the cross in the Coventry Pontifical c 1200, in L. and J. Riley-Smith, 1981: 139

[40] And, of course, many Jews, heretics and Eastern Christians

[41] Meier, 2000: 53ff.

[42] See the discussion in J. Riley-Smith, 1986: 24ff.

[43] L. and J. Riley-Smith, 1981: 118

the crusade rhetoric played on the fact that Christ's blood was shed there in Jerusalem, which must be won back for Him. The imitation of Christ implied that shedding blood for His sake in Jerusalem was an act of devotion, and, once again, accessed the benefits of the Cross. The Patriarch of Jerusalem's 1098 plea to the Western Church expresses such an idea:

> In behalf of God and ourselves, I, apostolic Patriarch, the bishops and the whole order of the Lord, urgently pray, and our spiritual Mother Church calls out: 'Come, my most beloved sons, come to me, retake the crown from the bands of the sons of idolatry, who rise against me - the crown from the beginning of the world predestined for you.' Come, therefore, we pray, to fight in the army of the Lord at the same place in which the Lord fought, in which Christ suffered for us, leaving to you an example that you should follow his footsteps. Did not God, innocent, die for us? Let us therefore also die, if it be our lot, not for Him, but for ourselves, that by dying on earth we may live for God.[44]

At the heart of this plea lies a fourth and crucial clue: 'Retake the crown from the bands of the sons of idolatry, who rise against me.' The Muslims are seen not only as enemies to the Christians, but also as enemies of Christ. Where Christ allowed His enemies to nail Him to the Cross in order that He might offer them redemption, the crusaders took up the Cross against the Muslims in order that they might gain redemption for themselves. In their zeal to show their love for God, and for their fellow Christians under occupation, few recognised that God also loved the Muslims. It is interesting that it was not immediately obvious to European Christians that they should fight the Muslims. One crusade sermon notes: 'Some will say: The Saracens have not done me any harm.Why should I take the cross against them?'[45] The sermon goes on to aver that the Saracens' actions are a great insult to all Christians, and to cite the zeal of the Maccabees in re-claiming the temple for God's people.

One of the questions implicit in current interactions between Islam and the West is the extent to which violence is religious. The question of the Islamic roots of terrorism is seriously considered. But the question of the Christian roots of Western response is, perhaps, even more urgent, because, if my 21st century call to take up the Cross is accurate, then the 11th century alternative is a travesty of what Christ actually died for and, therefore, a greater danger to His kingdom and His world than any so-called Islamic terrorism could ever be.

Many of the 11th century crusaders were, no doubt, sincere in their personal faith and their devotion to Christ crucified. However, so immersed were they in their own context that, with few exceptions, they were unable to discern the economic and political forces that drove them, or to see beyond their concern for their own salvation and community to God's concern for the Muslims'

---

44 The Patriarch of Jerusalem to the Western Church, Antioch, July 1098, Krey, 1921: 142-44

45 'Eudes of Chateauroux', in Meier, 2000: 141

salvation and community. Given the economic and political forces that drive our world, how can we hope to do better?

Perhaps the place to begin is in seeing ourselves on the Cross - recognising that we, just as much as the Jewish leaders of 2000 years ago and our Christian brothers and sisters of 1000 years ago, are likely to yield to the interests of self and of nation and do violence to Christ. The four clues offered here might help us to discern why we are doing this:

Firstly, do we seek to earn spiritual merit in our relationships with Muslims? Indulgences are things of the past, and attaining heaven by martyrdom is seen as Islamic rather than Christian. But how often do Christians make spiritual, moral or even material capital out of confrontation with Islam? And what about the movements that use Middle Eastern tensions to stir Christian emotion and devotion? Do not the various attempts to fulfil prophecy by assisting the Jews' return to Jerusalem and re-build the temple encourage an involvement in the salvation of the world that is rightly God's alone?

Secondly, do we martial Christian faith for the propagation of temporal power? In 11th century Christendom, the link between religion and temporal power was assumed. In the 21st century West, the opposite is often assumed. Christian faith tends to be seen as a private matter, and it is unclear how the faith of the individual relates to the politics of the nation, even when that individual is president or prime minister. It is at least arguable that this very separation of faith and power can give rise to unconsidered or unrecognised use of the Christian faith for economic or political ends.[46]

Thirdly, how does our understanding of Jerusalem affect our faith and actions? In the 21st century as in the 11th century, the 'Holy Land' stirs emotions, and is cited as central many current tensions. Where does 21st century Christian Zionism repeat the errors of the Crusades?

Fourthly, where have we fallen into seeing Muslims as the enemy? Are we in danger of dividing humanity into two categories: ourselves, for whom Christ died, and the enemies of the Cross, who are also our enemies? And is there a tendency to categorise Muslims as the latter?

The above 'Cross-reference theology' refutes and refuses such categorisation. It insists that Christ died for the very people who were His enemies, and that He died in forgiveness rather than in hatred. Christians can see themselves in the enemies who put Christ of the Cross; and they can see Muslims as people that 'God so loved' (John 3: 16) that He gave His Son to die for them.

I have suggested that thinking about the Cross in the context of Islam leads us to seeing ourselves anew. Thinking about the Cross and Islam in historical perspective makes us wonder how people will see us from the perspective of the 22nd century, and how God sees us from the perspective of eternity.

---

[46] Northcott, 2004 analyses such dynamics in the contemporary American context.

God, the Beneficent-the Merciful, and Jesus' Cross: From Abstract to Concrete Theologising

Rollin G. Grams

Dr Rollin G. Grams was Research Tutor in Biblical Studies at the Oxford Centre for Mission Studies, UK. He is Associate Professor of New Testament at Gordon-Conwell Theological Seminary, SIM-USA Theological Education Coordinator and Director of the Robert C. Cooley Center for the Study of Early Christianity.

Introduction

This essay brings together a discussion on the nature of theology, the cross in the New Testament, and Islam. The topics are not unrelated. Liberal theology and Islam equally dismiss the importance of the cross (Sura 4.157).[1] The argument I present here is that both suffer from theological abstractions, and that there is no greater theology of love than that which finds concrete expression in the cross of Jesus Christ. Specifically, the notion that God is Beneficent and Merciful is present in the concrete theological narrative of the cross.

Abstract Theologising

Nineteenth and twentieth century Liberal theology proved to be an experiment in theological abstractions. Three significant examples over one hundred years might be given to make this point. Consider the crest of the wave of Liberal theology in the summary of 'Christianity' presented by A. von Harnack in 1900 in his *What is Christianity?*[2] Harnack summed up the essence of Christian theology as the Fatherhood of God, the brotherhood of mankind, and the infinite worth of the human soul. Each of these points were universally applicable, and so any specific people of God or the Church, any concrete work, such as salvation or mission, or any particularity in the person and work of Jesus Christ, was eliminated. Not only was a community's specific self-identity omitted from the description; the historicity or unique tradition of the Church was equally dismissible.

Indeed, this was the age of seeking the 'essence' of religion. D.F. Strauss

[1] *The Koran*, 2005

[2] Harnack, 1900

had sought the same project in his *Life of Jesus* some sixty-five years earlier (1935), in which he distinguished 'myth' from historical fact. For Strauss, 'myth' was the historical garb in which the religious ideas of Christianity were dressed. It could be discarded in all its particular, concrete claims so that the essence of faith might be disclosed. Thus, while he allowed in this work that one could speak of the historical Jesus - whom he claimed to have been a thoroughly eschatological figure making messianic claims and expecting the coming of the Kingdom of God - by 1864, his representation of Jesus excluded any eschatological perspective. The dismissal of the particularities of Jesus' eschatological ministry opened the way for Strauss to concentrate on the Idea of Christianity.

But from whence will such an encapsulation be derived? Inevitably, as in all such instances, it is found in some reigning philosophy of the day. For Strauss, the philosopher providing this enlightenment was G.W.F. Hegel. The Christian Idea was that Jesus was God made man, or, in more Hegelian terms, Absolute Being made manifest in nature. Strauss 'handed over' the historical questions surrounding any such claim to historical criticism without the slightest concern over what it might find regarding the historicity of Jesus: the philosophical notions, not the historical facts, were his concern. Hegel spoke of Being made manifest in nature and of Spirit made manifest in the human spirit or the state. Such manifestations were never perfect, but according to Strauss 'in Jesus the idea of God-manhood was perfectly fulfilled and in a certain sense intelligibly realised.'[3]

One hundred years later, the programme of abstraction from historical particularity found its voice in R. Bultmann's writings. Bultmann argued that the Christ of faith was not dependent upon the Jesus of history. He spoke of 'demythologising' the Gospel records in the same sense that Strauss dismissed the historical garb in which the Gospels represented abstract truths.[4] His *Theology of the New Testament* began with these words:

> *The message of Jesus* is a presupposition for the theology of the New Testament rather than a part of that theology itself.... [Jesus] was first ...proclaimed in the kerygma of the earliest Church, not in the message of the historical Jesus.[5]

Theology, then, has little relationship to history. It is about ideas expressed in the message of the early Church, for which the message of Jesus (not the historical Jesus) was significant. This permitted Bultmann to explore the essential kernel of Christian teaching through the philosophy of his day: not by Hegel but by Heidegger. Existentialism could take the message of Jesus and find there its own teaching: Jesus' message was a call away from legalism to

---

[3] Schweitzer, 1968: 114

[4] See Bultmann, 1972

[5] Bultmann, 1951: 3

obeying the will of God, and God's will or demand was to love. But Bultmann rejected the idea that God's demand of love aims to form human character or shape human society.[6] Jesus, as eschatological preacher, presented God as imminent and as making demands on people in the last days. The particularities of this were false, claimed Bultmann: the end did not come. But the message is of lasting significance: God stands right before each of us as Absolute Demand, calling for decision. Even as the historicity of all this is made irrelevant, so also are the content of God's demands, the commandments of Jesus in the Gospels. Any focus on these would be to turn Christianity into Pharisaic Judaism for Bultmann and so to reject an existentialist reading of Jesus and Christian theology.

The early Church's following of God's demands, continued Bultmann, had to overcome the scandal of the cross: do such demands not lead to the cross? While on the one hand Bultmann insisted that in Paul's theology grace is not a quality but an event,[7] he equally insisted that this grace-event is a kerygmatic, not historical, event. In two paragraphs, Bultmann argued that Paul was not interested in the historical (particular, concrete) Jesus except insofar as he existed. Bultmann concluded as follows:

> Any 'evaluation' of the historical person Jesus according to human categories [*e.g.*, the historical Jesus] would be a *kata sarka* (flesh-wise) regarding of Christ and hence would mean seeing him as a *kata sarka* Christ.[8]

Bultmann distinguished two concepts of 'faith-belief': one which assents to the veracity of events such as the incarnation, crucifixion, resurrection; and one which is a 'self-surrender to the grace of God and which signifies the utter reversal of a man's previous understanding of himself - specifically, the radical surrender of his human 'boasting'."[9] The latter notion is what Bultmann found in his innovative and influential reading of Paul: it fits perfectly with his existentialist philosophy. God stands before humanity with the Demand to give up boasting and surrender life to Him. He writes:

> The union of believers into one *soma* with Christ now has its basis not in their sharing the same supernatural substance, but in the fact that in the word of proclamation Christ's death-and-resurrection becomes a possibility of existence in regard to which a decision must be made, and in the fact that faith seizes this possibility and appropriates it as the power that determines the existence of the man of faith.[10]

---

[6] Bultmann, 1951: 19

[7] Bultmann, 1951: 288f.

[8] Bultmann, 1951: 294

[9] Bultmann, 1951: 300

[10] Bultmann, 1951: 302

For one at home in existentialist philosophy, this way of speaking of the death and resurrection of Christ is understandable, but others will forever wait for an explanation with more substance, if not historical then at least some concrete action to be taken in light of the message. There is no such thing to be found. The most we ever hear about the 'decision-question' found in the 'word of the cross' (not the actual event) is something such as the following:

> This is the decision-question which the 'word of the cross' thrusts upon the hearer: whether he will acknowledge that God has made a crucified one Lord; whether he will thereby acknowledge the demand to take up the cross by the surrender of his previous understanding of himself, making the cross the determining power of his life, letting himself be crucified with Christ… The fact that this acknowledgement does take place demonstrates that Christ's death is a 'cosmic' event; *i.e.* that it may no longer be considered as just the historical event of Jesus' crucifixion on Golgotha. For God made this event the eschatological occurrence, so that, lifted out of all temporal limitation, it continues to take place in any present moment, both in the proclaiming word and in the sacraments.[11]

The theological landscape is literally littered with examples of theology as abstraction, with notions that have been 'lifted out of all temporal limitation' before being contextualised in some philosophy of the day. Harnack, Strauss and Bultmann are simply easy examples from the past to make the point. Today, however, the abstraction of theology is alive and well, even in some postmodern theologies which claim to take the local, historical, and particular more seriously.

So, for example, Jesus' concrete commands to turn the other cheek when slapped is abstracted into a call to love rather than seek revenge. But then a call to love others becomes the basis for 'Just War' advocates: love for an attacked third party may stir one to fight against the aggressor. Abstraction thus moves one from obeying Jesus' command to turn the other cheek to slapping the other back in the name of someone else.

Consider further contextual theologies. On the one hand, cultural theologies (e.g., African, Asian) begin with some abstract notion (e.g., a Creator God) that is then contextualised (the local theology's deity who is also said to be Creator). So long as the notion is abstract enough, the Christian theology can be correlated with the local theology, which becomes a concrete version of the abstract notion. Bultmann's theology is a prime example of a contextualised theology. Ideological theologies, such as Liberation Theology, also understand theology as Ideas. Liberation theology, of course, claimed the opposite. It sought to begin theology with praxis such that theologising became a reflection upon practice. But this actually means relegating theology other than practice to the most abstract level of thinking: so that the concrete might be action-focused, thought had to be kept in its most abstract form. The connection

[11] Bultmann, 1951: 303

between the two came from a reigning social philosophy of the day: Marxism. Something that is abstract can be filled in with whatever is at hand, as we have seen with Strauss and Bultmann. The principle of 'Liberation' was kept as unfocussed as possible, unrelated to the particularities of Biblical exegesis. Values, principles, metaphorical or symbolic theological ideas and the like could be given their concrete form not by means of Biblical interpretation but by means of Marxist philosophy.

A final and pervasive example in the West today is at play in the area of ethics. The concrete commands in Scripture to avoid homosexual practices are abstracted to mean that relationships should be monogamous, binding, and equal (hence ruling out pederasty, temple prostitution, or sexual acts outside committed relationships). So abstracted, the ethic can then be made to encompass rather than reject homosexual practices, so long as they are performed in 'homosexual marriage'! The game of theology as abstraction is not subtle or sophisticated; it can be played by anyone.

What this discussion of theologising has to do with the cross of Jesus Christ is just this: for Paul, the cross and resurrection of Jesus Christ stood as the concrete truth which always undermined theology as abstraction. I do not mean to suggest that the cross is the only concrete feature giving a focus to Christian theology, but it is an important example of how Christian theology is made concrete in the narrative of Jesus Christ.[12]

The Cross as God's Concrete Love

In this section, I will turn to how Paul uses the concrete reality of the cross and resurrection of Jesus Christ to overturn theology as abstraction in his letter to the Romans. Here we see how the notion of 'love' - abstract in itself - is given specific meaning when it is understood in terms of the cross of Jesus Christ.

In the context of a passage dealing with present suffering in the world - Romans 8.31-39 - Paul holds out a hope to Christians that is based on God's love and explores the implications of God's love through a series of questions: 'What then are we to say about these things? If God is for us, who is against us? He who did not withhold his own Son, but gave him up for all of us, will he not with him also give us everything else? Who will bring any charge against God's elect? It is God who justifies. Who is to condemn?...' (NRSV). God's love for believers in Christ means that: there is no reason for concern about what others who are against them might do (v. 31); there is no reason for concern about those who would bring a charge against them (v. 33); and there is no reason for concern about those who might condemn them (v. 34). The

---

[12] In speaking of the cross as a focus for Christian theology and ethics, I am close to a point made by Hays, 1996. Hays argues that there are three 'focal images' that help synthesise the New Testament documents and theology: creation, the cross, the new community.

reasons given for not being so concerned point to Christ and his work in these verses, and they are summed up in a final question in verse 35: 'Who will separate us from the love of Christ?' The answer is that nothing can separate us from God's love in Christ Jesus our Lord (v. 39).

Thus in these verses Paul ties together two thoughts: God's love - an abstract notion - and Christ and his work on our behalf, its concrete reality. God's love in Christ is stated in various ways: Firstly, if God has not withheld[13] His own Son on our behalf, there is no end to what He will give us (v. 32). Secondly, God justifies us (v. 33). Romans 1.18-5.21 points out that this justification involves making sinners righteous. In a conclusion to this first major section of the letter (Romans 5.1ff), Paul states: 'But God proves his love for us in that while we still were sinners Christ died for us' (Romans 5.8). God's work of justification is not raw justice but a work of His love, yet it is a love concretely at work through Christ's death on the cross for us, which fulfils the requirements of retributive justice. Thirdly, God's love is also shown in His not condemning us (v. 34). Romans 8.1 states that 'There is therefore now no condemnation for those who are in Christ Jesus.' And to be 'in Christ Jesus' is to participate in His death and resurrection (cf. Romans 6.1ff).

There is here no abstract notion of God's love, which could be understood in conflicting ways whenever anything concrete is under consideration. In this passage we see that God's love means that we need not fear human or Divine justice and condemnation. God's love is now understood concretely with respect to Christ's sacrificial death.

Thus love cannot be set over against justice. It would be possible to understand love without any connection to justice, as when one simply overlooks wrongs committed. Is this what it might mean to speak of God as beneficent and merciful? A vizier may show mercy to a thief in order to secure his allegiance or to demonstrate his authority even over the law. This is how personal power works in many political systems. But the cross is a concrete narrative that disallows such an understanding of God's love. Love and justice are inseparably related and come into focus by means of the cross of Jesus Christ.

For example, Paul writes in Romans 3.25 that God put Christ forward as a sacrifice of atonement for sinful humans, as an expression of His grace (v. 24), as we have already seen in Romans 8. But he continues in v. 26 to show that love and justice are, through the cross, related notions: '[I]t was to prove at the present time that he himself is righteous and that he justifies the one who has faith in Jesus' (Romans 3.26).

The cross, as a sacrifice for sins, satisfies any demand for justice. But as a sacrifice for others, it is equally an expression of love. Love and justice meet in

[13] D. Moo (following others) points out (correctly, it seems to me) that Genesis 22 lies behind this language of 'not withholding' a 'son'. See Moo 1996: 540 n.18. The notion of sacrifice is therefore close to the surface in this choice of words.

the cross. Without the cross, love becomes permissive antinomianism and fails to right any wrongs. Without the cross, justice becomes vengeance, unredemptive punishment, or pious purity, the practice of which makes one impure and offers no transformative hope to the enemy. Indeed, the cross is the opposite of violence, and so Christians can live a life of love that assumes the cross at every turn, as Paul shows in his description of the Christian community in Romans 12.9-21.

Romans 12.9-12 includes what most likely are some of Jesus' teachings even though Paul does not state their source. For example, 'Bless those who persecute you; bless and do not curse them' is close to what we find in Matthew 5.44: '[L]ove your enemies and pray for those who persecute you' (cf. Luke 6.27f). As M. Thompson notes, calling on people to bless their persecutors and revilers is without parallel in pre-Christian Greek literature.[14] 'Do not repay anyone evil for evil' and 'overcome evil with good' are parallel to Jesus' teaching in Matthew 5.38-47 ('Do not resist an evildoer;' 'Love your enemies and pray for those who persecute you'), along with examples of overcoming evil with good [turn the other cheek, go an extra mile when forced to go one mile to carry something (most likely for a soldier), give to one suing you, begging from you, or wanting to borrow from you, pray for your persecutors]. The specific example of feeding a hungry enemy or giving him something to drink if he is thirsty is already part of Jewish ethics (Paul here quotes Proverbs 25.21-22a) even if the law of retaliation ('an eye for an eye') is also to be found there. Jesus overturns the law of retaliation and, by his own example, shows a transforming alternative that stops cycles of violence,[15] which in this passage becomes the pattern for the Christian Church.

In 'associate with the lowly,'[16] 'do not repay anyone evil for evil,' 'never avenge yourselves,' and 'overcome evil with good' we can detect the pattern of Jesus' own life, climaxing in his death on a cross.[17] Thus both in Jesus' teaching and example a cruciform existence for the Christian community is set out. It can be summed up in terms of 'love,' but without the particular teaching of Jesus and his particular cruciform narrative the nature of this love would not have been understood. Also, as noted earlier, here too Paul understands that such love is related to rather than opposed to justice. We are free to act with a

---

[14] Thompson, 1991: 97ff.

[15] The choice of terms in this sentence comes from the argument presented by Stassen and Gushee, 2003.

[16] *Tois tapeinois* could be either 'lowly things' (neuter) or 'lowly persons' (masculine) or both, if the neuter is used to encompass both options. The main point is that Christians should regard themselves as equal to one another rather than wise in themselves.

[17] Jesus' prayer for his enemies from the cross sums up this ethic (Luke 23.34). See also Luke 22.50f, Matthew 8.28-34; Matthew 15.21-28, Matthew 8.5-13, Luke 7.2-10 and Luke 17.16.

cruciform love because we are not responsible for bringing enemies to justice: God will do that (Romans 12.19).

The cross permits believers to forego their own rights. Notice how Paul uses Jesus' example when exhorting Roman Christians who have the right theology to please those with a wrong theology and inferior practices. He offers the example of Jesus Christ in his sufferings:

> We who are strong ought to put up with the failings of the weak, and not to please ourselves. Each of us must please our neighbour for the good purpose of building up the neighbour. For Christ did not please himself; but, as it is written, 'The insults of those who insult you have fallen on me' (Romans 15.1-3).

In such ways, then, love (and justice) are made concrete in Paul's theology. What determines its concrete character is the cross of Jesus Christ. Thus when Paul speaks of love as the fulfilling of the Law (Romans 13.8-10), he is not offering an abstract theology (the principle of love) in place of the very concrete theology of the Old Testament laws. Rather, he is offering a new concrete theology of the cross as a definition of love.

Naming God and the Particularity of the Cross

Islam speaks of the ninety-nine names of God. The trajectory of Biblical revelation, however, is not some abstraction from narrative descriptions of God in a collection, large as it may be, of names for God. Rather, any naming of God is given concrete expression in the narratives themselves such that thick descriptions of those names may be revealed and false understandings omitted. Names for God can be a theologising by abstraction, even if multiple names are able to restrict the abstractness of Divine attributes to some degree. Without concrete narratives, however, single-word attributes of God will remain dangerously abstract. Chapters of the Qur'an typically open with the words, 'In the name of Allah, the Beneficent, the Merciful.' The language of mercy, beneficence, grace and forgiveness appears throughout the Qur'an.[18] One of the many examples is from Sura 2.160: 'And your God is one God! There is no god but He; He is the Beneficent, the Merciful.'

In all this Islam can have an encouraging dialogue with Christian theology as it is practised as abstraction, in the way it has been in Protestant Liberalism. Protestant Liberalism encouraged correlational theology (so Paul Tillich): abstract theological notions could be compared favourably between religions. But Christian theology is concrete precisely because it begins with and never lets go of the concrete fact of the cross and the resurrection of Jesus Christ.

[18] The electronic version of *the Koran,* 2005 shows the following number of hits for such words in English translation: forgiving (97), mercy (151), merciful (259), grace (71), gracious (8).

This can never be abstracted; it cannot be ignored or made irrelevant. It undermines all tendencies towards abstractions just as it enlightens and directs abstract attributes of God so that they cannot be bent by human wisdom.

The Power of a Concrete, Cruciform Theology of God's Love

Underlying the motives of those who have thought abstract theological ideas, under the name of whatever philosophy, is the desire to find a more potent theology. Bultmann, for example, thought that a concrete theology of the cross in the context of first century Palestine could not speak to twentieth-century, scientifically-minded Europeans. Only through an existential abstraction of the message in that context could the preaching of the early Church still have a power to speak to present-day society.

However, quite the opposite is true. By abstracting the message it loses all its potency, and the real power of the contemporary message is found in the reigning philosophy of the day. A concrete theology, on the other hand, is potent precisely in its challenge to reigning philosophies. It comes as something foreign, an alternative to solutions on offer, a clear challenge to all else. What is needed is not an abstract theology that can speak to any context but a concrete theology that has so potent a message that it cannot be eclipsed by any other message. The concrete theology of the cross of Jesus Christ comes as a truth whose power is 'greater than which there is no other.'

This language of 'greater than which there is no other' comes from Anselm's (Archbishop of Canterbury, 1093-1109) ontological argument for God's existence.[19] His argument sought to prove God's existence by exploring the need for a definition of God that could not be eclipsed by a definition that is still better. If one gave a definition of God that lacked any reference to the necessity of His existence, that definition could be eclipsed by another that did include such a reference. Thus 'God' must necessarily exist. The problem with Anselm's argument is that all he proves is that the definition of 'God', not God Himself, must include the necessity of existence. By this argument, the further question as to whether or not there is a God has not even been broached. This type of argument, however, is not faulty for our purposes in this essay and is, in fact, better suited for it than an argument for God's existence. Any account of God's beneficence and mercy, I would maintain, that lacks reference to the cross, is an account that can be eclipsed by one that does include reference to the cross.

What love can be greater than a love that gives life to others by giving one's own life? What love could be greater than a father's love for his only son than

---

[19] The argument can be found in various books. See e.g., *St. Anselm, Basic Writings*, 1962. The argument entails the following statement: 'God cannot be conceived not to exist. God is that, which nothing greater can be conceived. That which can be conceived not to exist is not God.'

a love in which a father gives his only son for others? A father would willingly die for his son, but what kind of love is it for which a father can give his son's life?[20] Permissive love may be a great form of love that persists even when wronged, but a love whose power can transform the sinner, and one which can at the same time satisfy justice, is a love beyond which there is no other. A human dying for another is truly an act of love, but no greater notion of love could there be than that God the Son dies for others. 'Indeed, rarely will anyone die for a righteous person - though perhaps for a good person someone might actually dare to die. But God proves his love for us in that while we still were sinners Christ died for us' (Romans 5.7f). To die for one's beloved is a great love, but even greater still is a death for one's enemies. There is no love greater than the death of the righteous one for the unrighteous, to bring them back to God (1 Peter 3.18). 'In this is love, not that we loved God but that he loved us and sent his Son to be the atoning sacrifice for our sins. Beloved, since God loved us so much, we also ought to love one another ' (1 John 4.10f).

Conclusion

There is no greater revelation of God the Beneficent, the Merciful than at the foot of the cross of Jesus Christ. The concreteness of the cross closes off misconceptions of love, misconceptions such as a divorce of love from justice or an understanding of love as for one's own ethnic group, people, or religion and not also encompassing one's enemies. Cruciform love rejects holy war - the Crusades entailed one of the most profound misunderstandings of Christianity the world has witnessed. But there have been other misunderstandings, such as when various Church officials sought to make peace with Nazism in the 1930's and 1940's in the interest of self-preservation, or when Apartheid theology in South Africa understood love as caring for inferior beings marked off by their colour. But a true understanding of Divine beneficence, mercy and love is to be found in the story of the cross of Jesus Christ. Its concreteness aborts malformed notions of love that only lead to a perpetuation of injustice and cycles of violence. The cross offers an interpretation of Divine love beyond which there can be no greater understanding.

[20] Of course, Jesus is not God's Son in any human sense of procreation. 'Isa's denial in Sura 5.116 that he and his mother Marium were two gods alongside God is also correct: Jesus is neither a physical son of God nor a second God (and so also Sura 4 171 is correct - there are not three gods but One).

A Christian Response to the Absence of the Cross in Islam

Clinton Bennett

Dr Clinton Bennett was Senior Lecturer at Westminster College, Oxford (1992-1998), Associate Professor of Religion at Baylor University, Texas (1998-2001) and is currently teaching world religions at Barrytown, New York

The Cross as Foolishness to Muslims

What follows describes my own wrestling with the problem and challenge to my faith of the apparent lack of the Cross in Islam. It shows how my thinking about this issue changed between writing my book, *In Search of Muhammad*[1] and my book *In Search of Jesus*.[2] Both texts sought to create dialogue between my own faith and that of Muslims, although the second book had a wider scope, also exploring Jewish, Hindu, Buddhist and humanist images of Jesus. For Christians, the Muslim denial of the Crucifixion is deeply problematical since Christians believe that Jesus' death and salvation are inseparably linked; the Cross was no mere historical accident but part of God's redemptive plan.

I am not claiming to have worked out a solution to Christian-Muslim disagreement regarding the Crucifixion of Jesus. On the other hand, I am offering the following as a positive contribution towards some sort of rapprochement. From the Christian point of view, Jesus' death on the Cross is taken to be so central to Christian thought, to the Christian doctrine of salvation, that it can be regarded as the cornerstone of Christianity itself. On Calvary, according to Christians, one who was sinless and who, therefore, did not deserve death, took upon Himself the sins of all humanity, making atonement and human-divine reconciliation possible. St. Paul put it like this, 'for as in Adam all die, so in Christ will all be made alive' (1 Corinthians 15: 22)'. Not to preach Christ crucified was to not to preach the Gospel. Paul preached 'Christ crucified, unto the Jews a stumbling block, unto Greeks foolishness' (I Corinthians 1: 23). It is this intimate relationship between the Christian doctrine of atonement and the Crucifixion that, as Deedat (1918 -

[1] Bennett, 1998

[2] Bennett, 2001

2005) put it in his hugely popular *Crucifixion or Cruci-fiction*?[3] produces the equation, 'in a nutshell, No Crucifixion, No Christianity.'

For Zwemer, (1867-1952) who spent his life attempting to reach Muslims with the gospel, what Islam needs most of all is the very Cross which it not only rejects, but sees as 'foolish'; 'If the Cross of Christ is the missing link in their creed, then the preaching of the Cross, although it may seem to them foolishness, will yet prove among Moslems the wisdom of God and the power of God.'[4] Zwemer was well aware of the argument that if the Crucifixion did not happen, the Christian doctrine of atonement loses the ground from under its feet. Thus, 'the bitter attacks of Islam on Christianity in the Moslem press of Egypt and India nearly always find their centre in the Deity and the atoning work of Jesus.'[5] Zwemer also pointed out that Muhammad is said to have had 'such a repugnance to the sign of the cross that he destroyed everything brought to his house with that figure upon it' and cites the *Hadith* that upon his return, Jesus will 'break the crucifix.'[6]

Zwemer wrote two books on the Cross, *The Cross Above the Crescent*[7] and *The Glory of the Cross.*[8] More recently, Cragg describes the Cross, which is 'the redeeming deed of Christ' in terms of 'cosmic' significance.'[9] It is a matter of profound concern that, in its rewriting the story of the Cross, Islam 'offends deeply against all that the gospels disclose about the self-giving of Jesus.'[10] Yet, Cragg continues, Islam says that this re-writing is in 'the interests of God's glory', as 'God cannot be honoured in the victory of a prophet's foes.'[11]

Stressing the 'why' not the 'what' of Christian Belief

Twenty-five years or so of engagement in Christian-Muslim dialogue leads me to agree with my missionary predecessors that the issue of the Cross is of central importance. I am also of the opinion that of all the issues in the dialogue between Christians and Muslims, most of which have been with us from the very first historical encounters, the Cross is the most challenging and difficult of them all. Other issues on that agenda, such as the Trinity, Jesus 'Divine

[3] Deedat, 1978

[4] Zwemer, 1912: 181

[5] Zwemer, 1912: 117

[6] Zwemer, 1905: 86-87 cited the *mishkat-ul-misabih* 23: 6 using Captain A.N. Mathew's 1809 translation. The *hadith* is also found in Bukhari's *Sahih*, Book LV (The Book of the Prophets), Chapter 44, hadith number 657. See Khan, 1987: 4. 436-7

[7] Zwemer, 1941

[8] Zwemer, 1928; reprinted 1982

[9] Cragg, 1985a: 271-272

[10] Cragg, 1985a: 267

[11] Cragg, 1985a: 268

Sonship, the character of Muhammad, and the status of the Qur'an are also challenging but I am convinced that, by following the advice of L.B. Jones (1880-1960) - another life long missionary to Muslims - some sort of mutually acceptable understanding is possible. I discovered the writing of Jones during my first year as a student at the Centre for the Study of Islam and Christian-Muslim Relations, Selly Oak, Birmingham in 1978-9 before proceeding as a Baptist missionary to Bangladesh, and since then I have been guided by his suggestion that, in conversation with Muslims, we should stress not the *what* but the *why* of our convictions. Human language, he said, is always inadequate as a description of our inner spiritual experiences.[12]

Christians chose certain language, such as sonship, hypostasis and *homoousios* to express their experience and conviction that Jesus, the Holy Spirit and the God of Creation are intimately related. Comparison with Muslim belief in the attributes (*sifat*) fails (although perhaps there is more common ground here than we often admit) because, as Ibn Taymiyya (1263-1328) argues, the Spirit and the Son exist *independently* of God, while the attributes *wholly subsist* in God. On the other hand, while Taymiyya regards the terms Spirit, Son and Father as Christian innovations or inventions, he also criticizes Christians for limiting God's attributes to three. Yet, as Tom Michel suggests, who knows Ibn Taymiyya better than most of us:

> A more accurate statement of what Christian faith says of the Triune God can be achieved by use of the term *hypostasis* defined by the early Councils, which can perhaps best be translated as 'mode' (or manner) of subsisting which Rahner prefers, or 'mode of being' as suggested by Barth. Speaking of the one God who subsists in three distinct modes is incidentally closer to the traditional Arab Christian formulation of one God with three essential characteristics or *sifât.*[13]

Therefore, some rapprochement appears possible. Similarly, vis-à-vis Muhammad, some Christians can affirm that he was a genuine prophet and that God has a message for us through him. Their appreciation of Muhammad may fall short of Muslims' appreciation yet more common ground can thus be claimed. However, such a movement towards rapprochement seems impossible vis-à-vis the cross, on which either Jesus *was* or *was not* crucified. I also wish to avoid playing the tit-for-tat game of accusing the other party of possessing an imperfect scripture, even if they say that mine is corrupt. I am persuaded that if I want Muslims to respect my belief that God disclosed God's-self in Jesus, I must in turn respect their belief that the Qur'an is God's infallible and perfect revelation.

---

[12] Jones, 1938: 95

[13] D'Arcy Lectures, Oxford, 2000

Some Preliminary Explorations

By reflecting on the problem of the Cross, I have read Muslim and Christian writing in an effort to find a way of somehow reconciling apparently irreconcilable convictions. Much writing simply takes the view that one side is right and one wrong. Obviously, although the Muslim argument that Christians have corrupted their scriptures may solve the problem from a Muslim perspective - that is, Christians are indeed wrong - this solution is unacceptable to Christians. Conversely, the argument that the Qur'an is wrong lacks appeal for Muslims! No Muslim will accept that the Qur'an is anything less than infallible. For Muslims, the Qur'an is verbatim God's speech, incapable of error. It is the immutable, final, definitive, comprehensive disclosure of God's will and word. A traditional Christian argument has been that many of the Qur'an's criticisms of Christian teaching were directed at heterodox Christians in Arabia who really did believe in a Trinity of Father, Son and Mary (Sura 5: 116), for example, or in a Jesus who only appeared to die on the cross.

Zwemer believed that Muhammad had sufficient opportunities to acquaint himself with orthodox Christian teaching but chose not to do so, while W.H.T. Gairdner (1973-1928) argued that 'the only way by which the 'Christianity' of that time and place reached the Arabian prophet was through false 'gospels' and the other literature of some heretical sects, which denied the divine sonship and the redeeming death of Christ'.[14] In this view, Sura 4: 157 is derived from Docetic beliefs in a Jesus who only seemed to be human who, therefore, did not die or suffer on the Cross. Islam, for Gairdner, represented a 'rebuke' to Christians, because had Christians of Muhammad's time borne him authentic witness, he would have been a Christian.[15]

St. Clair-Tisdall (1859-1928) agreed that Muhammad never had 'contact with pure gospel Christianity', and that it was largely due to the 'false forms which the faith had then almost universally assumed that the rise of Islam is really due.'[16] The source of Jesus' creating a bird from clay (Sura 3: 43), suggested Tisdall, was the *Arabic Gospel of the Infancy.*[17] The argument, however, that Muslims criticize only heterodox and not orthodox Christian beliefs is difficult to sustain, given such sophisticated and detailed refutations of Christian beliefs as Ibn Taymiyya's, which distinguishes clearly between the beliefs of various Christian churches, such as the Nestorians, the Melikites, Jacobites and Arians. Ibn Taymiyya considered belief in Jesus' Crucifixion, Trinity, divine Sonship and many Christian rituals, to be post-gospel innovations.[18] On the issue of the Crucifixion, he was fully aware that some

---

[14] Gairdner, 1920: 39

[15] Gairdner, 1920: 19

[16] Clair-Tisdall, 1905: 140

[17] Clair-Tisdall, 1905: 175; see Arabic Gospel of the Infancy 2006:36

[18] Michel, 1984: 236-237

Christians 'hold that the one crucified was not the Christ, but someone similar as Muslims say' but that orthodox Christianity teaches that Jesus died on the Cross. Taymiyya states the Muslim position thus: 'In the Qur'an (Sura 4:157) God has made it clear that He has raised up Christ alive and saved him from death.'[19] The generally accepted Muslim view, of course, shared (as Taymiyya says) by some Christian groups, is that someone else, probably Judas, died instead of Jesus.

The *Gospel of Barnabas*, popular among Muslims, has Judas die in Jesus' place.[20] Taymiyya says that - although perhaps not deliberately - the Christians got the story wrong. The apostles themselves did not witness the event. The crucifixion did not happen. Something did happen, as the Qur'an confirms but the Christian belief in the Crucifixion may well have been the result of Jewish boasts that 'they had crucified Jesus'. He pointed out that, unlike the Qur'an, which is purely divine speech the gospels contain not only what *Jesus said* but also what *people said he said*. They thus resemble the *sunnah*; 'they transmit some things from the speech of Christ and some things from his deeds and miracles…' and so are 'similar to the biography, the books of *hadith*, and books like these'.

Cragg, for his part, is insistent on the historicity of the Crucifixion, asking, 'Is historic Christianity, in short, explicable on the hypothesis of a substitute crucifixion?'[21] Zwemer thought Muslims too influenced by the *hadith*. More progress would be made, he believed, if Muslims 'dig beneath the rubbish of tradition;'[22] his section heading is 'Back to Muhammad and away with tradition' and looks instead at the Qur'an, which, he argued, contained 'unintelligible' and 'contradictory' material on Jesus' death, so that the process of interpreting and making 'clear by means of tradition' had been inevitable.[23] According to Zwemer (who cites Muir) tens of thousands of *hadith* are forgeries.[24] What Zwemer meant here was that such Qur'anic verses as 19: 34 and 3: 55 at least leave open the possibility that Jesus did die, though perhaps not on the Cross. Muslims traditionally believe that Jesus' death (about which the Qur'an speaks in these verses) will take place in the future, after his Second Coming. Ibn Taymiyya takes this to be the clear meaning of such as text as 4: 159, 'There will not be any of this People of the Book but will believe in him before his death'. Thus, 'God states that they will put their faith in him when he descends to earth…he will descend to earth before the Day of Resurrection and then he will die'.

---

19 Michel, 1984: 306

20 Gospel of Barnabas, 2006. Zwemer also refers to this text's popularity in the Egypt of 1912.

21 Cragg, 1985a: 267

22 Zwemer, 1912: 187

23 Zwemer, 1912: 53

24 Zwemer, 1912: 56; Zwemer cites Muir, 1858: V1.Xlii

However, as my own thinking developed on this contentious issue, I have begun to see some merit in Zwemer's suggestion that a focus on the Qur'an, rather than on traditional Muslim belief, may be fruitful. Zebiri similarly comments that the fact that 4:157 is 'not grammatically straightforward or entirely free from ambiguity' has allowed Christians, and some Muslims, to offer 'divergent interpretations.'[25] Below, I show how my thinking on the problem of the Crucifixion in Christian-Muslim dialogue has changed.

My Journey Begins - My first effort at a response to the lack of the Cross

When I wrote *In Search of Muhammad*, I realized as I started to work on my conclusion that I had not dealt with the issue of the Crucifixion. In a sense, I did not have to since the book's aim was an attempt at a Christian reappraisal of the character, sincerity and religious significance of Muhammad, much maligned in Christian discourse. However, I was also writing the book as a contribution to Christian-Muslim dialogue, so some recognition of the Crucifixion issue seemed appropriate, however brief. Therefore, I did turn, finally and rather inadequately, to that issue. I stated that for me as a Christian, 'Muslim denial of Christ's crucifixion was problematical because the 'event is central to my faith'. Observing that one possible response is to declare the Qur'an wrong (a strategy noted above), I said that I wished to avoid this and instead suggested that Muslims look again at what the Qur'an says, 'they did not kill him, nor crucified him, but it was made to appear to them (Sura 4: 157).' [26] I then asked whether the text really denies Jesus' crucifixion or does it rather 'suggest that attributing blame for his death is complex and contentious'. The 'they slew him not' (or 'they did not kill him, nor crucify him') refers to the Jews. Indeed, I went on to say, it was not the Jews who killed Jesus (although charged with deicide by Christians in days past) which does not actually fit Christian understanding of atonement. If 'Christ's death was no accident', I continued, 'but part of God's redemptive plan, so that there was 'no other way', no human agent or agents can properly be blamed'. The blame, I stated, 'rests with us all', by which I meant that it was human sin, human rebellion against God that crucified Jesus. Nonetheless, the 'I slew him not remains difficult to gloss (and we cannot ignore the almost universal Muslim conviction that Jesus did not die).[27]

In arguing the above, I was close to G. Parrinder (1910-2005) and R.C. Zaehner (1913-1974), who have also argued that, 'There is a parallel to this interpretation in sura 8, 17 when the Muslims were rejoicing over the victory at

---

[25] Zebiri, 1997: 216

[26] The Qur'anic citations not taken from secondary sources are guided by 'Ali (AY), 2001. See also Sura 5: 110 for a verse that appears to say that God protected Jesus from the Jews who wanted to kill him.

[27] Bennett, 1998: 238-9

Badr and taking all the credit to themselves'. They were, Parrinder points out, 'sternly reminded that…'ye did not kill them but God killed them'…'God can destroy the Messiah (5, 19).[28] What I did not do in *In Seach of Muhammad* was discuss other verses in which Jesus' death is referred to in the Qur'an, such as Sura 4: 159 or 19: 33.

Subsequently, I have explored Muslim and non-Muslim interpretations of these verses. Two factors here appeal to Christians - firstly, the most widely cited verse is, in its original Arabic, subject to a linguistic analysis that can support different interpretations (Sura 4: 157):

> That they said (in boast), 'We killed Christ Jesus the son of Mary, the Apostle of Allah;' but they killed him not, nor crucified him, but so it was made to appear to them, and those who differ therein are full of doubts, with no (certain) knowledge, but only conjecture to follow, for of a surety they killed him not:
>
> وَقَوْلِهِمْ إِنَّا قَتَلْنَا الْمَسِيحَ عِيسَى ابْنَ مَرْيَمَ رَسُولَ اللَّهِ وَمَا قَتَلُوهُ وَمَا صَلَبُوهُ وَلَـٰكِن شُبِّهَ لَهُمْ
>
> وَإِنَّ الَّذِينَ اخْتَلَفُوا فِيهِ لَفِي شَكٍّ مِّنْهُ مَا لَهُم بِهِ مِنْ عِلْمٍ إِلَّا اتِّبَاعَ الظَّنِّ وَمَا قَتَلُوهُ يَقِينًا

Secondly, other verses unambiguously speak of Jesus' death. However, as noted above, Muslims understand these to refer to a *future death*. Several verses also refer to God raising Jesus up, just as Christians believe happened after the Crucifixion (although the Qur'anic event is more like the Ascension). Ibn Taymiyya reflects the typical Muslim belief when he says that God, 'raised up Christ alive and saved him from death' (306). Thus, Jesus' ascension was like Enoch's or Elijah's (Genesis 5: 24; 2 Kings 2: 11-13). The death referred to in the verses cited above has not yet happened. However, the more I examine the various texts, the more it seems to me that 19: 33 suggests that Jesus' death precedes Resurrection, or Ascension, 'So peace is on me the day I was born, the day that I die, and the die that I shall be raised up to life (again)'.

> وَالسَّلَامُ عَلَيَّ يَوْمَ وُلِدتُّ وَيَوْمَ أَمُوتُ وَيَوْمَ أُبْعَثُ حَيًّا

Here we seem to have the traditional Christian order of events, the very 'mystery of our faith' proclaimed in the Eucharist - Jesus was born, died and rose again. Jesus' resurrection is in the future with respect to his death. A small number of Muslims have accepted that Jesus died but was revivified by God, then taken up into Heaven. For example, Fahkr al-Din al-Razi (d. circa 1192) and Rashid Rida (1865-1935).[29]

On the other hand, 'I will take you and raise you to myself' (Sura 3: 55) seems to by-pass Jesus' death, as does the traditional view:

---

[28] Parrinder, 1977: 120; see Zaehner, 1958: 212; see also Basetti-Sani, 1977: 172

[29] See McAuliffe, 1991: 139-141

ذْ قَالَ اللَّهُ يَا عِيسَى إِنِّي مُتَوَفِّيكَ وَرَافِعُكَ إِلَيَّ وَمُطَهِّرُكَ مِنَ الَّذِينَ كَفَرُوا وَجَاعِلُ الَّذِينَ اتَّبَعُوكَ فَوْقَ
الَّذِينَ كَفَرُوا إِلَى يَوْمِ الْقِيَامَةِ ثُمَّ إِلَيَّ مَرْجِعُكُمْ فَأَحْكُمُ بَيْنَكُمْ فِيمَا كُنتُمْ فِيهِ تَخْتَلِفُونَ

Sura 5: 117's reference to God taking Jesus up (verb *rafa'*, raise) is open to various interpretations but Parrinder thinks that it can refer to Jesus' death on the Cross.[30] I find myself in sympathy with Parrinder, who concluded that the 'cumulative effect of the Quranic verses is strongly in favor of a real death, and a complete self-surrender of Jesus.'[31]

I am not fully convinced, however, that it will be easy to persuade Muslims to abandon their traditional beliefs and accept that Jesus really did die. Even if Muslims do accept the historicity of the crucifixion, the very different Muslim view of sin makes the Christian ideas of a substitutory, sacrificial atonement all but obnoxious. Marshall cautions us that:[32]

> even if it could be established that the Quran does teach that Jesus genuinely died on the Cross and was then raised to heaven, this episode would still have to be interpreted within the Quranic frame of reference, which has no place for ideas of atonement…the events of Jesus' earthly life would not be seen as the key moment in God's redemptive plan for humanity.

A Christianity without the Crucifixion?

Turning to write my book on Jesus, in which I discussed a range of images and views of my faith's central personality, I was surprised to discover just how many non-Muslims share a similar view, that Jesus did not die on the cross. Of course, one can think of Barbara Thiering (Jesus died somewhere in France) or even of Mirza Ghulam (1835-1908) (Jesus died and is buried in Kashmir), let alone of Hermann Samuel Reimarus (1694-1768) (who argued that Jesus did die but that the Resurrection was dreamt up and staged by the disciples) all of which are easy to dismiss as of dubious academic value. What fascinated me more was the possibility of a Christian faith for which Jesus' sacrificial death is not central. For example, those who believe that it was St. Paul who introduced such notions as divine sonship and a dying and rising saviour into Christianity from pagan sources and cults popular in the Greek-speaking world (which some Muslim and Jewish writers also advocate), thereby corrupting Jesus' original message (which pointed to God and not to himself, as the Qur'an says, 'It is Allah Who is my Lord and your Lord; then worship Him' (Sura 3: 51). What God requires of us is not 'belief in Jesus' death' but to do as Jesus did, to live for the sake of others. On the other hand, the idea of a sacrifice as a requirement for forgiveness of sin may derive from the sacrifices of Hebrew

[30] Parrinder, 1977: 107
[31] Parrinder, 1977: 121
[32] Marshall, 2001: 15

religion (see Leviticus 17: 11). Others stress that it was by entering the world that Jesus sanctified human life, indeed the whole world.

Something of this is hinted at in the *Gospel of Thomas*[33] from the Nag Hammadi Library, where Jesus says, 'I am the light that is over all things. I am all: from me all came forth, and to me all attained' and 'Split a piece of wood; I am there.'[34] It has been argued that the *Gospel of Thomas*' lack of a crucifixion narrative is not only due to its style of writing, which is a collection of sayings rather than a chronological account of Jesus life, but also because, whether it happened or not, the crucifixion was not essential to its theology. That which is spiritual cannot die.[35] Light is within all people.[36] Pagels points out that the cross was not used as a Christian symbol for several centuries.[37] As Gairdner said, there were Christians around at the time of Muhammad for whom Jesus' death was not significant.

In this understanding, it is Jesus' life as much as his death that mediates salvation. The 'blood' language of the New Testament (see Romans 3: 23-26, Hebrews 9: 22; 1 Peter 1: 2; Ephesians 1: 7) does not fit comfortably with my own conviction that God's love is strong enough to save without a price being paid. The New Testament writers lived in an environment where such language was commonplace. They knew that they were saved because of what Jesus had done, and were trying to make sense of this awareness, of this experience of spiritual re-birth. They expressed their ideas using available idioms and language. Nineteenth century hymn-writers picked up the 'washed in the blood' language enthusiastically but it does not speak to me. What I am saying, then, is not that I do not any longer believe in Jesus' death but that the Qur'an's apparent denial of Jesus' crucifixion may challenge a Christian over-emphasis on the need for a sacrificial, substitutary, atoning death that so many Christians for so long regard as essential to or the bed-rock of Christian belief. Thomas Fudge's work too, shows how Oneness Pentecostalism (developing from Acts 2: 38) does not necessarily require the Cross in any meaningful sense for salvation.[38]

By way of a conclusion, put simply, perhaps we can reflect on whether the absence of the Cross in Islam (or apparent absence of the Cross) must generate as much consternation among Christians as it has traditionally caused us.

---

[33] Pagels, 2003: 78 dates the *Gospel of Thomas* from around the same time as the Gospel of John and describes a struggle between these two schools for canonical acceptance. She and other scholars, including the Jesus Seminar who include it as a fifth gospel in Funk (ed.), 1997 regard the Gospel as authentic.

[34] Gospel of Thomas 2006:77

[35] Gospel of Thomas 2006:11

[36] Gospel of Thomas 2006:77

[37] Pagels, 2003: 41

[38] Fudge, 2003

THE QUR'AN AND THE CROSS - LESS ABSENT THAN YOU THINK

Kenneth Cragg

Bishop Kenneth Cragg served as Bishop in the Anglican Jurisdiction of Jerusalem and the Middle East and now lives in Oxford, UK

It is commonplace to hear in Christian circles that care about their Muslim neighbours: 'How sad it is that the Qur'an denies the crucifixion of Jesus.' There is grief, as perhaps sometimes harsh reproach, in their saying so. The Cross is truly at the heart of Christian faith and the very focus of its sacramental *anamnesis* in 'the bread and wine' of Eucharist. It is the central theme of New Testament witness in the very genesis of the Church, beginning at Jerusalem where all had begun.

We must concede that Islam had *a* sure instinct - if it meant radically to disavow Christianity - to eliminate Christ's Gethsemane and all that followed it, as the Gospels narrate it. The Cross of the Messiah (as with a partial meaning to the *al-masih* term in noting its 'Isa the Qur'an employs)[1] is indeed the one unthinkable thing for the Islamic mind as ever duly happening to a divinely appointed 'messenger.' Or perhaps we had better say, it is *verboten* as ever in the context of an Incarnation of 'the Word made flesh' - that other utterly excludable dimension for Muslim theism. A faith that could say: 'Born of the Virgin Mary' and promptly follow with: 'Crucified under Pontius Pilate' was totally estranged from divine ways. It was typical irony when a noted South African Muslim preacher coined his witticism: 'Crucifixion-cruci-fiction.'[2]

We need hardly stay to observe how this 'rejection' of the Cross has underwritten so long an enmity between mosque and church, with measures of disdain on the one part, studied antipathy on the other. Muslims have unwittingly or deliberately obscured significances in their own Qur'an, in their antagonism to the hated symbol, their vehement exclusion of it from all their art forms. Christians, responsively, have often re-asserted the reality of the Cross of Jesus in terms that darkly compromised the very term in which Jesus

---

[1] The several references *to* Jesus *in* the Qur'an use the *matronymic*, *ibn maryam* with *al-masih* following. The sense, however, is not the Biblical one - we may characterize as the divine agent as answer *to* the human (the Jewish?) need of salvation in the light of creation, covenant and exile. *Al-masih* for the Qur'an is the anointed messenger, 'Isa, whose anointing is to that vocation.

[2] As noted in this book by the paper of Clinton Bennett.

suffered it. The issue of this ancient legacy has been a heavy liability on a sane introspection either way.

But, 'verily' as the Gospels loved to say, is Jesus' crucifixion really 'absent from the Qur'an? The question may seem to be mischievous or wayward and such it might be until and unless we look further and more patiently. So much we aim here to do.

It is noteworthy that the three passages in the Qur'an that relate to 'Isa and, ambiguously, the Cross, do so in the broad Christian sequence of 'born, dying and being raised.' This is significantly so in Sura 19.33 which tells of the infant, cradled, saying: 'Peace upon me the day I was born, the day I die and the day of my being brought back alive,' In the same Sura v. 15, Zechariah uses the same formula for his son John the 'Baptist' to be, where it surely refers to physical death. The v.73 of Jesus is traditionally understood as the ultimate natural death due to follow his return to earth (as a Muslim) and his eschatological role in the destruction of Al-Dajjal. His being 'raised up' thus refers to what - as in Suras 3.55 and 4.157 - is taken to be his rapture' to heaven from the danger which his ministry finally encountered.[3]

This scenario, however, much repeated in modern Muslim accounts of 'Isa, is wholly absent from the Qur'an.[4] It belongs only with Hadith and must be assumed to have been necessitated by the traditional reading of that danger as never culminating in crucifixion because the will to do this, in the Gospel context, was circumvented by divine intervention via 'rapturing' rescue into heaven. That rooted Hadith apart, 19.33 would fit exactly into the summary brevity of the familiar Christian creed: 'Born, dead, buried, raised up.' The explicit echo here must always remain significant.

Nevertheless, the more loaded passage is that in 4.157-59 with its insistence that the crucifying of 'Jesus' was only in the realm of 'seeming,' and its firm denial that 'they' (whether Romans or Jews) did not 'kill him,' did not crucify' him. Even the pronoun is 'hidden' in the verbs and the repetition of the synonyms reinforces the strength of the negation. 'Assuredly they did not crucify him' adds a further emphasis, observing - for better urging - that much 'surmise' had for long dogged the situation.

Indeed, 'surmise' has abounded and - to quote the text - 'there is a lot of doubt about the matter among those who are at odds about it.' It is not seldom that a *parti pris* uses such language about those with whom they are in dispute.

---

[3] Attempt was made in Cragg, 1985b, to examine the complexities of Islamic exegesis of these passages and, notably, the readings of crucifixion as 'only in the realm of seeming.'

[4] Found in Muslin Tradition it may be seen as an effort to 'place' a 'dying' on the part of Jesus in a far eschatological future, seeing that - while the Qur'an requires it to happen - its historic eventuation in the New Testament narrative had to be excluded to retain an 'Isa who never suffered. The eschatology thus turns, not on an achieved redemption, but on *a* resumption of earth-dwelling on return from 'rapture' in heaven.

But a charge of confusion is a double-edged weapon and may recoil on those who would wield it. As we must see later, there were more than historical reasons why Islam denied the crucifixion - reasons which plainly had their place in the verdict about the facts.

Even so, the historical has first priority. Three points call immediately for iteration. Even the Qur'anic 'seeming' indicates a 'dying' issue deeply present. Even something of this order allegedly 'illusory' requires a context in which such deception can occur. Secondly, there is in the long rooted actuality of Christian *confessio* about 'Jesus crucified,' with the ever added sequence '…and was buried.'[5] Thirdly, there is the plain witness to that confession of Roman historians like Tacitus and Pliny. Thus, however controversially, the Cross is present in the Qur'an. We must reckon positively with Sura 4.157-159.

Moreover, it is present in evidently Christian terms as being squarely implicit in those terms themselves. For, by their very negative shape, they necessitate two things. One is an 'Isa/Jesus whose death the powers and society around him expressly sought and for which they deeply conspired . The other is that Jesus/'Isa in this situation was he who came into it with a courage that had not flinched. On both counts we have - emphatically we have - the Jesus of the Gospels.

The hypothesis of rescue in and at a climax means a *mise-en scène* just like the New Testament, *i.e.* a ministry of deed and word, of moral challenge to 'establishment,' which drew down upon itself a deep adversity, a malign resistance, crying: 'Let him be crucified!' There is nothing 'only apparent' in this aspect. It is only too evident. 'Isa/Jesus, on any guess of ours, could only be aware of this 'gathering storm,' seeing that tokens of its brewing had been growing throughout his Sirah, his serving ministry. Yet he had not antecedently trimmed his sails, abandoned his vocation or made his own safe exit into safety over Jordan, putting himself 'out of harm's way'. This evident fact makes him - whatever 'rescue' might supervene - the Jesus who could say: 'The cup my Father gives me I must drink.' Who then wants to say that the Cross is 'absent from be the Qur'an? In the will to crucify 'the sin of the world' is there and so also, in fact though not in doctrine, is 'the Lamb who bears it'.

It would be possible to align this aspect with the Qur'an's own Sura 3.55 where God is telling 'Isa: 'O 'Isa, I am causing you to die…'[6] - a verse hard to reconcile with the tradition (to which we have yet to come) about some post-

---

[5] That clause was always of vital significance for the Gospel' narrative and e.g., for Paul in 1 Corinthians 15, it passed firmly into the classic Creeds as clear repudiation of any 'unreality' about Jesus' death. It was an essential safeguard against Gnostic notions disparaging things physical in a firmly incarnational *and* sacramental religion.

[6] The verb *mutawaffika* with the attached pronoun means, 'I am calling you to account,' i.e. to death, on which accounting will ensue. This marks the culmination of mortal liability and means the ultimate finality of dying as the business of that moment. It must surely then imply a vivid consciousness on the part of 'Isa of impending demise, as evident in the mounting of opposition to his mission.

millennial demise he will eventually undergo. It reads much more sanely as relating to a crisis within a prophethood.

But the pivotal passage remains that in Sura 4. What, we have to ask, is the 'apparentness' about the crucifying of Jesus. The translations vary. Only a likeness was shown' (Arberry); 'It only seemed to them as if...' (Asad); 'He was counterfeited to them' (Bell); 'it was an illusion for them' (Abd al-Latif).

The crucial verb is *shubbiha lahum*. It is reflexive and passive from the root meaning 'to resemble, or 'made to seem'. The agent is 'hidden' in *the* verb and could be either 'he ' or 'it,' *i.e.* crucifixion. Having 'it' - as the Ahmadis do - would mean that the actual Jesus was crucified himself but that somehow he did not succumb but was salvaged still living from burial to have a subsequent career in Kashmir. The ambiguity on this score is then between crucifying and actually causing to die, thereby, the verb *salaba* meaning either.

The wide consensus, however, in mainstream Islam rejects this 'heresy' reading and has *ma salabuhu* as meaning the actual crucifying of 'another than 'Isa who, meanwhile, was - raptured into heaven so that he was himself ever unscathed. But this alternate victim was only so by mistaken identity, having been taken, by divine intent, as if he were 'Isa, and, for the time being (all that was left to him) vested in the very image of the real Jesus. The perpetrators intended Jesus as their prey (a vital point) but were thwarted in their intent, though *de facto* there was, by that intent, 'a Jesus-cross.'

It is, therefore, ambivalently that it is said: 'Jesus was not crucified', if we are dealing in history. A 'fictional' Jesus was killed but only because an anti-'Isa conspiracy was no fiction. Any inclusive denial of the event flouts the very thesis on which its partial 'denial' alone rests. In crucial measure we do have the Jesus of the Gospels in quite a central element of the Christian dimensions of his narrative, his death included. It is therefore lamentable that, for too 1ong and too casually, Christians have deplored what they have taken as a Qur'anic veto.

So much then - to proceed - caveat about the historical verdict: 'The Qur'an denies the Cross, but always there is more than the historical. It helps to read the Passion of Jesus as like a threefold cord. It brings in one the doing of humans in wrong; the act of Christ in grace and suffering; and the act of 'God in Christ reconciling the world.' For Christian faith these are entwined as one. The first two, as we have seen, are implicitly present in the Qur'an. The third emphatically is not. Indeed it is utterly excluded.

The reasons why it is so, take us beyond historical into the Christology for which the Qur'an bas neither place nor tolerance.[7] The grounds of Christology and, indeed, of its rejection are both moral and theological. It is the Muslim perception of these grounds which explains - in large part - the reasons for the

---

[7] Because of a sustained veto on 'Incarnation' as never an option - still less a strategy for the omnipaten, if by 'Christology' what Christianity means and not the limited *masih*-ness Islam allows. Cf. note 1 above which might be loosely thought *a* Christology.

reading of the history. It was, and is, not so much that the Gospel 'history' *into* and after Gethsemane was insecure or 'fictional,' but that it was essentially unwanted. There is irony in the fact that, for the mind of the New Testament. The history was/is altogether authentic because it was also so eminently 'desirable'.[8]

We can well preface the moral and theological motives here, between the two faiths, by musing on that *shuabbiha* root in Sura 4.157 f. It has an uncanny resemblance to the Greek verb *dokeo*, also meaning 'to seem' - the verb that gave name to an early Gnostic heresy about the 'seeming-ness' of the Incarnation and of the Cross in its train. Broadly, the acetic theme held that, if or since Jesus was divine, in being divine he could not suffer. To include the Cross, therefore, in his history for faith meant that it would have been 'in the realm of seeming,' a necessary facade to carry one 'truth' while obviating another. Jesus' suffering had only been apparent. He had not veritably 'been there' when it happened.

In its corporate mind, the early Church banned this 'make-belief' about the Cross as quite destructive of the very core of faith, of the truth that only by the love that suffers to forgive is sin opened to a 'forgiven-ness' that is honest and full. There was no classic truck with the forlorn and faithless Docetics, whose vagaries were, or would have been, a total de-validation of the Gospel. Hence the Creedal inclusion of '...and was buried' and the evidentiality of an empty tomb.

We cannot and need not, be sure of how there may have been any nexus between *shubbiha* and *dokeo.* The conceptual tally, however, is evident enough. Islam had its own innate reasons for the unwantedness of the death of Jesus, all historicity apart. They were different from those of the Docetics who disavowed it on incarnational grounds. But something of these attached in the Islamic idiom to 'messenger' also, as eminent 'agencies' in Allah's employ. It would be in no way condign for these to suffer, certainly not to the degree of humiliation explicit in a crucifixion.[9] Divine omnipotence could not be assumed incapable of due succour and proper vindication. 'Isa as we have seen, must surely have been validated, not by his redemptiveness but by his exaltation. There is, thus, a clear conceptual link between how Docetics thought and what the Qur'an affirms. Both, either way, are calling in question the

---

[8] 'Desirable ' in the Biblical sense of 'the desire of all nations' (Haggai 2.7) the long yearned-for 'answer' to our human hope. The point, too, is that the coming about of the faith was itself a fact of history and, thus, a new 'fact of the situation,' *It* is not that 'believing makes things so' but that 'things *so* believed make history.'

[9] *Allahu akbar*, 'God is greater' than that' might summarize the situation. The criterion of greatness, however, remains at issue. There might be a greatness of such a different order as to be capable of total self-expenditure in contrast to entire (and oblivious) self-sufficiency. What is at stake here is not the competence of divine power but the shape the divine nature might give to it. Why could it not be capable of love in kenosis as the New Testament believes?

reality of Incarnation and, still more, of its final measure in the Cross.

We return to the Islamic dimensions, whatever any causal interaction between. Theologies of what is apt for God responding to the human scene. Tersely, we may say that, for the Qur'an, a Christian theme of redemption via the Cross of Jesus is morally repugnant and theologically unnecessary. Much in the first sphere has followed from sadly deficient Christian trust with its own meaning, whenever that redemption has been told in terms of arbitrary substitutional suffering using the flawed analogy of Levitical sacrifice.[10] Islam feels that 'x' crudely immolated on behalf of 'another x' is immoral since our sins are our own and each bears its proper solitary selfhood. No 'scales' avail but our own and the 'load,' light or heavy, they weigh belongs to no other and is in no way transferable.

There is previous and valid insight in this Muslim rejection of a crude and arbitrary thesis of 'a' punished, 'b' freed. It never carried the very different truth of how 'suffering because of' can be borne in such a way as to be 'suffering on behalf of.' The 'father in the story of the wandering son is a good example. He 'bears' the pain of that 'Father, give me.. ' the abrupt departure, the 'grape-vine ' word, of what ensues. But he does not disinherit or repudiate. On the contrary, he continues to love and to yearn. In his heart he keeps open a home to which a returnee could look and come finally to say: 'Father I am no more worthy….' Then there is the welcome, the robe and the feast.[11] They, Father and son, have the *status quo ante* back again (as we never do after retaliation) enriched the more by the deep experience of forgiveness and of being forgiven. So it is between us and God on Christian ground. The wrong is 'borne' only to be thus 'borne away.' God is alike 'faithful and just to forgive.' There has been no cheap condoning in that patient yearning: only a potential and finally actual and real 'overcoming of the evil with good.' It is important for Christians to be wise in their presentation of Christ's redeeming Cross. There was nothing less like a helpless scapegoat than Jesus in Gethsemane. All is volitional and only so, salutary or salvific. Islam's moral antipathy to the Cross is based on a misreading of the very nature of pardon, its cost and its conditions. What might seem morally reprehensible, duly discerned, is known

---

[10] Animal sacrifice, a mere ritual, bears no comparison to one who recognises 'a cup his Father gives.' In Isaiah 53 ('The Lord has laid on him the iniquity of us all') the meaning can never be that of a hand with a formula pushing the scapegoat out into the wilderness. In the Isaiahan sense it can only be how the very will of Yahweh coincided redemptively with the costly bearing, in some Jeremiah's fidelity, of the deep wrong-doing of His people and by that very ' bearing ' bringing truth' through to victory.

[11] The point *is* the more graphically underlined by the contrasted attitude of the elder brother who 'would not 'go in.' When the father pleads with him in terms of 'this thy brother,' he retorts pointedly with 'this thy son.' He has not kept faith with relationship. One has to realize how different a 'father' the younger son has in mind between saying: 'Father, give me…' to his later plea: 'Father, make me one of your hired servants…Father, I am no longer worthy…'

to be morally authentic.

But Islam has other grounds on which to repudiate the Gospel about the Cross - the ground of a theology for which it is superbly unnecessary. Omnipotence just forgives. A means to do so is quite superfluous, still more a 'Saviour' enabling it somehow. Forgiveness, like the creation, is divinely effortless. He only says: 'Be and it is.' If, naively, Christians are heard saying: 'God forgives us because of Jesus, 'they will be heard saying: 'God otherwise is inadequate.' Communicators need always to anticipate prejudice.

But this is to belittle both sin and Allah. For, if forgiveness is effortless, it does not matter. Instead it is about wrong and guilt. It has to do less with what I did but with whom I am. It has to do with character beyond deed, the self in relationship beyond events. This the Qur'an knows well with its radical concept of *zulm al-nafs* nad *marad fi qulubina.*[12] These are costly to resolve, to heal and redeem.

Thus the point about forgiveness through Christ and the Cross answers the 'whether' of forgiveness only because it has to do with 'how.' It is a divine adequacy itself at grips with what asks of God for more than our education, more than our direction, nothing less than our conversion, the remaking of our character. There is no task more fitting for divine omnipotence. Far then from being theologically improper or morally repulsive, a suffering love at the heart of a divine-human forgiveness is blessedly apt for both grace in Him and need in us. Only so, furthermore, does it become a paradigm of what ought to obtain between us humans also, so that we learn 'to love as He loves us,' and only because He showed the way and we perceived how to make it ours. For to know ourselves redeemed, is to become in turn redeemers, 'bearers of wrong' for this ever vulnerable, self-hurting world. Only intelligent witness takes due care of deep meanings. When the moral and theological 'case' within the Cross of Christ is seen and heard can we resolve also the puzzle - which only some have mis-guardedly found - concerning its historicity. For of that, history leaves no doubt, the dubiety being itself the fruit of a resistant ethic and a less than profound theology.[13]

That there is justice in this conclusion might be told another way - the way in which history and theology unite here is being each other. The emergence of Christian faith in the Cross of Jesus, as redemptiveness on divine part, was

---

[12] Both are frequent allusions in the Qur'an. *Zulm* is dire wrong-doing, truth-scorning in what realm - social, political, commercial, spiritual. Self-wronging is the inward perversity that destroys personal integrity, one that has to cry: 'O wretched man that I am.' wrong in being, not only in behaving. That private evil is like a disease implies much about a need for cure, beyond the reach of education, or command and prohibition. 'Heart-disease' *is* a malady calling to 'the great physician.'

[13] Or, in other words, history has its origin not in some genuine historical disquiet about evidences (these being elsewhere so unanimous) but in theological motives deriving from Muslim pre-possessions about Allah's power and 'messenger' status as its instrument.

itself a fact of history no less than the content of that Cross. It did so emerge against all the odds of how dire a tragedy was a 'crucified Messiah' when the expectation had been of another 'Son of David,' a subduer of the nations and their power in political terms. That strange reversal of the very content of faith ensued upon the disciples' own desperate failure at the last. The faith itself was a 'resurrection' of them as of the one about Jesus. That it ever came to pass makes a further credential concerning the realities in Jesus which enacted it - ministries antecedent and compassion-in-the -Passion at the climax.

There was thus a double sense in which history underwrote theology and theology became history. It is possible for Christian faith to tell with reverent authority that 'God was in Christ' and 'in Christ this way,' as thereby 'the Christ in God.' The third vital strand in the threefold cord we noted is restored, whereby what humans did in sin and 'Jesus did in love is also 'God's action' as 'doing what He does that He may be who He is.'

There is, however, yet more to propose about the absence of the Cross in the Qur'an and to explore it briefly can only help to bring home the other argument from within the New Testament. What should we think of things in the Sirah of the Meccan Muhammad analogous in part to the experience of Jesus in Galilee and Jerusalem? There was something of the same - if differing - obduracy in the immediate community, a similar encounter with 'established mind-set.' In the Meccan case it was that of the pagan Quraish, with sanctions of local prestige and custodial privilege around the Ka'bah and its 'liturgy,' its watering even, and its management and truce-provision and the attendant authority/control. All was a pagan 'Temple-area.' The analogy with Judaic Jerusalem only seems remote. It was valid enough to make Muhammad a potential 'martyr.' What of Sura 18.6 telling Muhammad: 'Is it that you are distressing your very soul over the way they are? - so unbelieving of the message.' We find him in 25.30 saying: 'Lord, my people have been altogether dismissive of this Qur'an, ' only to be reminded that such was the way it had always been among God's messengers. It is clear that something coming to seem a *via dolorosa* was emerging during the Meccan Sirah.

Clearly, the Hijrah needs an explanation, never being expressly commanded in the Qur'an but pragmatically undertaken, on Muhammad's own initiative. It was a decision surely not of cowardice - for it needed great fortitude - but of courage and strong resolve. That it happened and a Medinan Islam ensued are plain index to a Meccan situation of chronically resistant unbelief and of 'gathering storm.' There was reason for 76.24 to admonish: 'Await with patience what your Lord determines.' Did he not in fact continue doing *so* until, the Hijirah, since 'he had in hand a great undertaking' (68.4) and had six times been warned: 'Your sole liability is the *balagh*, the message preached.'

That *qul yaqulun* refrain through the Qur'an, the command to 'say', because 'they are saying' is witness to a steady encounter with an obloquy that had to he rebuffed - 'he is a mad sorcerer;' 'he disrupts our traditions;' ' he vexes our morale;' 'he has his folly about dead bones revived;' 'he gets it from strangers;'

and the like - it is all evidence of a hard experience demanding great hardiness and fortitude. Would it be wrong to see it as at least a potential Gethsemane, 'a burden breaking down the back' (94.3 albeit an early Sura)?

We cannot banish the question from any realist reckoning with the Meccan Sirah of Muhammad nor with the urgent logic from it that proposed the Medinan sequel. As with our analysis of the Gospel, there was/is, no point in rescue in the non-existence of danger and anti-conspiracy. Muhammad had been in a like-Jesus situation, *mutatis mutandis* and his Hijrah radically altered the sequel.

Islam in its Medinan idiom reached for the political solution which Jesus had resisted in the third *peirasmos*, the third 'trial' with Satan in the wilderness, the Power of the political order. The *vaquluna fa qul* formula became *ha jadu wa jahadu* — 'they went out and they struggled.' The concept of *fitnah* - a close parallel to *peirasmos* - passed through three significant changes of meaning. *Fitnah*, as what 'tested', was first the persecution that vexed *a* minority faith and became at length in late Medina the 'subversion' that tried *a* victorious majority via the machinations of 'hypocrites.' In between, it had meant the temptation to shrink from battle out of fear to leave widows bereft, and orphans behind, or simply reluctance to die. Medina brought its own tests but they were different sharply from those of the Meccan years. The Muhammad who had been 'distressing his very soul' as 'only a messenger' was steadily surmounting distress in its martial form at Badr and Uhud and beyond, in different terms - terms which obviated all analogy with a Gethsemane. Islam had opted, via the Hijrah, for a corroboration of 'persuasion' - if such be possible - by one of implied 'coercion,' insofar as 'surrender' (*islam*) might and did happen prior to belief conviction.[14]

Nevertheless, if we are speaking of a cross in the Qur'an it is right to have in perspective the genuine tribulation which Muhammad endured with tenacity during his Meccan mission. It holds great potential for Islamic relevance to the current global scene and the vocation of religions within it to be, not enmity brooding and breeding identities, but saving sharers in the imperatives of peace.[15]

---

[14] As happened, e.g., in Sura 49 where certain 'desert Arabs' surrendered to Muhammad politically but were told that 'faith had not entered their hearts, not allowing them to say: *amanna*, 'We have believed.' There is a vital distinction between *islam*, as personal devotion and Islam as the institutional frame thereof.

[15] The whole theme enshrined in Sura 4.157-159 and, with *it*, the issue of *the* threefold 'elements' in *a* 'Christ crucified' has been remarkably explored from within Islam by the scholar and surgeon, Muhammad Kamil Husain of Cairo. Essentially, he omitted the third dimension of 'God in Christ,' but uniquely in Islamic range he explored the other two, *i.e.* an 'Isa willing to face the dying implied in a society's will to have him die. That rejection was, for Kamil Husain, a symbol of all human wrongness *in* its quality of enmity to truth and love. In Husain, 1954 (the work in question), the author 'identified in that enmity a willful suppression of the role and duty of 'personal conscience' in

That hope returns as squarely to the perennial meaning of Jesus in and through his Passion and to how it gave credence to God Himself, 'God in Christ,' as truly 'acquainted with grief for ever embracing the world in the meaning of the wounds of Jesus.'

---

human affairs. Jews and Romans perverted rights and justice because they let their private conscience be over-ridden by the counsels of establishment, bent on its own wrong 'interests' of power and authority. Husain, 1966 uses a Qur'anic phrase and applies it to Jerusalem on that Good Friday making *it* 'the darkest day in human history.' In this work, *zalimah* is the 'doing' participle derived from *zalama*, the verb and *zulm*, the noun. There are several issues of the English translation of this work; see e.g., Husain, 1995. See also Cragg, 1985c: 126-144 or more fully in Haddad (ed.), 1995: 411-425.

Christology in an Alternative Islamic Theological Structure[1]

David Emmanuel Singh

Dr David Emmanuel Singh is Research Tutor at the Oxford Centre for Mission Studies, UK

Introduction

The Bible and the Qur'an may have similar narratives but they have different purposes/messages.[2] 'The Parting of Ways' (to use Kenneth Cragg's phrase) between Christians and Muslims is inevitable if the context for Christian engagement is the Traditional Structure. For most Christians, the Bible contains a single narrative just as for many Muslims the Qur'an contains a single purpose/message. The Bible is read by many Christians as portraying a unique 'salvation history' culminating in the incarnation of the Son of God as Jesus of Nazareth and, through his Cross, the possibility of salvation for all beings. The Traditional Structure has a different goal: it is to demonstrate the truth about the Prophet Muhammad being the Messenger of the One God whose message, the Qur'an, leads the erring to 'the straight path'. All the examples of the prophets and their prophecy, including Jesus, thus serve to support the Prophet Muhammad's claim to be the final Prophet and the Qur'an being the final revelation of this One God. The possibility of a God-human association is impossible, sin is not central, and the Cross represents a typical 'unbelief' and corruption of the revelation of the Gospel by Christians. According to this, the fundamental nature of the Christian corruption of the Gospel was that the Prophet Jesus was believed to be the 'Son of God' and was made to die on the Cross.

There are two issues here. Firstly, that a human prophet is said to share in the divinity of God. Sharing the nature of God contravenes the Traditional Structure. It is not hard to understand why to most Muslims, the Christian faith in Jesus being 'the Son of God' appears blasphemous. Secondly, that the Prophet Jesus is made to die on the Cross. The image of the Cross in itself is not problematic. The Cross did exist and the Jews did attempt to put Jesus on the Cross but, God could not let his servant, the Prophet Jesus, suffer such an

---

[1] This paper is being published with permission from Koninklijke Brill NV. It was originally published as Singh 2006:239-260

[2] Singh, 2000: 60-72 and Singh, 2001: 177-197

unnecessary humiliation. The Cross bearing Jesus would be a sign of God's failure and, indeed, his powerlessness to protect his Prophet. But as God cannot cease to be who he is, the suggestion that Jesus died on the Cross is incomprehensible to many Muslims.

This paper assumes two broad categories of theological structures in Islam: Traditional and Alternative. The main argument is that the Alternative Structure is rooted in Islamic mysticism and affords greater flexibility for the development of a Christian theology of Islam. The approach adopted in this paper reflects J. Hick's reading of Islamic mysticism. The main aim of the paper is to present some reflections on two of the main problems of Christian theology in Islamic contexts - the person of Jesus and his Cross - in terms of a key Islamic mystical notion, 'the Perfect Man' (PM).

The Perfect Man in the Alternative Structure

Although, the idea of the PM existed before 12th century CE, it was fully developed by Ibn 'Arabi, the 'greatest mystic-master' (*al-shaykh al-akbar*), to denote the 'totality of divine attributes' or the Creator of all beings and the source of all knowledge (Cf. Singh, 2003a). God as the Majesty (*al-jalal*) (a parallel to the idea of God-in-Himself) was transcendent. The Creator was denoted by the term 'Beauty' (*al-jamal*) (a parallel to the idea of God-for-Us).[3] Greek Neoplatonism transformed the concrete Traditional Structure in Islam just as it influenced Christian theology. Neoplatonism originally conceived the process of creation in terms of the impersonal concept of emanation as a spontaneous overflow, a deluge of Being (Genequand 1996: 795). Islamic Neoplatonism conceived of Being's emanation or *fayd* as an overflow that brought things into existence. Human beings were the last to be created but were the first to be conceived. This 'first conception' was, therefore, represented in terms of the PM and the intrinsic connection between the PM and human beings explained the reason why mystics had spiritual knowledge and were able to relate to this 'God-for-Us', variously conceived as the *logos,* the 'Word of God', the Creator.[4]

The details of Islamic Neoplatonism can be found in I.R. Netton, S.H. Nasr and S.M. Stern's works.[5] A brief overview is in place here. Ishma'ilism is a branch of Shi'ism but represents a significant aspect of philosophy in Islam.[6] The earliest Ishma'ili philosophical works date back to the 10th century CE. The Qur'an was the corporeal representation of the Word of God, the Creator [also called the 'Mother of the Book' (*umm al-kitab*) or the preserved heavenly tablet (*lawh al-mahfuz*)] (Sura 36:12). The Ishma'ili goal was to reach out to this

---

[3] See Burrell 1986 for a discussion of 'God-for-Us' and 'God-in-Himself'.

[4] Netton, 1989: 116, 165 ff.

[5] Netton, 1982, Nasr, 1993 and Stern, 1983

[6] Poonawala, 1988: 200-23

Book, the very source of the creation and revelation. The physical Qur'an pointed to the hidden (*batin*) source of all knowledge and existence, namely the Word of God.[7]

It has been pointed out that the group of unidentified authors (Ikhwan al-Safa') of a work called *rasa'il* (epistles) were Ishma'ilis.[8] The *rasa'il* is a collection of 52 epistles dealing with varied subjects. The work divides itself into four parts dealing with mathematics, nature, psychology and metaphysics. I.R. Netton points out that the Ikhwan were specially influenced by Plotinus, a Greek philosopher whose relatively simple structure of the emanation of being (called 'the One') into the Intellect and the Soul was expanded by the Ikhwan.[9] The Ikhwan conceived of 'the One' emanating into the Intellect, the Soul, the Prime Matter, the Nature, the Absolute Body, the Sphere, the Four Elements and finally the Beings of this World.[10] They believed the human intellect to be the means of reaching out and knowing the 'highest' state of knowable being, the Supreme Intellect. Similar to the Ishma'ilis and the Ikhwan, the Sunni Arab philosophers were generally influenced by Neoplatonism.

The predecessor of Hamid al-Din al-Kirmani (d. ca. 412/1021), a well known Ishma'ili philosopher, namely Abu Ya'qub al-Sijistani (d. ca. 361/971), begins with what has been described by A. Nanji as 'the doctrine of *ibda'*(creation through 'eternal existentiation') (cf. Sura 2:117)[11]. This creation was not unconscious. It was a deliberate act of the Creator (*mubdi'*). Al-Sijistani conceived of a series of emanations beginning with 'the Word of God', 'the Intellect' or 'the Soul' and ending with the corporeal world.[12] S.H. Nasr points out that in Islamic philosophy, this Word or *logos* a parallel to the Neoplatonic idea of the Supreme Intellect, the source of all wisdom (*hikma*).[13] Al-Kirmani proposed that the first level of being's emanation was the Chief Intellect (*al-aql al-awwal*). This highest state of being's emanation further overflowed into a series of 10 spheres, the last of which was the earth.[14] The human soul being part of the same substance as the Creator reaches out to him, in an immediate or direct manner.

It is this combined tradition of the Islamic Neoplatonism/Arab philosophy that Islamic mysticism acquired and developed. Muslim mystics or the Sufis replaced the non-personal epistemological imageries of the 'Word' and 'Intellect' with the personal ontological imagery of the PM connected often to

---

[7] See Singh 2003a:51

[8] Nètton, 1982: 95-104. See for an ideological connection between the Ishma'ilis and the Brothers of Purity in Nasr 1993: 36; also Zimmermann (ed.), 1983: 5.325-337

[9] Netton, 1996: I.222

[10] Netton, 1996: I.227-8

[11] Nanji, 1996: I.149

[12] Netton, 1989: 213 and 221

[13] Nasr, 1996: I.21 and 34

[14] Netton 1989: 228

the supreme examples of perfection in Islam: the Prophet Muhammad or the Saint of Saints, Jesus. The historical Muhammad and Jesus were then connected ontologically to the pre-existing 'Spirit of Muhammad' or 'Spirit of Jesus' in an attempt to authorize the particular Islamic tradition and broader mystical traditions represented by their own discourses.[15]

Selected Sources of Islamic Mysticism

I have selected two particular Islamic mystics, al-Ghazzali and Ibn 'Arabi. My reasons for this selection are twofold: Firstly, whilst al-Ghazzali is known as the great reconciler of Alternative and Traditional Structures, Ibn 'Arabi's thought is known to have influenced much of the Islamic mysticism or Sufism in Syria, Turkey, North Africa and South Asia and, hence, both of these are significant representatives of the Alternative Structure. Secondly, in recent literature on the Christian theology of Islam, J. Hick follows al-Ghazzali's position on Jesus being a metaphor and Ibn 'Arabi's idea of *al-haqq* (the Reality) as a synonym of his 'the Real'. He defends the use of the mystical tradition in Islam as a partner in dialogue with Christianity and, I think, he is right in this choice.

Al-Ghazzali

Al-Ghazzali is known to be one of the most important Islamic mystic-philosophers (d.1111 CE).[16] He represents a less 'hard-line' view on the Christian doctrine of the divinity of Jesus. In his book on the 'refutation of the divinity of Jesus' referred to by M.A. Sirry, he rethinks the doctrine of Jesus' sonship in figurative or symbolic terms. This is to him more consistent with his mystical worldview which recognizes the hidden world behind the literal. If, therefore, Jesus' sonship was symbolic then his death on the Cross too was a figure of something beyond its concreteness. The Cross itself was not significant but what it signified.[17] Sirry refers also to M.M. Watt who speaks of al-Shahrastani (d. 1153) as another sympathetic Muslim thinker in line with al-Ghazzali. It is suggested that M. Ayoub represents these sympathetic traditions when he speaks of sonship in terms of the term *ibn* (denoting relationship of love or adoption). In contrast, the term *walad* refers to biological generation. Jesus was a son in the former sense, suggesting a sense of his special status before God by virtue of his proximity to him.[18]

But al-Ghazzali goes beyond Sirry's characterization of his thinking on this issue. M. Takeshita has in his work examined some of the works of al-Ghazzali to recover his thinking on a tradition of the Prophet Muhammad, which speaks

---

[15] Singh, 2003a

[16] For more on Al-Ghazzali, see Knysh, 2000: 142-49

[17] Sirry, 2005: 371 and see also Leirvik, 1999

[18] Watt, 1983a: 249-59 and see also Ayoub, 1995: 65-81

of a human correspondence with God.[19] The tradition in question is as follows: 'whoever knows himself knows God.' Takeshita examines some of the major works of al-Ghazzali and concludes that there are two types of God-Man correspondences in al-Ghazzali: firstly, Moral-Ethical: this suggests that it is possible to find certain similarities in God and man since, like God, man also possesses the qualities of 'goodness' and 'mercy' etc. and, secondly, Spiritual: this suggests that the God-Man correspondence lies in the idea of the Spirit breathed into man by God. As this Spirit belongs to God, the God-Man intimacy is essential and ontological.

Man combines in himself both the characteristics of divinity and of corporeality, the transcendent world and the corporeal world. Hence, al-Ghazzali speaks of man as a miniature of the universe (macrocosm), a microcosm. Man as microcosm, contains within him aspects that correspond to the world and his nature reflects both the characteristics of divinity and corporeality. This status of man is rooted in the fact of his possession of the 'Transcendental Spirit' which was breathed into Man by God. Thus, by his essential nature man is capable of 'ascending' towards God and mystics are an example and evidence of this being true. Al-Ghazzali, however, rejected the idea of the 'descent of God'. If mystics like al-Hallaj made such claims, they were not necessarily wrong but were simply in illusion or were confusing an upward movement of the human spirit with the downward movement of the Spirit of God. This was an important point for al-Ghazzali for, as a Muslim, he had to guard against any suggestion of his acceptance of the Christian doctrine of the special incarnation (*hulul*) of Jesus.[20]

The idea of the PM, however, was developed far beyond al-Ghazzali's 'spirit' that generally defines man. This development was in accepting the possibility of the existence of the PM, a 'synthetic' being who combined two diametrically opposite aspects of the divine reality, the body and spirit, the physical world and the spiritual world. Thus, the PM is the 'actual' Creator of all beings, the quintessential model of perfection and source of knowledge of all 'perfect men', the Saints.

The key questions are: who is this metaphysical-pre-existent PM to be identified with, what is his role and how does this help us understand the Cross? Not all of these can be answered fully but a beginning can be made.

Ibn 'Arabi

G. Webb, M. Takeshita and T. Burckhardt have already noted the centrality of man in Islamic mysticism in general and in Ibn 'Arabi in particular.[21] It has been argued that the supposition about man's centrality seeks to answer two questions: how does man know God and who is man? Ibn 'Arabi's Alternative

---

[19] Takeshita, 1987

[20] Gairdner, 1924: 61-62

[21] See Singh 2003 for details of these references.

Structure presupposes two fundamental polarities: *al-haqq* (the Reality) and *al-khalq* (the Creation). *Al-haqq* to him is Sheer Being (*al-wujud al-mahd*) and, thus, nothing can be said either positively or negatively about it. *Al-khalq* is primarily the *imkan al-mahd* (Sheer Possibility) of the Creation and only in a conditional sense, the actual creation. Ibn 'Arabi thinks of this Sheer Possibility as God, the Creator, the *logos*, and one who relates to man. This Creator is thought of in terms of the image of the 'spirit of Muhammad'.[22] In another paper I have discussed the distinction between Sheer Being and Sheer Possibility in Ibn 'Arabi and have argued that these are parallel to the broader mystical ideas of God-in-Himself and God-for-Us, i.e. God who is utterly transcendental and the God who creates and relates to what he creates.[23]

This God-for-Us is often represented in terms of 'the spirit Muhammad' in Ibn 'Arabi, which is the reason why A. Jeffrey, in his introductory notes to the translation of the *shajarat al-kawn* (the Tree of the Universe),[24] suggests that Ibn 'Arabi here was trying to make a contribution to the general trend towards the glorification of Muhammad and was attempting to enhance Muhammad beyond Jesus, the *logos.*[25]

According to Ibn 'Arabi the universe was not directly created by Being (God-in-Himself). The universe is the actualization of Being's Will or Knowledge. This Will/Knowledge corresponds to the Neoplatonic Supreme Intellect and is conceived of both in terms of non-personal and personal images. One of the personal images for this 'derived being' is that of the Creator or the *logos*. As this idea is used in an Islamic context, the *logos* is identified with Muhammad and not Jesus. 'Muhammad' here is therefore, a traditional label referring to the pre-existential source of being and knowledge - the bridge between man/universe and God-in-Himself.

I have argued in a paper that to Ibn 'Arabi, the priority of Muhammad and his pre-existence was not absolute. I think A. Jeffrey was wrong in supposing that in using Muhammad's name to denote the Creator, Ibn 'Arabi was attempting to exalt Muhammad over Jesus, the *logos* of Christianity. The name Muhammad was used by Ibn 'Arabi as merely a traditional label to denote his Alternative Structure with the PM at the centre.[26]

The central place accorded to Muhammad and the use of traditional language in Sufism is hardly surprising. The presence of traditional role models, conventional vocabulary etc. is essential to determine the identity of

---

[22] Singh, 2004: 275-301

[23] Singh, 1999: 295-306

[24] Jeffrey, 1959: 43-77 and 1959: 113-160. This was reprinted in Lahore by Aziz Publishers 1980. See also Ibn 'Arabi 1968/1388

[25] Jeffrey, 1959: 45, 46. Jeffrey has attributed the motive for the veneration of the prophet 'to interpret the significance of their prophet as unique not only in his own community but also in cosmic history.'

[26] Singh, 2004: 286-288

any religious group. On the other hand, embellishing all radical thinking with traditional language was necessary if one wished to remain within Islam.[27] We know for instance that one of the concerns of Ibn 'Arabi was to show how the knowledge gained by the mystics was of a higher order than that gained by the prophets. Ibn 'Arabi circumvented the problem which generated a traditional reaction by positing that Muhammad also had two levels of knowledge: firstly, prophetic (for the Muslim community); secondly, saintly (for the saints are not necessarily bound by any religious boundaries). This made it possible to speak of an alternative and a 'superior' way to God [though veiled], whose leadership was not in Muhammad, the historical prophet, but in Jesus, 'the seal of the Universal Sainthood', and thus, it is to this we now turn.[28]

Jesus and the Cross: A Position

Our discussion above shows that traditions or 'shades' other than the Traditional Structure exist in Islam. This plurality shows promise for Christians who seriously wish for a respectful engagement with Islam. In this context, the idea of the PM may be especially helpful. A supposed 'pre-existential Muhammad' is often identified with this idea. We have argued that the name 'Muhammad' may have been used merely as a traditional label to mask the radical nature of the meaning of this symbol within an Alternative Structure. As such, the idea of a pre-existential Muhammad is parallel to the Christian *logos* and is part of a wider Islamic mystical notion of the PM. This PM is the face of God for man – one who 'associates' with man, one who is not limited by his transcendence to vulnerability, change and suffering. He is the Creator, the revealer and the immanent God. The argument below is that this, as opposed to the Traditional Structure, is potentially a promising framework for a Christian theology in some Islamic contexts.

Jesus and the Cross in the Traditional Structure

In the historic Christian Faith, the Cross is worth nothing without the faith in Jesus, the Son of God and the bearer of the Cross unto death. The key purpose of this Son is not the performance of miracles to assure himself or others of his status (Matthew 4.3ff.) but to lay down his life (Matthew 16.16, 21). Traditional Islam denies both Jesus, the Son of God (that he was not God in human flesh) and his Cross (that Jesus, the Prophet did not die but was rescued by God from the Cross). In the Christian engagement with traditional Islam, historically, there have been a number of key problems.

Firstly, there has been the issue of the identity of Jesus. The Christian notion of Jesus' 'sonship' has been one of the bones of contention in the theological encounters between Christianity and traditional Islam which go back in time to

---

[27] Stroumsa, 1999

[28] See more on Jesus in Ibn 'Arabi, D'Souza 1982: 185-200 and Ibn 'Arabi 1981

the first four centuries of Islam. M.A. Sirry has in his paper approached this from the point of view of 'the development of Muslim perceptions of Christian doctrines and practices', [29]whereas M.I. Beaumont views this from the point of view of the Christian interlocutors in the early theological dialogue between Christians and Muslims.[30] Jesus' sonship was assumed by Muslim partners in dialogue to be 'biological' and not 'spiritual'. In the concrete worldview of their time, the term, *ibn* (son) as the possession of the owner (God) meant that 'God married a woman and begat a son'. The idea of a biological begetting of Jesus involving God and a woman was not only considered illogical because the eternal could not be born in time but also blasphemous as begetting presupposes sexual intercourse. The Qur'anic ideas of the Messiah being only a 'Messenger' (Sura 4.171) and God being different to humanity in not begetting or being begotten' (Sura 112.3) is stressed as the final arbiter of truth in respect of this Christian doctrine.

Assuming that Jesus is the 'son', traditional Muslims have held that the final proof of corruption in Christian beliefs is that Jesus died on the Cross: he could not have been God or his son, as God cannot die. In their dialogue with Muslims, Christians have relied on the Qur'anic idea of Jesus being 'His word' (which he conveyed unto man) and a 'spirit of Him' (Sura 4.171) and they have at the same time emphasized the orthodox Christian doctrine of Jesus being both human and divine in equal measure. Traditional Islam, with its 'concrete' worldview, does not see any possibility of this association. Superior and inferior beings simply do not unite as this would imply change in God and affect his unity. As history shows, the issue of Jesus' identity has been impossible to resolve.

Secondly, there has been the issue of the Cross. The traditional Islamic conception of God is that He is one who is absolutely powerful and merciful, thus, his servants (prophets and messengers), cannot conceivably be subjected to unreasonable suffering and certainly not death. This is evident in the story of Abraham and his sacrifice (Sura 37.83-113. Cf. Genesis 22.1-19). This story in the Qur'an is set within the context of the prophetic ministries before Abraham. Abraham follows in the footsteps of Noah in obeying God and fulfilling his role as a prophet despite his many sufferings. But, as prophets perform their ministries, rejection (by people) and suffering (at their hands) follow. Those that come near to dying God rescues as when people 'build him a furnace' to throw Abraham 'into the blazing fire'. The experience of death, suffering and alienation is displaced from the prophet Abraham through the symbolic sacrifice of his son which Muslims all over the world celebrate in the festival of *id al-adha* (the feast of sacrifice) lasting for 4 days at the end of the Hajj on the 10th day of the 12th month of the Islamic calendar.

Jesus was a prophet like Abraham and others in the Qur'an and thus could

[29] Sirry, 2005: 361-376

[30] Beaumont, 2005a: 20-27 and 2005b: 195-202

not have died on the Cross because God rescues his prophets from such a fate. In the particular case of Jesus, the Cross would be meaningless also because firstly, human sacrifice, even if it involved a messenger or a prophet, would be limited to his immediate time and people; secondly, it would be pointless for the lack of a good enough reason for it. Human sin is marginal and, therefore, even if it were possible for God to allow his prophet or son to die there would be no purpose for this death. The Cross would be utterly futile. The Christian idea of sin being a collective human rebellion against God would not mean much notwithstanding stories in the Qur'an of the particular sins of people like the Pharaoh. Islam does not think of such a rebellion in terms of 'collective and original sin' for which God needs to be expiated and propitiated. God is independent of any such compulsions for His power gives him the capacity to forgive or punish as He chooses without having to do anything more than this. His word makes things happen.

Thirdly, the argument that the universal efficacy of Jesus' death is based on the assumption about his divinity also fails because it leads to the problem of change in God. The NT is full of references supporting the idea that Jesus' status as the Son makes his death as the universally valid means to life. John 3.16 is a well known verse. It speaks of God loving 'the world' so much that he sends his only Son to die on the cross. 'Anyone' who believes is promised eternal life. John 3.18 speaks of belief in Jesus the son of God as a way for all to freedom from condemnation. John 3.36 speaks of belief as a way to 'everlasting life'. Clearly, the concrete worldview of traditional Islam is incapable of appreciating the possibility of incarnation, divine suffering and its universal validity. The Alternate Structure and in it the idea of 'Complex Unity' may hold promise. It cannot resolve all the points of differences but it can provide a more sympathetic environment in which to conduct theological dialogue.

An Alternative Theological Structure

The idea that Jesus is the *logos* who bridges the ontological gap between God and man, the world of eternal life and the world of suffering and death, would not seem blasphemous when seen in the context of the theological structure being outlined below.

A Dialogue with J Hick

J. Hick uses the idea of 'the Real' as the basis for the plurality of religious phenomena. In a rather Neoplatonic sense, Hick thinks of 'the Real-in-itself' as ineffable and, thus, beyond human experience. The ground for all human experience of God is 'the Real-for-us' (subject to human experience/relations). This is clearly different to Otto's idea of *noumena* which is itself the ground of human experience of awe and pleasure, repulsion and attraction.[31] The source

---

[31] Otto, 1968

of Hick's idea appears to be Neoplatonic (the One-Soul/Intellect distinction). In his dialogue with Islam, Hick deliberately chooses Islamic mysticism and defends its use against the critique of mainstream Muslim scholars who think of Sufism as a marginal phenomenon.

I agree with Hick in this defence, although I know his reason for the use of this tradition is to support his pluralist theology.[32] To me, Sufism is important not because religious experience underlies all religious phenomena but because some aspect of Sufism defines Islam all over the world. Thus, it may be marginal in respect of its presence in the dominant institutions but it represents the majority of Muslims and their way of life. In this sense it is a mainstream tradition. The particular theological tradition Hick chooses is that of the 12-13th century Spanish Muslim mystic-philosopher-theologian, Ibn 'Arabi. Hick's approach to the Cross, however, is akin to the 12th century Muslim mystic-philosopher-theologian, al-Ghazzali.

Hick uses Ibn 'Arabi's *al-haqq* (the Truth/Reality) as the Real-in-itself and distinguishes it from *allah*.[33] It is worth noting here that in my studies on Ibn 'Arabi I have not come across this distinction. *Allah*, as many of Ibn 'Arabi's sources would show, is the *haqq,* the ineffable essence. *K. al-jalal wa-l-jamal,* for instance, would speak of this essence in terms of the 'Majesty' and of God subject to human awareness as 'the Beauty' corresponding to the ideas of God-in-himself and God-for-us. The *shajarat al-kawn* speaks of *al-haqq* as the *allah,* the God-in-Himself and God-for-us in terms of the 'Spirit of Muahmmad', a phrase parallel to the Christian idea of *logos* (as Jeffrey argues). Ibn 'Arabi uses several other terms to refer to the non-relational and the relational God of the Complex Unity which I have described in my book.[34] Hick is therefore rightly critiqued by M.S. Reçber for making a distinction between the *haqq* and *allah* although his reasons for this are different to Ibn 'Arabi's.[35]

In the context of this Alternative Structure, Hick concedes that Jesus is central to Christianity but only in al-Ghazzali's sense of being a religious symbol or a metaphor and not as the Christ, the God-for-us of the Complex Unity. The Muslim scholar, M. Ayoub, would appear to be closer to the historic Christian confession of Christ than Hick. With all his suspicion about mainstream Islam, on this most central of Christian confessions, Hick shares the traditional Islamic understanding of Jesus being 'a great prophet rather than the second person of a divine Trinity incarnate'. Hick says, 'The Qur'an is deeply opposed, as a form of *shirk,* to the idea that God has a son, and I share that view....This understanding of Jesus as a great prophet and in a

[32] Hick 2005: 14

[33] Hick 2005: 11-14

[34] Singh, 2003

[35] Reçber, 2005: 3-10. His reasons are based on the Traditional Structure which is to say that *al-haqq* is an attribute of the owner, Allah.

metaphorical sense a son of God...should I think, be something that Muslims can share.' In the same breath, consistent with the traditional Islamic position, he also rejects the historic Christian belief that this prophet, Jesus, died on the Cross.[36] Shorn of divinity, the death of Jesus on the Cross would not have any meaning beyond his immediate religio-political context; his death would also be a theological problem (how can an all-powerful God allow his servant to suffer and die such an ignominious death?), rather than being a solution for the most complex of all predicaments (according to Christian theology), human sin.

The point is that Hick's choice of the Alternative Structure is motivated by his pluralist hypothesis. Ibn 'Arabi has been styled as a pluralist, but his pluralism never loses sight of the Traditional Structure. The Qur'an and Muhammad are central to his thinking. Despite this, Ibn 'Arabi creates a space for thinking about Jesus in terms that are a far cry from the Traditional Structure. Jesus could be in his system like the spirit of Muhammad, the God-for-us. Indeed he is more 'expansive' than Muhammad in being the ground for the universal phenomena of sainthood whereby mystics realize the possibility of 'friendship' and intimacy with this God. Hick obviously chooses to ignore this part of Ibn 'Arabi's Alternative Structure despite having read and quoted from his *fusus al-hikam* in his response to M.S. Reçber.[37]

Jesus, the PM?

It is the nature of God to be 'Complex' rather than 'Simple.' Islamic Neoplatonism, Ishma'ilism and Sufism represent strong and inwardly developmental traditions which are rather more beholden to the notion of a Complex Unity. Christian faith regards Jesus as the God-for-Us. The scriptures testify to him being the *logos* who creates and the Son who reconciles man with God, the Father through his incarnation and cross. Can we call Jesus the PM of the Christian faith? This is not an extremist view even within the context of the Alternative Structure of Islam and possibly holds some promise for Christian engagements with Muslims.

In Christian traditions, Christology has been viewed from both ends of humanity and divinity. The Chalcedonian formula (CE 451) emphasized the idea of 'fully God and fully man'.[38] The mainstream early church in the East was concerned to show Christ's authentic divinity. Both his divinity and humanity were affirmed and Jesus was thought of being a perfectly integrated person. Two early centres of Christianity debated the nature of this integration. The Alexandrian School agreed with the idea of the perfect union of God and man. The Antiochene School agreed with the idea that divinity dwelt in the Jesus of Nazareth. Both Schools had Biblical foundations for their Christological perspectives. The Alexandrian School took John 1.14, 'And the

---

[36] Hick, 2005: 11

[37] Hick, 2005: 14 and Ibn 'Arabi, 1981

[38] Neuner and Dupuis, 1996

Word [*logos*] became flesh and dwelt among us' as the basis for its position on the God-Man union and the Antiochene School's thinking was founded on such scriptures as Colossians 2.9, 'For in him the whole fullness of deity dwells bodily….' The former conceived of the 'priority' of the pre-existing Christ as the *logos* who descended to assume embodiment, whereas, the latter began with the notion of a true humanity being indwellt by divinity.

Both of these positions are found in Indian Christian theology which makes a serious attempt to connect with spiritualities within Hinduism where man seeks perfection on the model of Jesus, the *avatara* (incarnation) and the *nara-hari* (Man-God).[39] These are also found in some traditions of Islamic mysticism: Firstly in conceiving the PM or the God-for-Us who is akin to the *logos* of Christian faith. This PM is especially identified in some traditions with the 'Spirit of Muhammad' and 'the Spirit of Jesus' who are actualized as historical prophets. Secondly, in regarding saints as those who are intimate with God and, thus, as it were, bear God. The Alexandrian position appears especially similar to the idea of the PM used in relation to Jesus and the Muhammad of Islamic Mysticism. The PM, like the *Logos,* is assumed to be an eternal hypostasis who descends as an actuality in history and then ascends. In thus descending and ascending, the PM becomes the 'Seal of Sainthood' - a model for humanity to follow (saints are said to be examples of this).

One of the main characteristics of the PM is his capacity for 'intimacy'-'association'. He expresses this through his mercy-love. The grounds for this are in his pre-existential experience of the Complex Unity. The notion of mercy (*rahma*) is as important to Islam as love (*agape*) is to Christian faith. Two of the many names that describe God in the Qur'an are *al-rahaman* (the Compassionate) and *al-rahim* (the Merciful). That God loves and loves enough to send his only Son to be our friend, brother, saint-guide-teacher (*wali*) and to die for us to be reconciled with God is fundamental to the NT faith. In the Qur'an, all chapters, except Sura 9, begin with the phrase *bismillah al-rahman al-rahim* (in the name of compassionate and merciful God). God 'grants forgiveness' and 'bestows mercy' (Sura 2.286). This idea of mercy and compassion sits awkwardly in the Traditional Structure that presupposes a strict Transcendental Unity of God (*tawhid*). How does God show mercy and compassion without *being* merciful and compassionate and how does God *be* merciful and compassionate within the 'Simple Unity'? The idea of the Complex Unity in the Alternative Structure takes care of this problem in presupposing essential and ontological relations within Godhead. It renders the central Islamic concept of *rahma* and indeed the Qur'anic notion of the 'names' of God fully meaningful. In other words, mercy and compassion are relational concepts and their existence in the Qur'an increases the plausibility of the Complex Unity and aligns these traditions of Islam nearer to Christian faith than we realize.

[39] Boyd, 1991

Suffering in this context would not necessarily be negative as it would be an extension of the Merciful God who experiences it first within the Complex Unity before He 'grants forgiveness' and 'bestows mercy' upon His creation. To show compassion and mercy is to sacrifice and in the Complex Unity, there exists a timeless and transcendentally perfect sharing of mercy and, hence, God remains forever and immutably One. The Cross can remain as the ultimate evidence of divine compassion and mercy. To suggest God cannot suffer would limit God and his power who exercises his limitless compassion and mercy 'inside' His being before He shares it with beings 'outside' His being. Nothing would ennoble the godliness of this God and nothing would endear Him to his creation more than His willingness to suffer for them. God is as one who is at once exalted and yet humble, immutable and yet capable of suffering, different and yet one with us, God-for-us.

The historic Christian faith takes the mercy of God and the Merciful One to the highest and the noblest level presupposed by these most central of Islamic notions about God. God is Merciful and His mercy is not merely an exercise of His power to forgive, but an exercise of His power for His Self to fulfil the demands of His justice. This is why Jesus is central to the Christian faith. The Christian idea of sin as human rebellion is not marginal but central to the human attempt to 'acquire divinity'. The divinity of Jesus is not something he acquires through his obedience even unto the cross, but is an ontological state in God's Complex Unity. Whereas nothing may be said of the ineffable God Himself, Jesus, the PM as God-for-us, is totally just. Man must die for laying a claim on God's divinity which properly belongs only to Jesus. But God is totally merciful and, hence, man must have an opportunity to live. This opportunity to live is presented to man through the PM, Jesus, whose death on the Cross reconciles God's justice and his mercy. This PM, Jesus, is the God-for-us; he is the model for man to aspire to be like him in obedience and not in acquiring his divinity.

The Cross in this context is not a symbol of conquest as many of my Muslims friends think of it. It is rather the very opposite of the exalted nature of the PM, Jesus; the ultimate form of humiliation he chose to suffer for the extreme imperfections of man (Philippians 2.5 ff.), his creation; a means by which he lead the way for Man to actualize the highest possible state of intimacy *(uns)* with God-for-us (Romans 5.10; John 14);[40] the extreme extent of his descent into the world of sin and suffering, a threshold for his ascent to the exaltation of his glory and a way for sinful man towards eternal life *in* him (Cf. Acts 3.13 & 3.26). The Cross shows that true humanity is not that of 'living in flesh' but 'living in Spirit' Romans 1.4; Galatians 2.20, Galatians 4.6). True humanity is realized, reached, or received in man's 'ascent' through Jesus who

---

[40] The word used in Romans is 'reconciled' which I think roughly is parallel to the idea of *uns*.

first 'descended' and then 'ascended' (John 20.17).[41] It also shows that the human ascent with Jesus has to do with the spirit, the seat of being, which communes with the glorified Jesus who has ascended to God where he belongs. The faithful will eventually meet this Jesus face to face and indeed be with him in perfect communion. Seeing Jesus will be like seeing God (but only as the God-for-Us), the Father, however, remains beyond human reach/sight (Cf. John 14; Exodus 19.20ff.).

Conclusion

This paper addresses the problem of Jesus and his Cross in Christian-Muslim relations from a personal and confessional point of view. There is a fundamental parting of ways between historic Christianity and traditional Islam. The paper argues that in Islam, the plurality of Theological Structure offers a possibility of a new level of interfaith dialogue. The Traditional Theological Structure posits God as the 'Simple Unity' whereas the Mystical-Philosophical Structure thinks of God as 'the Complex Unity' thus locating the experience of relationship and its demands in the very heart of God. The idea of the PM, as God-for-us is central to the notion of a Complex Unity.

In this context incarnation is not as blasphemous as it is supposed by some Muslims and the Cross can receive a more sympathetic treatment. By virtue of his position in the Complex Unity, the Cross of the PM can have a universal relevance for man beset by sin that causes the 'straying'. Prophecy is fulfilled by the PM who addresses sin, the root cause of man's habitual straying from God. True existence is in man when living in obedience to God. If sin is understood as the human rebellion against God, its consequences must be separation from God and the cessation of true existence. The PM, God for-us, knows about the relationship and its demands as these are essential to the experience of the Complex Unity. Thus the Cross could well be possible as a fulfilment of the demands of the divine love/mercy and justice on behalf of man who is destined to die.

[41] The idea is likely from the OT: Exodus 19.18 and Proverbs 30.4

BIBLIOGRAPHY

Abraham, J.
'Liberation of the Oppressed through Conversion,' in *Integral Liberation* (4) 4, 251-261

Agwal, H. 2001
'Christian Responses to Islam', an unpublished essay, MA in Mission at Selly Oak, Birmingham

Ahmed, A.S. 1984
'Religious Presence and Symbolism in Pukhtun Society' in A.S. Ahmed & D.M. Hart (eds.) *Islam in Tribal Societies, From the Atlas to the Indus* (London: Routledge and Kegan Paul) 310-330

Alavi, K.K. n.d.
kutafuta uhakika (Nairobi: Njia ya Uzima)

Ali, A. 1978
Islam- Ideology and Leading Issues (Lahore: United Ltd.)

Ali, H.A. et. al 1970
The Meo of Mewat: Old neighbours of New Delhi (New Delhi: IBH Pub. Co.)

'Ali, A.Y. (trans.), 2001
The Qur'an (8th ed.) (New York: Tahrike Tarsile)

Amhad, M.G. 1978
Jesus in India Qazi Abdul Hamid (trans.) (London: Ahmadiyya Muslim Foreign Mission; English 1944; Urdu original 1889)

Anderson, J.W. 1978
'There Are No Khans Anymore: Economic Development and Social Change in Tribal Afghanistan' in *Middle East Journal*, 32 (2), 167-183

St. Anselm, Basic Writings 1962
Proslogium, Monologium S.N. Dean (trans.), Introduction by C. Hartshorne (LaSalle, IL: Open Court Publishing Co.)

Arabic Gospel of the Infancy 2006
At http://wesley.nnu.edu/biblical_studies/noncanon/gospels/infarab.htm accessed 27/02/2006

Armerding, C. 1945
'The Brazen Serpent' in *BS* (102), 110-116

Assad, Y. 1996
Ezat an al-salib [Preaching about the Cross] (Cairo: Youssef Assad's Sons)

Austin, R.J.W. (trans.) 1981
The Bezels of Wisdom (*fusus al-hikam*) (Ramsey, N.J.: Paulist Press)

Atayee, M.I. 1979
A dictionary of the terminology of Pashtun's tribal customary law and usages Shinwari, A.M. (trans.). (Kabul: International Centre for Pashto Studies, Academy of Sciences of Afghanistan)

Athanasius 2006
'Athanasius on the Incarnation' at http://www.spurgeon.org/~phil/history/ath-inc.htm, Accessed 22/02/2006

Ayoub, M.M. 1995
'Jesus the Sond of God: a study of the term bn and walad in the Qur'an and tafsir tradition in Y.Y. Haddas and W.Z. Haddad (eds.) Christian Muslim Encounters (Gainsville: Florida University Press) 65-81

Ayoub, M.M. 1978
Redemptive Suffering in Islam (The Hague: Mouton)

Ayoub, M.M. 1980
'The Death of Jesus: Reality or Delusion,' The Muslim World (70) 91-121

Aziz, Sheikh. 2006
'Pashto Music' (excerpts from 'The Richness of It All') at http://www.khyber.org/culture/music/pashtomusic.shtml. Accessed 14 /01/2006

Baker, D.L. 1991
Two Testaments, One Bible rev. ed. (Leicester: IVP)

Barrett, C.K. 1978
The Gospel According to St. John: An Introduction with Commentary and Notes on the Greek Text, 2nd edition (London: Fortress)

Barth, F. 1981
'Pathan Identity and Its Maintenance' in *Features of Person and Society in Swat: Collected Essays on Pathans. Selected Essays of Fredrik Barth* (London: Routledge and Kegan Paul [1969]) 103-120

Bartlotti, L.N. 2000a
Negotiating Pakhto: Proverbs, Islam, and the Construction of Identity among Pashtuns, Ph.D. thesis, University of Wales

Bartlotti, L.N. 2000b
'The Pashtun Peace Ritual of Nanawati: Ambiguity and Variability in Folklore Praxis', an unpublished paper

Bartlotti, L.N. 1992
Qurban de shum (May I Sacrifice Myself for You): The Story of the Promised Sacrifice of God (Peshawar: Roshan Books)

Bartlotti, L.N. & Khattak, R.S. 2006
Rohi Mataluna (Pashto Proverbs). Revised and expanded edition, based on the 1st edition, M.N. Tair, & T.C. Edwards (eds.) (1982) (Peshawar: Peshawar University/InterLit Foundation)

Basetti-Sani, G. 1977
The Koran in the Light of Christ: A Christian Interpretation of the Sacred Book of Islam (Chicago: Franciscan Herald Press)

Bashier, Z. 1983
The Hijrah, Story and Significance (Leicester: The Islamic Foundation)
al-Basri, 'Ammar 1977
'Kitab al-Burhan' M Hayek (ed.) in *'Ammar al-Basri: Apologie et Controverses* (Beirut)
al-Basri, 'Ammar. 1977
'Kitab al-Masa'il wa-l-ajwiba,' in M. Hayek (ed.) in *'Ammar al-Basri: Apologie et Controverses* (Beirut)
Bataille, G. 1989
Theory of Religion (New York: Zone Books)
Bataille, G. 1977
Violence and the Sacred (Baltimore: John Hopkins University Press)
Beaumont, M.I. 2005
Christology in Dialogue with Muslims (Carlisle: Regnum)
Beaumont, M.I. 2005
'Early Muslim Interpretation of the Gospels,' *Transformation* (22), 20-27
Bediako, K. 1995
Christianity in Africa: The Renewal of a Non-Western Religion (Edinburgh: Edinburgh University Press/Orbis Books)
Bell, R. 1970
Introduction to the Qur'an, rev. and enlarged by W. Montgomery Watt (Edinburgh: Edinburgh University Press)
Bellinger, C.K. 2001
The Genealogy of Violence: Reflections on Creation, Freedom, and Evil (New York: Oxford University Press)
Bennema, C. 2002
The Power of Saving Wisdom, (Tübingen: Mohr Siebeck)
Bennema, C. 2005
Excavating John's Gospel For Today: A Contextualized Commentary, (Delhi: ISPCK/Bangalore: SAIACS Press)
Bennett, C. 1998
In Search of Muhammad (London and NY: Cassell)
Bennett, C. 2001
In Search of Jesus: Insider and Outsider Images (London and New York: Continuum)
Bernard 2006
Bernard of Clairvaux *On Loving God* at http://www.ccel.org/ccel/bernard/loving_god.htm, Accessed 27/02/2006
Bidawid, R.J. (ed.) 1956
'Epistle 59' in *Les Lettres du Patriarche Nestorien Timothée I*, Studi e Testi 187, Rome
Blauw, J. 2003
Missionary Nature of the Church: A Survey of the Biblical Theology of Mission (London: Lutterworth)

Bornkamm, G. 1969
Early Christian Experience (New York: Harper and Row)
Bowen, J.R. 1993
Muslims Through Discourse: Religion and Ritual in Gayo Society (Princeton, N.J.: Princeton University Press)
Brombley D.G and Melton J.G. (ed.) 2002
Cults, religions and Violence (Cambridge: Cambridge University Press)
Brown, R.E. 1994
The Death of the Messiah: From Gethsemane to the Grave, 2 vols. (London: Geoffrey Chapman)
Bultmann, R. 1951
Theology of the New Testament (New York: Charles Scribner's Sons)
Bultmann, R. 1972
Kerygma and Myth (London: SPCK)
Burrell, D.B. 1986
Knowing the Unknowable God: Ibn Sina, Maimonides, Aquinas. (Notre Dame: The University of Notre Dame Press)
Burrows, E.W. 1974
'Did John the Baptist call Jesus 'the Lamb of God'' *Expository Times* (*ExpT*) (85) 245-249
Burrows, M. 1977
Jesus in the First Three Gospels (Nashville: Abingdon)
Carey, G.L. 1981
'The Lamb of God and Atonement Theories' in *Tyndale Bulletin* (*TynBul*) (32) 101-107
Caroe, O. 1985
The Pathans: 550 B.C.-A.D. 1957. 4th ed. (Karachi: Oxford University Press)
Chabot, J.B. 1899-1910
Chronique de Michel le Syrien, Tome III, Paris
Chabot, J.B. 1937
Anonymi Auctoris Chronicum ad annum Christi, 1234 Pertinens, CSCO 109, Louvain
Chapman, C. 1989
'The God who Reveals,' in Woodberry, J.D. (ed.) *Muslims and Christians on the Emmaus Road* (Monrovia, CA.: MARC)
Charny, I.W. 1973
'And Abraham went to slay Isaac: A Parable of Killer, Victim, and Bystander in the Family of Man' in *Journal of Ecumenical Studies* (10) 304-318
Cheikho L. (ed.) 1921
in *Al-Machriq* (19) 359-374 and 408-418
Chesworth, J. 1999
'Muslim Affirmation through Refutation: A Tanzanian Example', MA dissertation, University of Birmingham

Childester, D. 1991
Shots in the Street: Violence and Religion in South Africa (Boston: Beacon Press)

Childs, B.S. 1974
Exodus: A Commentary (London: SCM)

Chittick, W.C. 1989
Ibn al-'Arabi's Metaphysics of Imagination: Sufi Path of Knowledge (Albany N.Y.: State University of New York Press)

Clements, R.E. 1989
'The Messianic Hope in the Old Testament,' *Journal of the Study of the Old Testament* (*JSOT*) (43) 3-19

Corley, B. 1992
'The Trial of Jesus,' in J Green & S McKnight (eds.), *Dictionary of Jesus and the Gospels*, (Downers Grove Il: InterVarsity Press)

Cornell, V.J. 1998
Realm of the Saints: Power and Authority in Moroccan Sufism (Austin: University of Texas Press)

Coser, L. 1956
The Functions of Social Conflict (Glencoe, Il.: The Free Press)

Cosgrove, C.H. 1984
'The divine *Dei* in Luke-Acts: Investigations into the Lucan Understanding of God's Providence' in *Novum Testamentum* 26, 168-90

Cragg, K. 1984
Muhammad and the Christian - A Question of Response (London: Darlton, Longman and Todd and Maryknoll, N.Y.: Orbis)

Cragg, K. 1985a
The Call of the Minaret (Maryknoll, N.Y.: Orbis)

Cragg, K. 1985b
Jesus and the Muslim (Oxford: Oneworld 1999/George Allen and Unwin)

Cragg, K. 1985c
The Pen and the Faith (London: Allen and Unwin)

Cragg, K1986a
The Christ and the Faiths: Theology in Cross-Reference (London: SPCK)

Cragg, K. 1986b
The Call of the Minaret (New York: Oxford University Press)

Cragg, K. 2004
A Certain Sympathy of Scriptures: Biblical and Quranic (Brighton: Sussex)

Daly, R.J. 1977
'The Soteriological Significance of the Sacrifice of Isaac' in *Catholic Biblical Quarterly* (*CBQ*) (39) 45-75

David, M. 2002
'God's response to Suffering in the Old Testament' in M.T.B. Laing (ed.) *Persecution and Suffering Christian Reflection and Responses* (Delhi: ISPCK)

Deedat, A. 1978
Crucifixion, Or Cruci-fiction? (Durban: Islamic Propagation Centre International)

Deedat, A. 2005
At http://jamaat.net/crux/crucifixion.html, Accessed 05/05/2005

Dick, I. (ed.) 1959
'Deux Écrits Inédits de Théodore Abuqurra' *Le Museon* (72)

Dillon, R.J. 1987
'The Psalms of the Suffering Just in the Accounts of Jesus' Passion' in *Worship* (61) 430-440

Dodge, B. (ed.) 1970
The Fihrist of al-Nadim vol. I, New York

D'Souza, A. 1982
'Jesus in Ibn 'Arabi's *fusus al-hikam*' in *Islamochristiana* (8) 185-200

Dunn, M.C. 1994
'Islamic Activists in the West' in *Middle East Policy* (3) 1,

Du Plessis, P.J. 1986
'The Lamb of God in the Fourth Gospel' in Petzer, J.H. and Hartin, P. J. (eds.) *A South African Perspective on the New Testament: Essays by South African New Testament Scholars Presented to Bruce Manning Metzger during His Visit to South Africa in 1985* (Leiden: E.J. Brill)

Durham, J.I. 1997
Exodus: Word Biblical Commentary, vol. 3 (Dallas: Word Book)

Ebied, R. and Thomas, D. 2005
Muslim-Christian Polemic during the Crusades, the Letter from the People of Cyprus and Ibn Abi Talib al-Dimashqi's Response (Leiden: E.J. Brill)

Edwards, D.B. 1996
Heroes of the Age: Moral Fault Lines on the Afghan Frontier (Berkeley CA: University of California Press)

Eickelman, D.F. 1982
'The Study of Islam in Local Contexts' in Contributions to Asian Studies (17) 1-16

Eickelman, D.F. 1985
'Introduction: Self and Community in Middle Eastern Societies' in *Anthropological Quarterly*, 58 (4) 135-140

Encyclopaedia of Islam 1913-1934
M.T.H. Houtsma, T.W. Arnold, R. Basset *et.al.* (eds.) Vol. 1 (Leiden: E.J. Brill)

Engineer, A.A. 1989
Communalism and Communal Violence in India: An analytical approach to Hindu-Muslim conflict (Delhi: Ajanta Publications)

Esposito, J.L. 1992
The Islamic Threat: Myth or Reality? (New York: Oxford University Press)

Fierro, M. 1992
'The Polemic about the *karamat al-awliya'* and the Development of Sufism in al-Andalus (Fourth/Tenth-Fifth/Eleventh Centuries)' in *BSOAS* (55) 245 (236-49)

Finkel, J. (ed.) 1926
Fi al-radd 'ala al-Nasara in thalath rasa'il li-Abi 'Uthman al-jahiz (Cairo)

Finkel, J. (trans.) 1927
'A Risala of al-Jahiz', *Journal of the American Oriental Society* (47) 328-9

Firestone, R. 1990
Journeys in Holy Lands: The Evolution of the Abraham-Ishmael Legends in Islamic Exegesis (Albany, N.Y.: State University of New York)

Fredricks, J.L. 1998
'The cross and the begging bowl: Deconstructing the cosmology of violence' in *Buddhist - Christian Studies* (18) 154

Freed, E.D. 1983
'Psalm 42/43 in John's Gospel' in *NTS* (29) 62-73

Fretheim, T.E. 1984
The Suffering of God: An Old Testament Perspective. Overtures to Biblical Theology (Philadelphia: Fortress)

Fudge, T. 2003
Christianity Without the Cross: A History of Salvation in Oneness Pentecostalism (Parkland, FL.: Universal Publishers)

Funk, R.W. (ed.) 1997
The Five Gospels: What Did Jesus Really Say - The Search for the Authentic Words of Jesus (New York: Polebridge Press/Harper Collins)

Galtung, J. 1959
'Pacifism from a Sociological Point of View,' *Journal of Social Issues* (3) 67-84

Gardner, P., Green, C. and Wright, C. (eds), 2003
Fanning the Flame: Bible, Cross and Mission (Grand Rapids, MI.: Zondervan)

Gairdner, H.T. 1920
The Rebuke of Islam (5th edition of *The Reproach of Islam*) (London: United Council for Missionary Education)

Gairdner, H.T. (trans.) 1924
al-Ghazzali's Mishkat al-Anwar, [The Niche for Lights] (London: Royal Asiatic Society)

Gibson, M.D. 1899
A Treatise on the Triune Nature of God (London: C.J. Clay and Sons)

Girard, R. 1965
Deceit, Desire and the Novel: Self and Other in Literary Structure Y Freccero (trans.) (Baltimore: The Johns Hopkins University Press)
Girard, R. 1977
Violence and the Sacred (Baltimore: The Johns Hopkins University Press)
Girard, R. 1987
Les Choses caches depuis la Fondation du Monde (Paris: Grasset 1978); English trans. *Things Hidden since the Foundation of the World* (London: Athlone Press)
Girard, R. 1996
The Girard Reader J.G. Williams (ed.) (New York: Crossroad Pub. Co.)
Girard, R. 2005
'Violence, Victims and Christianity,' The D'Arcy Lecture. At http://theol.uibk.ac.at/cover/girard_oxford_video.html, Accessed 2004-2005
Goldin, H.E. 1952
Hebrew Criminal Law and Procedure (New York: Twayne Publishers, Inc.)
Gospel of Barnabas 2006
Gospel of Barnabas at www.barnabas.net 27/02/2006
Gospel of Thomas 2006
Gospel of Thomas at www.earlychristianwritings.com/thomas.html and www.gospelofthomas.com 27/02/2006
Graf, G. (ed.) 1951
Die Schriften des Jacobiten Habib Ibn Hidma Abu Ra'ita, CSCO, 130, Louvain
Griffith, S.H. 1998
'The Monks of Palestine and the Growth of Christian Literature in Arabic' in *The Muslim World* (78) 1-28
Grigsby, B.H. 1982
'The Cross as an Expiatory Sacrifice in the Fourth Gospel' in *Journal for the Study of New Testament* (*JSNT*) 5 (15) 51-80
Grima, B. 1993
The Performance of Emotion among Paxtun Women: 'The Misfortunes Which Have Befallen Me' (Karachi: Oxford University Press)
Grundmann, W.
'dei' in *TDNT*, II: 21-25
Guillaume, A. 1956
Islam (London: Penguin)
Guthrie, D. 1981
'The Lamb in the Structure of the Book of Revelation' in *Vox Evangelica* (12) 64-71

Haddad, Y.Y. and W.Z. (ed.) 1995
Muslim-Christian Encounters (Gainesville FL.: University Press of Florida)

Haenchen, E. 1971
The Acts of the Apostles: A Commentary, (Oxford: Basil Blackwell)

Hall, C.S. and Lindzey, G.1970
Theories of Personality, 2nd ed., (New York: John Wiley and Sons)

Hall, R. 1976
'For this you have been called: The Cross and Suffering in 1 Peter' in *Restoration Quarterly* (*ResQ*) (19) 137-147

Hamerton-Kelly, R.G. 1992
Sacred Violence: Paul's Hermeneutic of the Cross (Minneapolis: Fortress Press)

Hamerton-Kelly, R.G. 1988
Violent Origins. Walter Burkett, Rene Girard, and Jonathan Z. Smith on Ritual Killing and Cultural Formation (Stanford CA.: Stanford University Press)

Hanifi, M.J. 1976
Historical and Cultural Dictionary of Afghanistan (New Jersey: Scarecrow Press)

Harnack, A von. 1900
What is Christianity? T.B. Saunders (trans.) (New York: Harper & Row)

Hart, D.M. 1985
Guardians of the Khyber Pass: The Social Organizaton and History of the Afridis of Pakistan (Lahore: Vanguard Books)

Hayek, M. 1977
'Ammar al-Basri, theologie et controversies (Beirut: Dar El-Machreq Editeurs)

Hays, R.B. 1996
The Moral Vision of the New Testament: A Contemporary Introduction to New Testament Ethics (San Francisco: Harper Collins)

Hick, J. 2005
'Response to Dr Reçber' in *Islam and Muslim Christian Relations* (16) 1, January, 11-14

Hillenbrand, C. 1999
The Crusades: Islamic perspectives (Edinburgh: Edinburgh University Press)

Hillyer, N. 1967
'The Lamb' in the Apocalypse' in *Evangelical Quarterly* (*EQ*) (39) 228-236

Hooker, M.D. 1959
Jesus and the Servant: The Influence of the Servant Concept of Deutero-Isaiah in the New Testament (London: SPCK)

'How the Shepherd Saved the SEAL' 2005
The tale of an Afghan's amazing rescue of a wounded U.S. commando' in *TIME*, 11 July at http://www.time.com/time/magazine/article/0,9171,1081394-1,00.html accessed 16/07/2005

Huffard , E. 1989
'Culturally Relevant Themes About Christ,' in *Muslims and Christians on the Emmaus Road* Woodberry, J.D. (ed.) (Monrovia CA.: MARC) 161-74

Hughes, T.P. 1994
Dictionary of Islam, repr. (Chicago, IL.: Kazi)

Hujra 2006
'Hujra.net: Virtual Pashtoon Hujra on Internet' at http://forum.hujra.net/index.php?board=3;action=display;threadid=15, Accessed 14/01/2006

Husain, M.K. 1954
Qaryah zalimah, Cairo

Husain, M.K. 1966
City of Wrong: A Friday in Jerusalem (New York: Seabury Press)

Husain, M.K. 1995
City of Wrong. A Friday in Jerusalem, K. Cragg (trans.) (Oxford: Oneworld)

Ibn 'Arabi, 1968/1388
Shajarat al-kawn (Cairo: al-Halaby and Sons)

Ibn 'Arabi, 1981
Fusus al-hikam, Austin, R.J.W. (trans.) *The Bezels of Wisdom* (Ramsey, N.J.: Paulist Press)

Ibn Ishaq 1957
Sirat rasul allah, Guillaume, A. (trans.) (Oxford: Oxford University Press)

Ibn Khaldun 1958
Al-Muqaddimah, F. Rosenthal (trans.) Vol. 1 (Princeton: Princeton University Press)

Ibriy A.H. (trans.)
Imam Al-Ghazali: Hikmah dan Rahasia Haji (*Imam al-Ghazzali on the Wisdom and Inner Meaning of the Hajj*, (Surabaya: Penerbit Tiga Dua) Part 1, Book 7 of the *Ihya Ulum al-Din*) 136

Imran, M.S. n.d.
Mafundisho ya yesu kwa nuru ya qur'ani (Mombasa: Adam Traders)

Inkeles, A. 1999
What is Sociology? An Introduction to the Discipline and Profession (New Delhi: Prentice-Hall of India)

'Isa, n.d.
'Isa (yesu kristo) ndani ya kurani na biblia (Morogoro: TELM)

Izutsu, T. 1983
Sufism and Taoism (Los Angeles: University of California Press)

Jackman, M. 2001
'Licence to Kill: Violence and Legitimacy in Expropriative Social Relationships' in Jost, J.T. and Majors, B. (eds) *Psychology of Legitimacy: Emerging Perspectives on Ideology, Justice and Intergroup Relations* (New York: Cambridge University Press)

Jadeed, I. n.d.
Hapana! dini ya kristo haijabatalishwa (Nairobi: Njia ya Uzima)

Jeffrey, A. (trans.) 1980
Shajarat al-kawn in *Studia Islamica* (Leiden) (10) 1959, 43-77; (11) 1959, 113-150 [reprinted Lahore: Aziz Publishers]

Jones, L.B. (1938)
Christianity Explained to Muslims (Calcutta: YMCA Press)

Kakar, S. 1996
'The Construction of a New Hindu Identity' in *Unravelling the Nation: Sectarian conflict and India's secular identity,* Basu, K. and Subrahmanyam, S. (eds.) (New Delhi: Penguin Books) 206-210

Kateregga, B.D and Shenk, D.W. 1981
Islam and Christianity: A Muslim and a Christian in Dialogue (Grand Rapids MI.: Eerdmans)

Kearney, R. 1995
'Myths and Scapegoats: The Case of Rene Girard' in *Theory, Culture & Society* (12) 4

Khalid, K.M. 1958
Ma'an 'ala-l-tariq muhammad wa-l-masih, Cairo

Khalifé, I-A. & Kutsch, W. (eds.) 1959
Mélanges de L'Université Saint Joseph (36), 144, Beirut

Khan, M.M. 1987
Sahih al Bukhari (9 Vols.) revised ed. (Delhi: Kitab Bhavan)

Kraemer, H. 1938
The Christian Message in a Non-Christian World (London: Edinburgh House Press)

Krey, A.C. 1921
The First Crusade: The accounts of eyewitnesses and participants (Princeton N.J.: Princeton University Press)

Küng, H. 1977
On Being a Christian, E. Quinn (trans.) (London: Collins)

Ladd G.E. 1964
Jesus and the Kingdom (London: Harper and Row)

Lefebure, L.D. 1998
'Beyond Scapegoating: A conversation with Rene Girard and Ewer Cousins' in *Christian Century* (115) April, 372

Leirvik, O. 1999
Images of Jesús Christ in Islam (Uppsala: Swedish Institute of Missionary Research)

Levine, B. 1974
In the Presence of the Lord (Leiden: E.J. Brill)

Lewis, B. 1994
Islam and the West (New York: Oxford University Press)

Lindholm, C. 1982
Generosity and Jealousy: The Swat Pukhtun of Northern Pakistan (New York: Columbia University Press)

Little, D. 1996
'Religious Militancy' in Crocker, A.C. *et al.* (eds.) *Managing Global Chaos: Sources of and Responses to International Conflict* (Washington D.C.: US Institute of Peace Press)

Livingston, P. 1992
Models of Desire: Rene Girard and the Psychology of Mimesis (Baltimore: The Johns Hopkins University Press)

Love, R. 2000
Muslims, Magic and the Kingdom of God: Church Planting among Folk Muslims (Pasadena: William Carey Library)

Malina, B.J. and Jerome, H.N. 1991
'Conflict in Luke-Acts: Labelling and Deviance Theory' in Neyrey, J.H. (ed.) *The Social World of Luke-Acts: Models for Interpretation*, (Peabody, MA.: Hendrickson)

Mandav, P. 2000
Communalism in India: A Paradigm Shift to Indian Politics (Delhi: Authorspress)

Marshall, D. 2001
'Christianity in the Quran'' in L. Ridgeon (ed.) *Islamic Interpretations of Christianity* (London: Curzon)

Marquet, Y. 1982
'Les Ikhwan al-Safa et le christianisme,' *Islamochristiana* (8)

Masudi, S. 1991
Nuru ing'ayo gizani: ushuhuda wa kijana mwislamu aliyetafuta njia ya kweli, Simalenga, T. (trans.) (Morogoro: Tanzania Evangelical Literature Ministry)

May, E.E. 1947
Ecce Agnus Dei! A Philological and Exegetical Approach to John 1:29, 36. Vol. 5 (Washington D.C.: Catholic University Press)

May, R. 1953
Man's Search for Himself (New York: W.W. Norton)

McAuliife, J.D. 1991
Quranic Christians: An Analysis of Classical and Modern Muslim Exegesis (Cambridge: Cambridge University Press)

McCaffrey, U.P. 1981
'Psalm quotations in the passion narrative of the Gospels' in *Neotestamentica* (14), 73-89

McEvenue, S.E. 1984
'The Elohist at Work' in *Zeitschrift für die Alttestamentiche Wissenschaft* (*ZAW*) 33 (96), 315-332

McGarvey, J.W. 1963
Original Commentary on Acts (Bowling Green: Guardian of Truth Foundation)
Meier, C.T. 2000
Crusade Propaganda and Ideology: Model sermons for the preaching of the cross (Cambridge: Cambridge University Press)
Michel, T.A. 1984
Muslim Theologian's Response to Christianity: Ibn Taymiyya's Al-Jawab Al-Sahih (New York: Delmar Caravan Books)
Michel, T.A. 2000
Paul of Antioch and Ibn Taymiyya: The Modern Relevance of a Medieval Debate, The D'Arcy Lectures, Oxford University, At http://www.sjweb.info/dialogo/documents/doc_show.cfm?Number=5, Accessed 27/02/2006
Milgrom, J.
'Sacrifice', *Anchor Bible Dictionary*-CD-Rom (Logos Bible Software)
Miles, J.
'Lamb', *Anchor Bible Dictionary*-CD-Rom (Logos Bible Software)
Mingana, W.A. (ed. & trans.) 1928
The Apology of Timothy the Patriarch before the Caliph Mahd, Woodbrooke Studies, *Bulletin of the John Ryland Library*, Manchester, 137-298
Moffet, S.H. 1992
A History of Christianity in Asia: Beginnings to 1500 , Vol.1 (New York: Harper)
Moo, D.J. 1983
The Old Testament in the Gospel Passion Narratives (Sheffield: Almond Press)
Moo, D.J. 1996
The Epistle to the Romans (Grand Rapids MI.: Eerdmans)
Moucarry, C. 2001
Faith to Faith: Christianity and Islam in Dialogue (London: IVP)
Mowinckel, S. 1956
He That Cometh (Oxford: Blackwell)
Muir, W. 1858-61
The Life of Mahomet, 4 v. (London: Smith & Elder)
Muller, R. 2000
Tools for Muslim Evangelism (Belleville, ON.: Essence Publishing)
Musa, S. n.d.
Maisha ya Nabii Isa (Alahais Salam) (Mombasa: Adam Traders)
Musalaha
At www.musalaha.org
Musk, B. 1995
Touching the Soul of Islam: Sharing the Gospel in Muslim Cultures (Crowborough: Marc)

Nandy, A. 2002
Time Wraps: Silent and evasive pasts in Indian politics and religion (New Brunswick: Rutgers University Press)

Nasr, S.H. and Leaman, O. (eds.) 1996
History of Islamic Philosophy part II Routledge History of World Philosophies (London/New York: Routledge)

Nasr, S.H. 1993
An Introduction to Islamic Cosmological Doctrines (Albany: State University of New York Press)

Nielsen, K. 1992
'Shepherd, Lamb, and Blood: Imagery in the Old Testament - Use and Reuse' in *Studia Theologica* (46), 121-132

Neno, n.d.
Neno la mungu ndani ya torati, injili na kurani (Morogoro: TELM)

Netton, I.R. 1989
Allah Transcendent: Studies in the Structure and Semiotics of Islamic Philosophy, Theology and Cosmology (London/New York: Routledge)

Netton, I.R. 1982
Muslim Neoplatonists: An Introduction to the Thought of the Brethren of Purity (London: Allen & Unwin)

Neuner, J. and Dupuis, J. (eds.) 1996
The Christian Faith in the Doctrinal Documents of the Catholic Church (Banglore: Theological Publication in India)

Newbigin, L. 1989
The Gospel in a Pluralistic Society (Grand Rapids, MI.: Eerdmans)

Nöldeke, T. 1915
'Arabs (Ancient),' in Hastings, J. (ed.) *Encyclopaedia of Religion and Ethics,* Vol. 1, 659-673 (Edinburgh: T. & T. Clark) 665-666

Northcott, M. 2004
An Angel Directs the Storm: apocalyptic religion and American empire (London: I.B. Tauris)

O'Neill, J.C. 1979
'The Lamb of God in the Testaments of the Twelve Patriarchs' in *JSOT* (1) 2-30

Oswalt, J.N. 1997
The Book of Isaiah Chapters 40-66, The New International Commentary on the Old Testament (Grand Rapids MI.: Eerdmans)

Otto, R. 1968
The Idea of the Holy (Oxford: Oxford University Press)

Padwick, C. 1938
'North African reverie' in *International Review of Mission* (27) 107, 341-54

Pagels, E. 2003
Beyond Belief: the Secret Gospel of Thomas (New York: Random House)

Parshall, P. 1983
Bridges to Islam: A Christian Perspective on Folk Islam (Grand Rapids MI.: Baker Book House)

Parrinder, G. 1977
Jesus in the Quran (New York: Oxford University Press)

Peddiny, A. 1999
'Hindu Hate Literature against Muslims,' MTh thesis, Senate of Serampore College, Calcutta

Plumptre, E.H. 1959
'Acts,' *Ellicott's Commentary on the Whole Bible* C.J. Ellicott (ed.) (Grand Rapids MI.: Zondervan)

Poonawala, I.K. 1988
'Isma'ili *ta'wil*' in Rippin, A. (ed.) *Approaches to the History of Interpretation of the Qur'an* (Oxford: Clarendon Press) 200-23

Pope, M.H. 1986
'The Timing of the Snagging of the Ram, Genesis 22:13' in *BA* (49) 115-117

Puniyani, R. 2003
Communal Politics: Facts versus Myths (New Delhi: Sage Publications)

Puniyani, R. 2005
'Hindutva Offensive Social Roots: Characterisation,' in At http://www.foil.org/politics/hindutva/rampun1.html, Accessed 20022005

Putnam, H. 1975
L'Église sous Timothée I 780-823): Étude sur Église Nestorienne au Temps des Premiers Abbasides (Beirut: Dar el-Marchreq)

al-Qasim, 1921-2
'Reply to the Christians,' I de Matteo (ed.) as 'Confutazione contro I Christiani dello Zaydati al-Qasim b. Ibrahim' in *Revista degli Studi Orientali* (9)

Qur'an, 2006
Electronic English version' at http://www.hti.umich.edu/k/koran/simple.html accessed on 27/02/2006

Koran, 2005
At http://www.hti.umich.edu/k/koran/simple.html, Accessed 10/07/2005

Qurra, Abu 1904
'Maymar fi anna-hu la yaghfiru li-ahad khatiya-hi illa bi-awja' al-Masih allati hallat bi-hi fi sha'n al-nas' in C. Bacha (ed.), *Les Oeuvres Arabes de Théodore Aboucara Évêque d'Haran*, Beyrouth

Qurra, Abu 1959
'Confession of the Orthodox Faith' in Dick, I. (ed.) 'Deux Écrits Inédits de Théodore Abuqurra' *Le Museon* (72)

Ra'ita, Abu 1951
'Reply to the Melkites' in Graf, G. (ed.) *Die Schriften des Jacobiten Habib Ibn Hidma Abu Ra'ita*, CSCO 130, Louvain

Ra'ita, Abu 1951
'Al-risala fi-l-tajassud,' in Graf, G. (ed.) *Die Schriften des Jacobiten Habib Ibn Hidma Abu Ra'ita*, CSCO 130, Louvain

Read, K.A. 1987
'Human Sacrifice' in Eliade, M. (ed.) *Encyclopedia of Religion,* (New York: Macmillan) 515-518

Reçber M.S. 2005
'Hick, the Real and *al-haqq*' in *Islam and Muslim Christian Relations* (16) 1, January 3-10

Reim, G. 1974
Studien zum alttestamentlichen Hintergrund des Johannesevangeliums. SNTSMS. Vol. 22. (Cambridge: Cambridge University Press)

Reimarrus, H.S. 1970
Talbert, C.H. (ed.) *Fragments,* (Philadelphia: Fortress)

Reiss, M. 2002
'Ishmael, Son of Abraham' in *Jewish Bible Quarterly* (*JBQ*) (30) 253-256

Reumann, J.H. 1974
'Psalm 22 at the Cross' in *Interpretation* (28) 39-58

Ridgeon, L. 2001
'Christianity as portrayed by Jalal al-Din Rumi', in Ridgeon, L. (ed.) *Islamic Interpretations of Christianity* (London: Curzon)

Riley-Smith, J. 1986
The First Crusade and the Idea of Crusading (London: Athlone Press)

Riley-Smith, L. and Riley-Smith, J. 1981
The Crusades: Idea and Reality 1095-1274 (London: Edward Arnold)

Ringgren, H. 1956
The Messiah in the Old Testament (London: SCM)

Rissanen, S. 1993
Theological Encounter of Oriental Christians with Islam during Early Abbasid Rule (Åbo: Abo Akademi University Press)

Robertson, A.T. 1930
Word Pictures in The New Testament (Nashville: Broadman)

Roggema, B. 2001
'A Christian Reading of the Qur'an: the legend of Sergius-Bahira and its use of Qur'an and Sira', in D Thomas (ed.) *Syrian Christians under Islam, the first thousand years* (Leiden: E.J. Brill)

Rosenberg, R.A. 1965
'Jesus, Isaac, and the 'Suffering Servant'' in *Journal of Biblical Literature* (*JBL*) (84) 381-388

Runnick, C.T. 1968
'Feeding and Sacrifice: The Old Testament Background of the Fourth Gospel' in *ExpT* (79) 340-341

Rushdie, S. 1988
The Satanic Verses (New York:Viking)

'al-Salib' (the cross) 1960
in Bearman, P.J., Bianquis, Th., Bosworth, C.E. et. al (eds) *Encylopaedia of Islam* (second edition) vol. VIII (Leiden: E.J. Brill)

Samir S.K 2001
'The Prophet Muhammad as seen by Timothy I and some other Arab Christian Authors' in D. Thomas (ed.) *Syrian Christians under Islam, the first thousand years* (Leiden: E.J. Brill)

Samir, S.K. 1994
'The Earliest Arab Apology for Christianity (c.750)' in Samir, S.K. and Neilsen, J.S. (eds.) *Christian Arabic Apologetics during the Abbasid Period (750-1258),* (Leiden: Brill)

Sandy, B.D. 1991
'John the Baptist's "Lamb of God" affirmation in its canonical and apocalyptic milieu' in *JETS* (34) 447-459

Scholes R. and Kellog, R. 1968
The Nature of Narrative (London: Oxford University Press)

Schweitzer, A. 1968
The Quest of the Historical Jesus: A Critical Study of Its Progress from Reimarus to Wrede (New York: Macmillan)

Scott, A.R. 2000
The Ambivalence of the Sacred: Religion, Violence and Reconciliation (Lanham, MD.: Rowan and Littlefield)

Segundo, J.L. 1983
'Faith and Ideologies in Biblical Revelation' in Gottwald, N.K. and Horsley, R.A. (eds.) *The Bible and Liberation: Political and Social Hermeneutics*, (Maryknoll N.Y.: Orbis) 92-106

Shah, G. 2002
'Caste, Hindutva and Hideousness,' in *Economic and Political Weekly* (37) April 13, 1391-1393

Shihab, M.Q. 1999
Fatwa-Fatwa Seputar Ibadah dan Muamalah (*Fatwas Concerning Religious Acts and Duties* (Bandung: Mizan)

Shaheen, S. (ed.) 1984 & 1994
Pashto texts arranged alphabetically (Peshawar: Peshawar University Pashto Academy)

Singh, D.E. 1995
'Muhyil-Din Ibn al-'Arabi's Concept of *ma'ad* in the light of the Qur'an and the Hadith with special reference to the *barzakh*,' MTh thesis submitted to Serampore College, India

Singh, D.E. 1999
The Possibility of Having Knowledge of *al-wujud al-mahd* 'sheer being' According to Ibn 'Arabi's *Kitab al-jamal wa-al-jamal* in *Islam and Christian-Muslim Relations* (10) 3, October, 295-306

Singh, D.E. 2000
'Islam as a Context for Christian Theologizing: A Preliminary Search', in *Bangalore Theological Forum*, XXXII (2) December 60-72

Singh, D.E. 2000
'Abu al-Ala Mawdudi's Political Theory' in *Transformation* (17) 1, 6-13

Singh, D.E. 2001
'Radical Islamic Anthropology: Key to Christian Theologizing in the Context of Islam,' *Bangalore Theological Forum*, XXXIII (1) 1 June 177-197

Singh, D.E. 2003a
Sainthood and Revelatory Discourse (Oxford/Delhi: Regnum/ISPCK)

Singh, D.E. 2003b
'Hindu-Muslim Violence in Gujrat and a Profile of Christian Mission' in *Transformation* (20) 4, October 206-216

Singh, D.E. 2004a
'Beyond Controversy: Christian Mission and Communal Religious Violence in Contemporary India,' a lecture at the Divinity Faculty, University of Cambridge, UK, posted at http://www.martymission.cam.ac.uk/CDSingh.htm

Singh, D.E. 2004b
'An Onto-Epistemological Model: Adam-Muhammad as the Traditional Symbols of Humanity's All-Comprehensive Epistemic Potential' in *The Muslim World* (94) 2, April 275-30

Singh, D.E. 2006
'Rethinking Jesus and the Cross in Islam' in *Mission Studies* (23) 2, 239-260

Sirry, M.A. 2005
'Early Muslim-Christian Dialogue: a Closer Look at Major Themes of the Theological Encounter' in *Islam and Muslim Christian Relations* (16) 4, October 361-376

Snyder, H. 1988
'New Understandings of Two Genesis Passages' in *Journal of Reform Judaism* (35) 23-25

Spain, J.W. 1962
The Way of the Pathans (Karachi: Oxford University Press)

Stassen, G.H. and Gushee, D.P. 2003
Kingdom Ethics: Following Jesus in Contemporary Context (Downers Grove IL.: InterVarsity Press)

Stern, S.M. 1983
Studies in Early Ishma'ilism (Leiden: E.J. Brill)

Stroumsa, S. 1999
Freethinkers of Medieval Islam: Ibn al-Rawandi, Abu Bakr al-Razi and their impact on Islamic thought (Leiden: Brill)

Summers, R. 1965
'The Christ of John's Gospel' in *Southwestern Journal of Theology* (8) 35-43

Swanson, M. 1993
'Some Considerations for the Dating of *fi tatlit allah al-wahid* (Sanai Ar. 154) and *al-gami' wuguh al-iman* (London, British Library op. 4950)' *Parole de L'Orient* (18) 140

Swanson, M. 1995
Folly to the Ḥunafa: the cross of Christ in Arabic Christian-Muslim controversy in the eighth and ninth centuries A.D. (Rome: Pontificum Institutum Studiorum Arabicorum et Islamologiae)

al-Tabari, 'Ali ibn Rabban. 1959
'Al-Radd 'ala al-nasara,' Khalifé, I-A. and Kutsch, W. (eds.) *Mélanges de L'Université Saint Joseph* (36)

Tabory, J. 1996
'The Crucifixion of the Paschal Lamb' in *Jewish Quarterly Review* (*JQR*) (86) 395-406

Takeshita, M. 1987
Ibn 'Arabi's Theory of the PM and its Place in the History of Islamic Thought (Tokyo: Institute for the Study of Language and Cultures of Asia and Africa)

Tannehill, R.C. 1985
'Israel in Luke-Acts: A Tragic Story,' *JBL* (104) 69-85,

Taylor, J.V. 1980
'The Theological Basis Of Interfaith Dialogue' in *Chrsitianity and Other Religions*, Hick, J. and Collins, H. (ed.) (Oxford: One World) 212-233

Thanvi, A.A. 1990
Bahishti zewar, Ud-din, F. (trans.) (New Delhi: Taj Company)

Thiering, B. 1994
Jesus the Man (London: Corgi)

Tisdall, W. St. Clair. 1905
The Original Sources of the Quran (London: SPCK)

Thomas, D. 1992
Anti-Christian Polemic in Early Islam, Abu 'Isa al-Warraq's 'Against the Trinity' (Cambridge: Cambridge University Press)

Thomas, D. (ed. & tr.) 2002
Early Muslim Polemic against Christianity, Abu 'Isa al-Warraq's 'Against the Incarnation' (Cambridge: Cambridge University Press)

Thomas, D. 1996
'The Bible in Early Muslim Anti-Christian Polemic,' *Islam and Christian-Muslim Relations* (7) 29-38

Thomas, D. 2001
'Paul of Antioch's Letter to a Muslim Friend and The Letter from Cyprus' in D. Thomas (ed.), *Syrian Christians under Islam, the first thousand years* (Leiden: E.J. Brill)

Thomas, D. (ed.) 2003
Christians at the Heart of Islamic Rule: Church Life and Scholarship in 'Abbasid Iraq (Leiden: E.J. Brill)
Thomas, G. 1987
The Trial: The Life and Inevitable Crucifixion of Jesus (London: Bantam Press)
Thomas, J.C. 1991
Footwashing in John 13 and the Johannine Community (Sheffield: Sheffield Academic Press)
Thompson, J.A. 1980
The Book of Jeremiah (Grand Rapids MI.: Eerdmans)
Thompson, M. 1991
Clothed with Christ: The Example and Teaching of Jesus in Romans 12.1-15.13, JSNTSup 59 (Sheffield: Sheffield Academic Press)
Travis, J. and Travis, A. 2005
'Appropriate Approaches in Muslim Contexts' in Kraft, C.H. (ed.), *Appropriate Christianity* (Pasadena: William Carey Library) 397-414
Tucker, A. 1999
'Sins of Our Fathers: A Short History of Religious Child Sacrifice' in *ZRG* (51) 30-47
Van Rheenen, G. 1997
'A Theology of Culture: Desecularizing Anthropology' in *International Journal of Frontier Missions,* 14 (1) 33-38
Varshney, A. 2002
Ethnic Conflict and Civic Life: Hindus and Muslims in India (New Haven CONN.: Yale University Press)
Veijola, T. 1989
'Abrahams offer (Genesis 22) - *tid och budska* (Genesis 22): Date and Message' in *Svensk Exegetisk Arsbok* (54) 236-244
Waldman, M.R. 1987
'*Nubuwah,*' in Eliade, M. (ed.) *The Encyclopedia of Religion* vol. 11 (New York: Macmillan) 1-7
al-Warraq, Abu 'Isa 2002
Early Muslim Polemic against Christianity: Abu 'Isa al-Warraq's 'Against the Incarnation' D. Thomas (ed. & tr.) (Cambridge: Cambridge University Press)
Watt, W.M. 1983a
'Ash-Shahrastani's account of Christian Doctrine' in *Islamochristiana* (9) 249-59
Watt, W.M. 1983b
Islam and Christianity Today. A Contribution to Dialogue (London: Routledge)
Webb, E. 1988
Philosophers of Consciousness (Seattle: Univ of Washington Press)
Wenham, G.J. 1994
Genesis(16-50) in *Word Biblical Commentary* (Dallas: Word Books)

Wensinck, A.J. 1927
'Intercession' in *A Handbook of Early Muhammadan Tradition* (Leiden: E.J. Brill)

Wensinck, A.J. 1927
'Bridge' in *A Handbook of Early Muhammadan Tradition* (Leiden: E.J. Brill)

Westermann, C. (ed.) 1963
Essays on Old Testament Interpretation (London: SCM)

Whale, P. 1987
'The lamb of John: some myths about the vocabulary of the Johannine literature' in *JBL* (06), 289-295

Whiteman, D.L. 2004
'Anthropology and Mission: The Incarnational Connection', Part 2 in *International Journal of Frontier Missions* 21 (2) 79-88

Williams, J.G. (ed.) 1996
The Girard Reader (New York: Crossroad)

Williams, J.G. 1988
'The Innocent Victim: Rene Girard on Violence, Sacrifice, and the Sacred' in *Religious Studies Review* (14) 4, 320

Wingo, E.H. 1954
A Lawyer Reviews the Illegal Trial of Jesus (Hattisburg: E.H. Wingo Publications)

Woodberry, D. (ed.) 1989
Muslims and Christians on the Emmaus Road (Manrovia CA.: MARC)

Zaehner, R.C. 1966
Hinduism (Oxford: Oxford University Press)

Zaehner, R.C. 1958
At Sundry Times: An Essay in the Comparison of Religions (London: Faber and Faber)

Zebiri, K. 1997
Muslims and Christians Face to Face (Oxford: Oneworld)

Zimmermann, F.W. (ed.) 1983
Medieval Arabic and Hebrew Thought (London: Variorum Reprints)

Zuck, R.B. 1991
Basic Bible Interpretation: A Practical Guide to Discovering Biblical Truth (Wheaton, IL.: Victor Books)

Zwemer, S.M. 1905
The Moslem Doctrine of God (New York: American Tract Society)

Zwemer, S.M. 1912
The Moslem Christ (Edinburgh: Oliphant, Anderson and Ferrier)

Zwemer, S.M. 1954
The Glory of the Cross (London: Oliphants)

Zwemer, S.M. 1941
The Cross above the Crescent (Grand Rapids MI.: Zondervan)

SUBJECT INDEX

NAME INDEX

PLACE INDEX

GLOBAL THEOLOGICAL VOICES
Series Listing

David Emmanuuel Singh (Ed)

Jesus and the Cross: Reflections of Christians from Islamic Contexts

2008 / 978-1-870345-65-1 / x + 226pp

The Cross reminds us that the sins of the world are not borne through the exercise of power but through Jesus Christ's submission to the will of the Father. The papers in this volume are organised in three parts: scriptural, contextual and theological. The central question being addressed is: how do Christians living in contexts, where Islam is a majority or minority religion, experience, express or think of the Cross? This is, therefore, an exercise in listening. As the contexts from where these engagements arise are varied, the papers in drawing scriptural, contextual and theological reflections offer a cross-section of Christian thinking about Jesus and the Cross.

Sung-wook Hong

Naming God in Korea: The Case of Protestant Christianity

2008 / 978-1-870345-66-8

Since Christianity was introduced to Korea more than a century ago, one of the most controversial issue has been the Korean term for the Christian 'God'. This issue is not merely about naming the Christian God in Korean language, but it relates to the question of theological contextualization—the relationship between the gospel and culture—and the question of Korean Christian identity. This book examines the theological contextualization of the concept of 'God' in the contemporary Korean context and applies the translatability of Christianity to that context. It also demonstrates the nature of the gospel in relation to cultures, i.e., the universality of the gospel expressed in all human cultures.

Young-hoon Lee

The Holy Spirit Movement in Korea:
Its Historical and Doctrinal Development

2008 / 978-1-870345-67-5

This book traces the historical and doctrinal development of the Holy Spirit Movement in Korea through five successive periods (from 1900 to the present time). The first period (1900-20) was characterised by repentance and revival, the second period (1920-40) by persecution and suffering under Japanese occupation. The third period (1940-60) was a time of confusion and division while the fourth period (1960-80) was a time of explosive revival in which the Pentecostal movement played a major role in the rapid growth of Korean churches. In the fifth period (1980 to the present time), the Holy Spirit movement reaches out to all denominations. The book also discusses the relationship between this movement and other religions such as shamanism, and looks forward to further engagement with issues of concern in the larger society.

For the full listing of the Global Theological Voices Series, see http://www.ocms.ac.uk/docs/Global_Theological_Voices_Listing.pdf

In the present day, with so much tension between the Muslim world and the nominally-Christian West, it is important to hear the voices of Christians living within Islamic contexts. Such communities have developed strategies for co-existing with their more numerous Muslim neighbours. The Christian voices in this volume call for a spirit of reconciliation, drawing on their own experiences and finding inspiration in the message of the Cross. This is a call based on hope for the future, not despair for past conflicts. Such a call deserves to be heard.

Peter G. Riddell, Professor of Islamic Studies, and Director, Centre for Islamic Studies, London School of Theology

This work is a valuable reminder that the cross of Christ is relevant to all societies and cultures. It includes potential ways of communicating the meanings of the cross, and also reminders of the path of suffering which may need to be walked.

Martin Whittingham, Muslim-Christian Links

The book is an invaluable resource for reflection and study of the meaning of the cross in the world of Islam and in intercultural relations. I cannot recommend it too highly

Lamin Sanneh, D. Willis James Professor of Missions and World Christianity at Yale University

About the Editor

Dr David Emmanuel Singh is Research Tutor at the Oxford Centre for Mission Studies in the UK. He was Fellow of Redcliffe College and Crowther Hall in the UK and has served as Secretary of the North West India Auxiliary of the Bible Society of India and as Associate and Acting Director of the Henry Martyn Institute of Islamic Studies in India. He is the author of several papers and three books on Muslim-Christian themes.